The Mekong Delta:
Ecology, Economy,
and Revolution,
1860-1960

PIERRE BROCHEUX

The Mekong Delta: Ecology, Economy, and Revolution, 1860-1960

University of Wisconsin-Madison
Center for Southeast Asian Studies
Monograph Number 12

1995

Library of Congress
Catalog Card Number 94-69001

ISBN Cloth 1-881261-12-3
ISBN Paper 1-881261-13-1

Published by the
Center for Southeast Asian Studies
University of Wisconsin-Madison
Madison WI 53706 USA

Telephone: (608) 263-1755
FAX: (608) 263-7125

Designed by Ingrid Slamer

This monograph has been typeset in
11pt Garamond and Cochin

Contents

List of Figures

List of Maps

List of Photographs

List of Tables

Notes on Monetary Symbols

The currency used in Nam Bo during the period of French colonialism was the Indochinese piaster. Units of this currency were commonly represented by the symbol $, a convention followed in this text. Thus, this symbol should not be taken to represent dollars or to signify a conversion of the Indochinese piaster into an equivalent amount of U.S. currency.

Glossary

achar: Khmer layman venerated for his wisdom and piety

ấp: hamlet

bần nông: communist designation for a peasant too poor to support his family

bang (in French: *congrégation*): Chinese organization based on ethnicity or dialect, most prominently the Teochiu, Fujian, Hainan, Cantonese, and Hakka

bang trưởng: chairman of a *bang*

bình phong: Chinese traders who cooperated, not always voluntarily, with the Vietnamese Resistance, the so-called Viet Minh. (literally "folding screen")

bổn thôn điền: communal rice lands (alienable)

bổn thôn thổ: communal village forests, gardens, ponds, and fallow lands (alienable)

cái bồ: basket used for threshing rice

cái búa: harrow traditionally used to prepare soil for rice cultivation

cái caỳ: swing plough, traditionally used by peasants to prepare the soil for cultivation

canh nông: cultivator

chetty or chettiar: Indian from the cast of moneylenders

cố nông: communist designation for a landless peasant, a true proletarian

công: unit of land measure (see appendix 1)

công điền: communal village rice lands (inalienable)

công thổ: communal village forests, gardens, ponds, and fallow lands (inalienable)

conseiller colonial: elected member of the French colonial Assembly, the Conseil Colonial de Cochinchine

corvée: system of impressed labor

đàn: topographical feature, a mound or small hill

địa bộ: village land register

điền bộ: village rice-land register

điền chủ: landowner, landlord (riceland)

địa chủ: landlord

điền mại: agricultural loans secured by land titles

đình: temple, meeting place of village notables

đóc phủ sử: in Cochinchina (Nam Bô), the higher civil-service rank attainable by a Vietnamese under the French colonial administration

đồn điền: military settlements

ghe: boat, junk

giáo làng: village schoolteacher

gíap: mutual-aid association of the inhabitants of the hamlet, usually engaged in the organization of genius cults and funerals

giong: ancient beaches or dunes, a feature of the Nam Bô coastline between the mouth of the Mekong and the cape of Ca-mau

hội: association

hồi ký: memoirs

hương ca: chairman of the *notables,* or village council of elders

hương hào: chief of the village police

hương sư: second village vice-chairman, responsible for administering the budget

hương thân: *notable* charged with keeping order in a village, the middleman between the elders and the French administration

huyện: subprefecture, normally used to refer to the tri-huyên, or head of the subprefecture

khum: (Khmer) administrative subdivision composed of many *phum*

kỳ: country, a term used by the French colonial regime to designate Cochinchina, Tonkin, or Annam (Nam Ky, Bac Ky, or Trung Ky). The nationalists employed the terms *phần* or *bộ,* meaning "part of" or "segment of."

làng: village

mekhum: head of a *khum*

Minh Hương: offspring of a Sino-Vietnamese marriage

mục: cattle breeder

Nam Tiến: the historical southern migration of the Vietnamese people

ngư: fisherman

nông: farmer

nuí: hill or mountain

nước mắm: fish sauce, the national condiment of Vietnam

paddy: unhusked rice

phủ: prefecture, normally used to refer to the *tri-phu,* or prefect, both in the imperial bureaucracy and under the French regime

phum: (Khmer) village or hamlet

quốc ngữ: romanized transcription of the Vietnamese language devised by Jesuit missionaries

rạch: small watercourse with no discernable source

rẫy: slash-and-burn, or swidden, cultivation; also a swidden field

sĩ: literati

sou: five cents of a piaster

tá điền: tenant farmer

tập kết: regrouping of southern Vietnamese resistance soldiers and cadres in North Vietnam following the Geneva Agreements of 1954

thầy: a master or clerk, a "white-collar" worker

thợ: a mechanic or manual laborer

thông trưởng or xã trưởng: *notable* in charge of tax collection

thương: merchant

tiều: woodcutter

trát: edict

xã: rural commune (administrative unit)

xóm: village or hamlet

xứ: country, a term used by the IPC to designate Tonkin, Annam, and Cochinchina

xứ ủy: literally "committee of the country," the roster of the IPC in each *xứ*

Acknowledgements

I am very grateful to Professor Alfred W. McCoy whose friendly and tenacious support was crucial for the publication of this book. I am indebted towards Professor David Chandler who agreed to read and correct my clumsy English version. Many thanks to the two reviewers for their valuable, critical remarks on my manuscript and to the editors who performed thorough and careful work.

Last, but certainly not least, I wish to add to these acknowledgements my wife Michelle whose love and encouragement never failed.

Preface

A topic of research depends upon the researcher. In this case the relations between the two are not only intellectual but also existential. I chose the subject of the following monograph because I was born in Nam Bo, or Cochinchina, and I had the opportunity to travel around the Mekong Delta when I was young.[1] While growing up, I often overheard my family's stories of land disputes, land grabbings, children given to creditors to pay their parents' debts, and the exactions of mandarins and village elders upon the peasants. My childhood experiences ultimately led me back to Nam Bo to do my university research. I returned in 1960 and remained for eight years. But, because travel in the countryside had become much riskier due to the war, I was constrained to undertake far fewer trips than I would have liked. My mixed ethnic origin, half-Vietnamese, half-French, obliged me to be conscious from an early age of the racial inequality institutionalized by the French. This existence *entre deux mondes*—sometimes painful, sometimes rewarding, often uncomfortable—prompted me to scrutinize the society of Nam Bo with an especially critical eye.

The intellectual concerns that guided my research derive from the problematic character of Nam Bo in Vietnam's national history. Beginning in the seventeenth century, the Vietnamese migrated from the north and settled in this hydrographic basin long occupied by the Khmers, whose empire had once stretched from northern Thailand and southern Laos to the mouth of the Mekong River. This migration to the Mekong Delta is referred to as the "March to the South" or *Nam Tien*. By the turn of the nineteenth century, the Vietnamese were established in the central portion of the delta, known as Mien Trung, while the displaced Khmers had migrated to the western portion, Mien Tay. Chinese settlers and merchants, fleeing from Manchu invasions or searching for new markets, both preceded and accompanied the Vietnamese influx. They formed a significant part of the population in some of the delta's regions (especially in Bien Hoa and My Tho) even by the seventeenth and eighteenth centuries.

Nearly every feature of Nam Bo served as a contrast to the Red River Delta (Dong Bang Song Hong) of the north, from which the Vietnamese had migrated. Chief among these were ethnic diversity, the untamed hydrological environment, the absence of established villages, and the greater scope of mercantile activity. In his outstanding study, *The Birth of Vietnam*, Keith

Taylor emphasizes the complementarity of the two poles of the Vietnamese national character: "'Northern resolve and Southern release' towards the Chinese threat . . . [a] source of both irritation and creativity."[2] In contrast to the Red River Delta (the Vietnamese cultural and political center of gravity), Nam Bo raises a plethora of questions. The village is an essential complement of the national mythology of Vietnam, but how does the village in Nam Bo conform to the northern model? If the history of Nam Bo invalidates the model of the village as the central wheel of Vietnamese society, then what are the other institutions of social and cultural change? Are they patron-client relationships, class solidarities, renovated religious faiths, secret societies, or racial alliances? In Nam Bo's ethnically diverse society, what role, if any, does nationalist feeling play? And how much does nationalist feeling lessen class antagonisms within the Vietnamese community, while intensifying them in inter-ethnic relationships?

As they migrated further and further from their original homeland in the Red River Delta, the Vietnamese must have been concerned about their national cohesion. The unity of their state was endangered by wars between Trinh and Nguyen lords, the Tay Son uprising, the purported separatist rebellion of Le Van Khoi in 1833, and the French annexation of Nam Bo thirty years later. As a people distanced from their homeland, the migrants were more susceptible to being drawn away from it. The French began their political conquest of Vietnam in the south, taking Saigon in 1859, and they hoped to prolong it despite the post–World War II decolonization by forming an Autonomous Republic of Cochinchina in 1946. Even after the defeat of the French in 1954, the United States sought to maintain a separate political status for Cochinchina.

After the defeat of U.S. forces in 1975, Vietnam was reunified. But many problems have arisen with the reintegration of Nam Bo into Vietnam. Although the roots of these problems, to some degree, extend back centuries, Nam Bo's unique trajectory is clear. One of its most distinctive aspects is greater integration into the world market. Under French rule, the rapid acceleration of rice production for export transformed society, and much of the delta's land was converted to rice monoculture. Fortunes were made by Vietnamese landowners and Chinese merchants while many peasants suffered a nomadic and precarious existence. Unlike the relatively egalitarian landholding pattern prevailing in the north, many landowners in the south controlled thousands of hectares of land. Although trade was far from negligible prior to the late nineteenth century, the introduction of agricultural-export production provoked a qualitative change in both the magnitude and the direction of trade. The French were present less in the flesh than in their economic effects.

Of major concern in this study are the agricultural changes that occurred under French colonialism. Thus, the region of the Mekong Delta on which the study concentrates is the western portion, Mien Tay, where most of the agricultural expansion took place. The first half of the book is concerned with the agricultural transformation of Mien Tay while the second half addresses the politics and economics of Nam Bo as a whole. Prior to the French conquest, Mien Tay was the least populated region of the delta, with an environment extremely hostile to agricultural production. Much of the land was submerged under salt water for a good part of the year, subject to flooding by the Mekong, or covered with thickly rooted mangrove forests. French colonialism created a massive ecological, as well as economic, transformation. Thousands of miles of canals were dug to drain the swamps and vast stretches of mangrove were felled. Thus, Mien Tay was opened to large-scale human habitation and agricultural cultivation. Within a few decades it became one of the largest centers of export-rice production in the world. How this occurred and how it affected Vietnamese society are crucial questions.

Until four or five years ago, most Vietnamese and western historians had underestimated, if not ignored, these transformations in Nam Bo.[3] The strong nationalist bias in Vietnamese history books has prevented an examination of how France organized its Indochinese colonies—the actual modalities of colonialism. In these histories the terms *colonialist* and *colonialism* are employed more for derogatory effect than for their analytical content. The primary concern has been to strengthen national unity and downplay the differences between regions. A statement by Bui Huu Nghia (1807–72) is often heard today: "Nothing can shake the South; it is the pillar of our country."[4] While the Vietnamese are keenly aware that their common identity can bring them together to face an external threat, they are also beginning to realize that regional, class, and religious identities have been and continue to be divisive. Anthropologist Dinh Van Lien writes of the ethnic diversity of Nam Bo that "one legend on the origins of the Khmers clearly tells us that Viets, Khmers, Chams, and central highlanders were born from the same mother."[5] But, while the idea of a common ancestor may help sustain good relations between ethnic groups, it might also serve to justify an assimilationist policy whereby different cultures are homogenized into a single Vietnamese identity.

This study examines the French colonial period up to 1960, a terminal date dictated by two events. First, by September of 1960 almost all of the French-owned land in the Mekong Delta had been transferred to the South Vietnamese government in compliance with the terms of an agreement between President Ngo Dinh Ziem and the French government signed two years earlier.[6] Although the large rubber, tea, and coffee estates of Mien Dong, Nam Bo, and the central high plateau remained in French hands until 1975, we may consider 1960 as marking the end of French power in the delta. Second, 1960 witnessed the beginning of organized resistance to the United States' intervention in South Vietnam. The National Front for the Liberation of South Vietnam *(Mat Tran Zan Toc Giai Phong Mien Nam Viet Nam)* was proclaimed on 20 December of that year.

The work is based on my research in the archives of Vietnam and France. When I lived in Saigon I could take advantage of the riches of the library of the *Société des Études Indochinoises*. I was fortunate also to gain free access to the former archives of Cochinchina, the *Archives Nationales de la République du Vietnam*, the main interest of which lay in the sources relating to the provinces. In 1979, I had the opportunity to return and work in what had become the Archives of the Socialist Republic of Vietnam *(Luu tru 2)* in Ho Chi Minh City. For more than a decade, I have continued to work in the French colonial archives in Paris and Aix-en-Provence and the French Army archives in Vincennes.

Over the years I have been able to read and cross-examine a wide range of primary materials, French as well as Vietnamese, governmental as well as nationalist and communist, public as well as private. Along with archival documents, the importance of periodicals must be emphasized. French Indochina, and in particular Vietnam, had an early, lively, and opinionated press. It is worth remembering that Vietnamese modern literature was first published in its newspapers. Books, in both French and Vietnamese, also formed an important source of information. Many were published on the subject of Mien Tay during the colonial period and soon after. The region appealed to the imagination of the first French administrators and settlers, most of whom were sailors, naval officers, or former officials recently retired from government posts in France. For Vietnamese writers, Mien Tay also held a special attraction as a region possessing a pristine and generous nature and the promise of much wealth. Fictional works on Nam Bo's rural society are rare, however, even those bearing the realist stamp. In contrast to the abundance of northern novelists who wrote about village customs, mentalities, solidarities, and antagonisms during the 1930s, southerners have only Ho Bieu Chanh to cite, principally his *Nha Ngheo* (Born of the Poor). More recently, Son Nam, the most prominent historian of Nam Bo, has continued to evoke the region's frontier image, drawing vivid portraits of the early Vietnamese migrants as adventurous, tough, unsubmissive, blunt, and heroic (*anh hung*). His books are extremely important since by 1990 he was the sole Vietnamese using the colonial archives in Saigon and reproducing some of its documents.[7]

Still essential to any study of Nam Bo are books by the French agronomist, Yves Henry, and the geographer, Pierre Gourou.[8] The French administration also published informative monographs on the various provinces of Nam Bo from about 1907 onward, mimicking to some extent the tradition of chronicle writing maintained by the former Vietnamese imperial bureaucracy. Vietnamese writers such as Huynh Minh completed (by 1960) what the French ignored or misread. Finally, I have drawn heavily upon *hoi ky* (personal reminiscences), most of which were written by communist militants. But, while these are useful sources, one must be attentive to their interpretive framework: it must be remembered that communist historical writing follows the political line of the party, which imposes the choice of topics and the taboos to be respected.

CHAPTER 1

Ecology and Settlement

CONSECUTIVE WAVES OF Khmer, Vietnamese, and French settlement in the delta region of southern Vietnam produced a confusing array of names for the territory and the natural waterways that flow through it. The Khmers called the lower basin and the largest river branch flowing through it Bassac, while the Vietnamese referred to the delta as Cuu Long (Nine Dragons), the main tributary as Hau Giang, and the smaller river branch to the northeast as Tien Giang. The French applied the Thai name Mekong to both the delta and the river, but labeled its two main branches the Fleuve Postérieur and the Fleuve Antérieur. In addition, the French employed variations of the Khmer name for the river to describe two subregions of the delta with respect to their relative distance from the French presence in Saigon: Cisbassac and Transbassac.

French and Vietnamese administrative boundaries produced yet another set of labels. The southern part of Vietnam that the French called Cochinchina was known to the Vietnamese as Nam Bo and divided into eastern, central, and western parts: Mien Dong, Mien Trung, and Mien Tay. Naturally, the geographic and political divisions did not correspond perfectly. For example, the delta region, Cuu Long, falls within both Mien Trung and Mien Tay. And, while the Transbassac includes only the low-lying plain west of the Bassac, or Hau Giang, Mien Tay includes both the Transbassac and the Cisbassac, i.e., the land between the Hau Giang and the Tien Giang.

Not long before the arrival of the French, Mien Tay had been divided into three provinces: Vinh-long, An-giang, and Ha-tien. The French altered this division in 1875 by creating five districts subdivided into *inspections*. The names and extent of the districts were modified several times thereafter. By a decree of 1912 the region was divided into six provinces: Chau-doc and Long-xuyen (which protrude into the central delta), Can-tho, Bac-lieu, Rach-gia, and Ha-tien. Later the district of Ca-mau was detached from Bac-lieu and three others were created: Soc-trang, Tra-vinh, and Sa-dec. Ultimately the surface area of Mien Tay officially came to encompass 26,300 of the 56,400 square kilometers in all of Cochinchina.

To cut through the terminological imbroglio, I shall adopt the vocabulary of the ultimate winner. Hereafter Vietnamese terms will be used: Cuu Long, Mien Tay, Mien Trung, and, for the Mekong's two major tributaries, Hau Giang and Tien Giang. I will occasionally use the terms Mekong and Transbassac.[1]

An Amphibious Ecology

"In the beginning there was water" applies perfectly to the western part of the delta known as Mien Tay. There the Mekong River and the coastal sea currents of the South China Sea created the plain of the Transbassac. On a substratum of ancient origin, marked by the volcanic and granitic islets of Poulo Obi, Hon Da Bac, and Hon Chuoi, and the limestone peaks of Ha-tien and Chau-doc provinces, the great river, flowing from high Himalayan plateaus, accumulated alluvium to a great thickness. Borings taken in 1925 in the province of Bac-lieu revealed a thickness of more than 50 meters, while in 1931 it was found that the alluvial coverage exceeded 133 meters in Soc-trang Province and 197 meters in Ca-mau.[2]

Mien Tay resembles all the world's great deltas in that the boundaries between water and land are often indistinct. The osmosis between the two elements is such that the image frequently recalled in descriptions is that of a sponge. The main water course is the Hau Giang, one of the two major tributaries of the Mekong. Though it defines the eastern border of Mien Tay, it periodically leaves its proper limits. Gigantic and irregular, it regularly submerges most of the plain of Chau-doc under several meters of water for five months of the year. The rainy season, beginning in July, swells its waters so that by October it reaches its maximum level. As a rule the water runs slowly and poses little danger, as it is regulated by the great lake of Tonle Sap in Cambodia. Exceptions, when they occur, are often catastrophic. In 1904, for example, the river covered the province of Long-xuyen with four meters of water, submerging straw huts and drowning cattle and farm animals. At the multistoried administrative buildings of the province's chief town, the

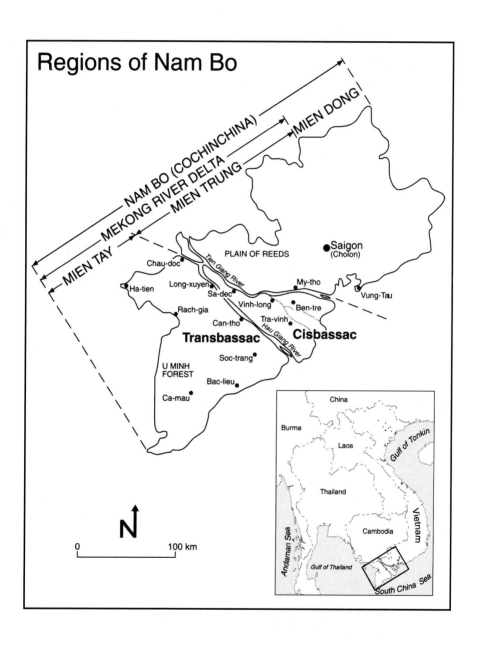

Regions of Nam Bo

NAM BO (COCHINCHINA)

MEKONG RIVER DELTA

MIEN TRUNG

MIEN DONG

MIEN TAY

PLAIN OF REEDS

Saigon
(Cholon)

Chau-doc

Tien Giang River

Ha-tien

Long-xuyen

Sa-dec

My-tho

Vung-Tau

Rach-gia

Vinh-long

Ben-tre

Can-tho

Tra-vinh

Hau Giang River

Transbassac

Cisbassac

U MINH
FOREST

Soc-trang

Bac-lieu

Ca-mau

N

0   100 km

China

Burma

Laos

Gulf of Tonkin

Thailand

Vietnam

Andaman Sea

Cambodia

Gulf of Thailand

South China Sea

occupants were forced to abandon the ground floor and move about in sampans. When the phenomenon was repeated in 1923, two-thirds of the rice harvest was destroyed. In 1937, when another flood inundated Chau-doc, Long-xuyen, Sa-dec, and Can-tho, even the crop of floating rice was lost.[3]

Mien Tay is drained by a system of *rach*, small water courses without any permanent source. The *rach* are shallow and nearly without slope due to the flatness of the land. Anastomosed to the point that it is almost impossible to distinguish their hydrographic basins, they form a magnificent network of waterways. As the tides wash through them two to four times a day, the flux and reflux imposes a rhythm on the movements of sampans and junks. The only obstacles to navigation are alluvium bars built up by the outgoing tides. The shifting alluvial deposits also make a mockery of human boundaries.[4]

The demarcation of land and water is just as uncertain along the coast where the sea penetrates by means of arroyos. The dry season favors the influx of brackish water, which in the rainy season is pushed a few kilometers out to sea. The coast is most unstable in the Gulf of Siam where violent northeasterly currents sweep away the alluvium and orient the hook of the point of Ca-mau toward the southwest. The coastline is remade quickly, as is evidenced in the village of Tom Bai Hap on the Bay of Cuu Long. Around 1915, the village was built on pilings by the sea; by 1930, it was found to be thirty-two meters from the beach.

The mangrove forest is the precious agent binding the silted land of Mien Tay. On each new accretion of land is found a strip of young mangroves, which gives the beach the appearance of beds of greenery arranged in regular tiers. The Bay of Cuu Long, which was depicted in the standard atlases of the early twentieth century, was by 1937 a forest reserve of twenty thousand hectares. On the coast south of Rach-gia, the U Minh is a vast flooded forest, saturated with water at the end of the rainy season. Everywhere of recent formation, the coast is low, swampy, and often arranged in a straight line. It only becomes picturesque between northern Rach-gia and Ha-tien where it is broken by heights and accompanied by rocky islets. Often less than a hectare in area, covered with luxuriant vegetation, and blessed with sources of fresh water, these islets once served as the lair of pirates and the refuge of exiles. They have served also, since ancient times, as staging posts for trading vessels and sites for fishing villages.[5]

The climate intervenes on the side of water in the land-water dialectic of Mien Tay. The west is dominated by the repetitive regime of the monsoons. Situated at the southern extremity of the Indochinese peninsula, the region is wide open to the southwest monsoon. But, while the violent winds

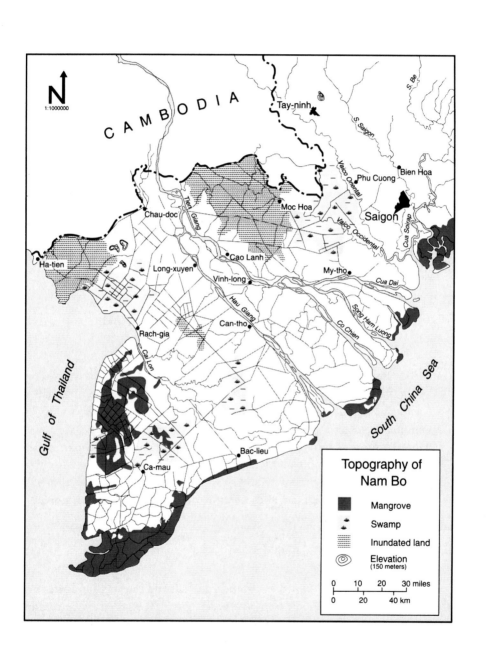

Topography of Nam Bo

Mangrove
Swamp
Inundated land
Elevation (150 meters)

and abundant rain impede maritime activity in the Gulf of Siam, they allow for agricultural work. The humidity, between 60 and 90 percent, and the temperature, between 25 and 35 degrees Celsius (77 to 95 degrees Farenheit), are propitious for rice cultivation, and generally the rains are abundant and relatively regular. Regularity does not prevent surprises, however, and the apparent fixity of the seasons conceals variations of some intensity.[6] Occasionally the rains are late, interrupted by the so-called little dry season of August and September. This is particularly dangerous for rice transplanted in August.

The reversal of the monsoon in October or November is rarely accompanied by typhoons in this part of Vietnam as it is elsewhere in Southeast Asia. The wind from the northeast brings a relatively cool, dry period, which grows warmer and dryer toward the month of April when the ground cracks and fresh water begins to run short.[7] In the absence of fresh water, water buffaloes succumb to disease. Their cadavers infect the air and the dangers of human mortality grow. During the dry season of 1921, a veterinarian, Le Louet, who directed the epizootic assistance for Cochinchina, went to the village of Thoi Binh (in Ca-mau) where an outbreak of cattle disease had been reported. Thinking that the epidemic would be over, he found it still in full force.

> I traveled in a motorboat. A few hours before arriving at my destination, I had incontestable testimony of the gravity of the epizootic: characteristic odors and flocks of crows permitted me to locate one of the numerous water buffalo corpses thrown in the muddy *rach* and the marshy forest. The corpses caught on the stumps and roots, choking the *rach*, submerged or floating, putrefied slowly in the nearly stagnant water, laden to the extreme with organic matter; these corpses remained at incubating temperature and constituted an excellent milieu, if not a culture, for the innumerable germs leaving the carcasses in profusion. . . . The birds of prey, the dogs, the fetid animals, finished this work of dissemination.[8]

Recently deposited alluvium, composed of silt and clay, predominates in the maritime provinces. Apart from stones and gravel, their finer elements are up to 50 percent clay and possess such great compactness that they require a preliminary soaking before the soil can be worked. Rich in humus and organic matter, easily recharged with nitrogen thanks to abundant rain and floods, and containing potash in sufficient quantities, the soil is ideal for rice culture (its youth, to a certain extent, compensates for its deficiency of phosphorus and lime). In the swampy zones of Chau-doc and Long-xuyen, on the other hand, the presence of iron sulfate and aluminum imparts acidity to the soil. In dry periods, salts come to the surface in fairly extensive efflorescences. In these areas fresh water is indispensable to wash the salts into the neighboring rivers so that the land can be worked.[9]

The mangrove tree provides a beautiful example of symbiosis between soil, water, and vegetation. All three varieties, the *duoc*, the *vet* (two rhizophoraceae), and the *mam*, are adapted to salt water. The *duoc*, with its flying-buttress roots exposed at low tide, and the *vet*, with its creeping roots, present curious silhouettes. In binding the alluvial mud these are the primary agents of the progression of the coast and the consolidation of the delta. Their presence corresponds to the pioneering phase of the fixation. Where the soil is exhausted, remaining wet but no longer very salty, there is a proliferation of the rear-mangrove, or *mam*, of which the principal tree is the *tram*.

In 1890, A. Henry, charged with surveying the forest resources of Mien Tay, estimated the area of the western forests at 1.9 million hectares, a plausible figure if one considers the enormous amount of labor later required to clear the forests. In 1938, of the 329,000 hectares of forest then documented in Cochinchina, the provinces of Ca-mau and Rach-gia together contained 170,000 hectares.[10] Accustomed to the stunted mangroves of the eastern provinces, early devastated by man, the first Europeans to arrive at Ca-mau were struck by the magnificent forests, as yet nearly untouched by man.

Every type of tree in Mien Tay is used for a variety of purposes. Mangroves are used for making charcoal, building houses (the *duoc* is rot-proof), and fashioning agricultural and fishing implements. They also serve as sources of tannin, oil, and fruit. The water palm is of such utility that "if the rural populations of the West were abruptly deprived of it, their life would be impossible." Not only do the forests feed the "civilization of the plants" but they are the foundation of a hunting and gathering economy: men were early attracted by hunting and by the search for honey and wax. Ca-mau was called by the Khmers Dei Kramuon, the "country of wax."[11] This amphibious environment is also the abode of fish, sea tortoises, edible fresh-water tortoises, reptiles such as the python and lizards, saurians such as crocodiles, birds (including many waders), and insects (the best known of which are the dreaded mosquitoes). Only the *nui*, or hills, shelter animals of the high forest: tigers, deer, and even elephants.

Almost everywhere in Mien Tay the altitude is no greater than two meters above sea level. Sunken landscapes are the most prevalent. The territory is dotted with immense basins, inundated and deserted. In the heart of the West, near Can-tho (in Phung-hiep District), the Xa No River brings together swamps intersected by occasional sandy ridges, the remains of ancient dunes, or *giong*, where a few trees thrust up in isolation. To the east of the U Minh forest, a vast undrained zone of some eighty thousand hectares is home to stagnant water, a few scraps of mangroves, and high grasses. Even in the month of March one can hardly move on firm ground there. As early as the end of April the expanse of black and spongy humus, water-logged and encumbered with reeds, is frequented only by the wading birds that give it one of its names, the Plain of the Birds. In Vietnamese it is known as Bien Lang (Tranquil Sea). In 1879, an administrator named Brière recorded the following description of an excursion through the plain between Bac-lieu and Ca-mau.

> Not a tree, much less a vestige of cultivation: a swarm of mosquitoes, without a break or respite, harass all humans who risk themselves in these inhospitable regions. I was obliged all day to keep up the fire constantly, around and beneath me, and to surround myself in a veritable cloud of smoke.[12]

At the approach to the Cambodian frontier the land rises. North of a hypothetical line drawn from Rach-gia to Can-tho the *nui* precede the Kampot Mountains in Cambodia. The *nui* thrust abruptly from the plain and the resulting contrast accentuates the impression of "mountains." Their altitude varies greatly, from Nui Sap (86 meters) and Nui Ba The (210 meters) in the province of Long-xuyen to Nui Sam (230 meters) and Nui Cam (880 meters) in Chau-doc. Although exploitable quarries and sources of fresh water have long encouraged a dense population at the base of each *nui*, the hillsides are cloaked in deep forest. In the early nineteenth century the mandarin Thoai Ngoc Hau described Nui Sap: "It is 2,478 *tam* in circumference and the aspect of its vegetation, which rises by stages, is of the most beautiful green. The undulations of its vegetation give it a resemblance to a dragon."[13]

Apart from the *nui*, the *giong* provide the only notable relief in Mien Tay. Composed of elongated hillocks of sand running parallel to the coastline, their successive alignments are testimony to the retreat of the sea. Sheltered from floods, the *giong* contain at some depth (where they meet the underlying clay) sources of fresh water. This has made them favored sites for human settlement. The landscape of sandy hillocks, wrapped in green groves, is evocative of oases.[14]

The climate of Mien Tay is not hostile to humans, for the heat and humidity are tempered by the proximity of the sea from which a breeze regularly blows. In 1937, an observer noted that fevers and epidemic illnesses were very rare in the province of Chau-doc: "The European can live there easily. The native himself is generally healthy and robust. Many live to an advanced age."[15]

The *monographie* of Bac-lieu Province, dated the same year, emphasizes the salubrity of the climate. But the minutes of the Provincial Council of Hatien carry a note of discord: apparently the salubrity of the country depends in large measure on the initiative of the inhabitants in altering the environment.[16] Endemic tropical diseases were noted by doctors on inoculation tours in the last quarter of the nineteenth century. The best-known diseases were malaria (which occurred principally in forests and swampy depressions),[17] amoebic dysentery, other intestinal parasites, dermatosis, opthalmic illnesses, conjunctivitis, trachomas, and bronchial diseases. Attacked by leeches, their eyes continually assaulted by the glare of the sun, the inhabitants worked the mire, their dwellings located above or near the water. This water served as an excellent vector of contamination, as the veterinarian Le Louet, writing on the subject of epizootics, vividly describes.

> The contaminated water inundates the soil, saturating it, penetrating it at all points. The animals of the riverine villages have nothing to drink other than the river water. There is no question of wells, the water is everywhere. The animals are not buried because they would be buried in the water, the hole is progressively filled in by water. It is the whole region, the whole plain, that must be condemned. The villages are semi-lacustral. . . . The inhabitants work with mud up to the belly.[18]

A priori, the climate and the natural environment of Mien Tay do not present insurmountable obstacles to human settlement. On the contrary, they offer rich agricultural possibilities. The climate and the soil are suited to flooded rice culture. But settlement is only possible if the water is controlled. Cultivation, whether irrigated or dry, can only be undertaken after the alum of the soil has been drained and the brackish water prevented from flooding the fields during the monsoon. The work is tremendous, for many canals and small channels must be dug to extend the natural waterways.

In the domain of rice culture, the regime of the water determines the mode of cultivation: floating rice sown directly or planted rice with one or two transplantings. It also affects the kind of rice cultivated: early rice, half-season rice, or full-season rice. Brière, one of the first administrators in Ca-mau, knew how heavily water weighed in the life of the population. In 1879, he noted the limited extent of rice cultivation within his district and the need to import it from Hai Nam. He attributed this insufficiency to the invasion of brackish water, which rendered cultivation unstable and blurred the limit of the fields.

> The cultivator is often forced to abandon his rice land after two or three years of cultivation, whether as a consequence of the infiltration of briny water or the impoverishment of the soil; and then must clear in the water palms or the neighboring forest a new *ray* [field]. . . . Nothing [is] more miserable than the sight of *ray* where it seems the stems of early rice must be choked by the more vigorous growth of the shoots of the water palm.[19]

Vietnamese Settlement

In 1818, the mandarin Thoai Ngoc Hau had engraved upon a stele at the hill of Nui Sap the words "At this epoch this was a 'veritable Eden'; the woods were thick and bushy and the fields were covered with grasses and served as a retreat for frisking herds of doe and stag." When he received an order to construct a canal from Long-xuyen to Rach-gia, he declared that "This sacred place, which had been hidden to the eyes, had not yet been trod by any human foot."[20]

He was not the only one to sense the virginity of the environment. In other regions of the West, the notes of the first administrators and settlers give the same impression. Yet recent discoveries, excavations, and interpretations of ancient Chinese texts have established that nearly two thousand years ago a kingdom known to the Chinese as Fou Nan and its successor, the "Tchen La d'Eau," extended into the Mekong Delta. A site near the village of Oc Eo, near the hill of Nui Ba The, was excavated during World War II by a team supervised by L. Malleret. Aerial photography revealed traces of an ancient hydraulic network, which allowed the archaelogists to speculate that during the second and third centuries Oc Eo was "a gateway through which Indianization extended into the heartland of Cambodia."[21] Was Oc Eo the seaport of the realm of Fou Nan identified by Chinese sources? Was this area under irrigated rice-cultivation by the fifth or sixth century? Were the canals revealed by aerial photographs in Rach-gia and Chau-doc provinces used for irrigation or only for circulation and transport? These matters have been debated without definitive conclusion. But it is not unreasonable to think that today the boats that circulate from the Gulf of Siam to the South China Sea by means of the *songs* (rivers) Ong Doc, Bay Hap, and Ganh Hao, to avoid the detour around the point of Ca-mau, sail in the wake of the sea junks of yesteryear. They illustrate the permanence of one of the paths of Chinese commerce of the "South Seas."[22]

Although settled to some extent since at least the second century, Mien Tay struck the eighteenth-century Vietnamese settlers as a new land. In 1757, when they reached Chau-doc, they were in the last stage of their Nam Tien (March to the South). Had the French not arrived, they would probably have continued in the direction of Cambodia. The character of the Nam Tien, progressive advance rather than brutal thrust, is most evident, perhaps, in the West.

At the end of the seventeenth century, a group of Chinese loyal to the Ming dynasty fled the Manchus and established themselves near My-tho, Vinh-long, and Sa-dec. In 1715, when a new wave of Chinese reached the region, the Vietnamese sovereigns residing in the north cleverly employed them to colonize the edges of their kingdom. One of these exiles, Mac Cuu, placed himself in the service of the king of Cambodia. On the coast of the Gulf of Siam he founded the settlement of Ha-tien, which he wished to make a port of entry for maritime commerce. Having created the port and cleared the surrounding land, he found himself at the head of a fiefdom in which commerce, occasional buccaneering, and gambling brought significant prosperity. But covetousness attracted the Siamese to Ha-tien, and in the face of a helpless Cambodian sovereign, the Chinese took service under the king of Vietnam. It is recounted that under the sway of the son of Mac Cuu, Mac Thien Tu, Ha-tien became not only a flourishing port but a renowned intellectual center.[23] The Vietnamese prince Nguyen Anh found refuge there, and later undertook the reconquest of his domain from this southern base. In the nineteenth century, when the Vietnamese combined this possession with their northern provinces of Gia-long and Minh-mang, they began to pay particular attention to the West.

The Vietnamese kings conquered and pacified the delta by digging canals, such as Vinh Te and Long An Ha (both constructed in 1819), and founding *don dien* (military settlements). Reviving, to their advantage, a proven method that the Chinese had once applied in the Red River Delta, the Vietnamese courts sent or encouraged the departure for the south of many unstable social elements that had lost or could not find a place in the villages. The construction of *don dien* allowed these settlers to defend themselves while ensuring that the central power would be able to preserve control over its subjects.[24] As soon as a group of settlers numbered fifty, it could apply for a concession of land that would be taxed for a period of only seven years. In exchange the settlers were obliged to perform guard duty and military service but they also enjoyed civilian prerogatives. Groups of settlers, installing themselves along the *rach* at the intersections of navigable waterways, gradually drove out the Cambodians.

While military colonization was not the only form of settlement employed in the south, it must have been the most common. When the French arrived in Mien Tay in 1867, there were about ten *don dien* in what was to become the province of Long-xuyen. Some of these were joined together and transformed into civilian villages; others were dissolved. Often cited is the example of Xom So village, in Bac-lieu Province, which was originally a *don dien* founded by the celebrated mandarin Nguyen Tri Phuong.[25]

The first *don dien* were founded in 1790 to defend the Nguyen lords' territories against the Khmers and Tay Son rebels. As the Nguyens' policy toward the Khmers varied with changing circumstances and reigns, the Khmer population's response differed as well. According to the historian Son Nam, himself quoting *Gia dinh Thanh Thong Chi*, in 1780 the Khmers of Tra-vinh revolted against Nguyen domination, and in 1816 the emperor Gia Long decreed that the Vietnamese must return confiscated land to the Khmers. He also forbade the Vietnamese to recruit Khmer servants, probably because he feared that they would be enslaved.[26] Nevertheless, during Gia Long's reign, the mandarin Thoai Ngoc Hau was famous for his harsh treatment of Khmers.

During the reign of Minh Mang (1820–42), the official policy became one of restoration. Convinced that Confucianism was the proper doctrine under which to organize the state and society, Minh Mang promoted the belief that Vietnamese culture was superior to those of its neighbors.[27] He ordered the mandarins to assimilate the Khmers. Implementation of *dong hoa* (assimilation) meant suppression of autonomy and Vietnamization of names and mores. As a result, from 1838 onward the Vietnamese were confronted with Khmer uprisings abetted by the Siamese. These spread into Cambodia and Mien Tay, and even into the central delta.[28] When the uprisings finally ended, the *don dien* were retained to "prevent latent troubles" instigated by the Khmers. In 1854 alone, the mandarin Nguyen Tri Phuong founded twenty-one *don dien* and a hundred villages.[29] These were placed in areas with a high density of Khmers. At the same time, in order to ensure peaceful coexistence between the two communities, Nguyen asked the newcomers to settle only on territory already inhabited by Vietnamese so that they could not be accused of usurping Khmer land.[30]

The geopolitics of these migrations help explain why in Chau-doc, Rach-gia, and Ca-mau, the Vietnamese settlements remained precarious. Though descended from agricultural people, the Vietnamese of Chau-doc remained principally fishermen and boatmen until 1902. That they did not take up land was probably due to Khmer dominance in the region. In Cambodia today, where the Vietnamese arrived more recently, a great many of the Vietnamese minority have devoted themselves to the occupations of fishing and transport. Can this not be seen as an image of the past?

The emperor Minh Mang tried to consolidate his power in the Mekong Delta through greater control over the tax system. In 1836, he appointed a commission to establish the *dia bo*, or land register. The lack of precise records had long resulted in disputes over land and levies. The emperor complained that

> Since time immemorial, cultivated lands have been registered with their area measurement given in detail [*mau, sao, thuoc, tac*]; this common rule has never changed. All the provinces of this country abide by this rule. Is there any reason why the six provinces of Nam Ky do otherwise? Is it an ancient custom? Few cultivated lands are measured; people simply describe them as "belts" or "plots."[31]

In 1836, Minh Mang sent a commission to Mien Tay to establish the *dia bo* (land register). But even as early as the nineteenth century the state found it difficult to implement its laws or persuade the populace to accept its social and political norms. Despite Minh Manh's attempts at reform, the administratively chaotic situation in Mien Tay lasted well into the French colonial period.

Later the *don dien* became the main focus of resistance to French conquest. Even after the treaty of "Peace and Friendship" was signed on 5 May 1862, the people of the *don dien* continued to fight. In Gia Dinh (in eastern Nam Bo) the war waged by the Nghia Quan (Army of the Righteous Cause) continued under the leadership of Truong Cong Dinh (whether on his own initiative or with the consent and support of the Court of Hue is not clear). Military operations spread to the center of the delta. After Truong Cong Dinh's death, Nguyen Ngoc Thang, Vo Zuy Zuong, and Doc Binh Kieu took advantage of the topography of places like the Plain of Reeds to harass French positions and communications. After King Tu Duc surrendered the delta to the French in 1867, the local insurgents still fought, retrenching in the U Minh forest, the hills of Chau-doc, and in Ha-tien. Nghia Quan fighters, sometimes numerous but not always coordinated, rose up under the banner of such heroes as Nguyen Trung Truc and Tran Van Thanh. In 1875, one of the final uprisings occurred under the leadership of Nguyen Huu Huan (Thu Khoa Huan) who raised the standard of revolt in Tan An and My-tho.[32]

A leading figure of the resistance against the French in the Mekong Delta was Tran Van Thanh. In her study of millenarianism, Hue Tam Ho Tai finds this man particularly illustrative of a cultural and political movement that emerged in the delta in 1849 and lasted throughout the French colonial period and beyond, the Buu Son Ky Huong (Strange Fragrance from the Precious Mountain). Its "millenarian world view and communitarian way of life" encompassed a tradition founded by a "mystic known as the Buddha Master of Western Peace/Phat Thay Tay An." The new faith was preached in the hills near the present-day Cambodian border. In this region of overlapping cultures, where Confucianism hardly influenced the population, the Buddha Master was receptive to an unorthodox Buddhism infused with superstition, magic, and healing practices rooted in autochthonous creeds and cults. As "an ideology of moral and cosmic integration," the Buu Son Ky Huong had relevance in a frontier society in which human relations were more tenuous than in the older settlements of northern and central Vietnam.[33] The Buddha Master retreated to the Seven Mountains of Chau-doc with his disciples, passing the time until Doomsday by contributing to land clearing and cultivation. Among his followers was a rich landowner, Tran Van Thanh, who became the master's heir. He came to lead the Dao Lanh (Religion of the Good), wearing amulets on which were printed the four ideograms *Buu, Son, Ky,* and *Huong.*

As early as 1862, Thanh participated in the resistance, fighting with Truong Cong Dinh, Vo Zuy Zuong, and Nguyen Trung Truc, and even establishing an alliance with the Khmer leader Po Kombo. In 1873, besieged by the French and their local auxiliaries in his fortified estate of Lang Linh, he was finally killed. The Dao Lanh sect continued the struggle until 1887, led by Nam Thiep, the second reincarnation of the Buddha Master of Western Peace, who allied himself with a Chinese secret society, the Thien Dia Hoi (Heaven and Earth Society), and with the Khmer monk Hien and the Khmer prince Si Votha.

From 1887 until the first decade of the twentieth century, Nam Bo remained relatively quiet despite a prophecy by Nguyen Trung Truc, uttered before his execution by the French at Rach-gia on 10 October 1868: "Unless the French uproot all the aquatic grass of Nam, there always will be Vietnamese to fight them."

Numerous Vietnamese and Khmers helped the French seize Nam Bo.[34] In the nationalist historiography they are branded as traitors. Three Vietnamese are held up for particular disdain: Huynh Cong Tan, Do Huu Phuong, and Tran Ba Loc. The first of these was the lieutenant who betrayed Truong Cong Dinh. He died at the age of thirty-seven, despised by the French officers to whom he had defected. Do Huu Phuong fought the insurgents from 1868 to 1881. He became a French citizen, traveled to France, and sent his two sons there for schooling. He is thought to have made his fortune while working as an administrator. It is known, for example, that Governor General Paul Doumer granted him 2,223 hectares of land.[35] Tran Ba Loc, born a Catholic, was "quite a praiseworthy man" in the eyes of the governor of Cochinchina. Vietnamese historian Son Nam describes him as a "very able, number one lackey."[36] Very ambitious, Loc became the best military commander conducting campaigns against the insurgents. For his services, he was appointed an administrator. Maintaining high-level connections with the French authorities, he amassed a fortune in land.[37]

CHAPTER 2

The Colonial Economy of Land, 1870-1929

ALTHOUGH NATURE ENDOWED Mien Tay with many waterways, over the centuries man has added canals. As the amphibious ecology impeded the construction of roads, canals were the only means by which people and goods could move through the region. The two major canals—connecting Ha-tien to Chau-doc and Rach-gia to Long-xuyen (thus joining the lower delta, or Bassac, to the Gulf of Siam)—were built for the transport of settlers. Their transverse routes are indicative of the aim of taking possession of the land rather than draining or irrigating it. These and smaller canals, dug by hand, were of relatively narrow gauge. Lacking upkeep, they rapidly filled with silt. The comings and goings of the tides through the network of *rach* and canals left *dos d'ane* (ridges), which led to frequent choking of the passageways and were often accompanied by the appearance of the *luc binh*, a hardy aquatic plant that impedes navigation. These early canals suited an economy in which exchanges were rudimentary and precise scheduling was not an essential factor.

Transforming the Land: Canal Construction

The exceptional economic importance of waterways did not escape the French but their initial concern with canals was primarily strategic. These were both the "arteries through which the poison of revolt circulates" and the "precious elements for the guarding and surveillance of this rich colony."[1] The French governor of Cochinchina, Admiral Duperré, named a permanent commission in 1875 to improve and complete the canal network between Saigon and the Bassac (Can-tho and Soc-trang provinces). At this time, military considerations prevailed.

Should one connect Soc-trang and Can-tho at Sa-dec by canalizing the parts of *rach* Cai Vom and *rach* Nha Man which are impassable at certain tides for the large junks? Or is it preferable to use the *rach* Tra On, Ba Ke, and Muong Thit to connect Soc-trang and Can-tho at Vinh-long and My-tho? The first is better from the commercial point of view but the Tra On way was chosen for strategic reasons.[2]

Military concerns declined in importance after Vietnamese resistance was quelled. In 1891, a cleansing canal dug on the Duperré canal proved to be an effective solution to the problem of *dos d'ane*. Though far from perfect, the procedure was practical and inexpensive.

After 1900, a new program was unveiled, and considerable sums were permanently allocated from the budget of the colony for its execution. In this second stage, both functions of the canals were prioritized: as a means of access to the area of settlement, and (through the construction of drainage channels) as a means of rendering the land arable. In 1908, three principal canals were completed in Rach-gia, Bassac–Long My, and Xa No. By 1930, linked to the arroyos, they formed a close checkerboard pattern over the whole expanse of the West, excepting the terminal triangle of the peninsula. Also in 1930, the Rach-gia–Ha-tien canal, begun in 1926, was opened. It was the last of these large works to be completed before the onset of the Great Depression and, as it turned out, the last to be constructed before the end of the colonial period. Measuring 81 kilometers in length and 3.5 meters in depth, it permitted the drainage of 220,000 hectares.

The digging and maintenance of such canals required a substantial labor force, and this was furnished by the *corvée*, a system of impressed labor. To maintain the canals, a dredger was introduced in 1884, and from the 1890s on they were commonly used, becoming a familiar silhouette on the plains of the West. Like large fish escorted by smaller, dependent ones, the dredger carried in its wake a crowd of sampans whose owners took immediate possession of the banks, unknowingly creating illegal and complicated situations. From 1883 to 1893, the works were executed by a public corporation; thereafter they were put out for bids. The first contract was awarded to the Montvenoux firm, which was succeeded in 1900 by the Société Française Industrielle d'Extreme-Orient. Its successor, in 1913, was the Société Française d'Entreprises de Dragages et de Travaux Publics, which still retained the contract in 1933. This company used more powerful equipment than had its predecessor: dredgers and appliances of extraction by suction and compression. The network of large canals was completed by the

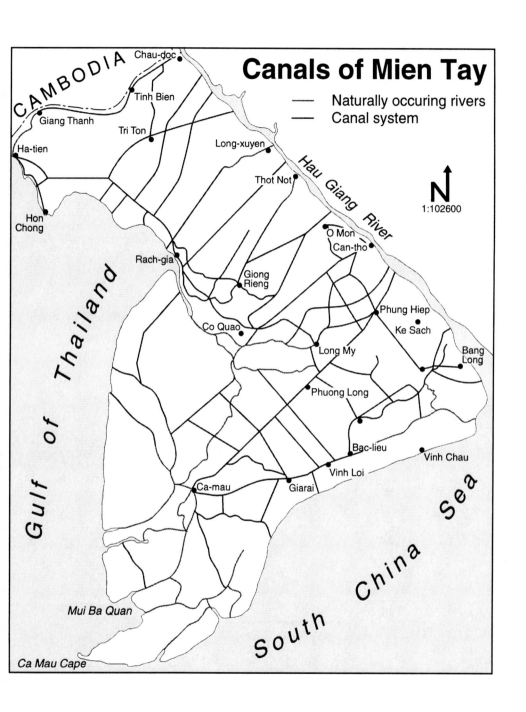

Canals of Mien Tay

Naturally occuring rivers
Canal system

N

1:102600

CAMBODIA

Chau-doc

Tinh Bien

Giang Thanh

Tri Ton

Ha-tien

Long-xuyen

Thot Not

Hau Giang River

Hon Chong

O Mon

Can-tho

Rach-gia

Giong Rieng

Phung Hiep

Ke Sach

Co Quao

Long My

Bang Long

Gulf of Thailand

Phuong Long

Bac-lieu

Vinh Chau

Vinh Loi

Ca-mau

Giarai

South China Sea

Mui Ba Quan

Ca Mau Cape

Figure 1

Amount of Dredging in Nam Bo, 1885-1924 (in cubic meters)

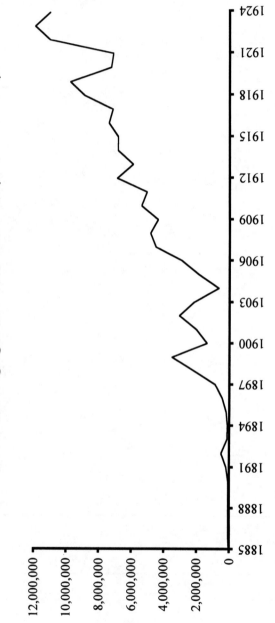

Source: P. Estebe, *Le Probleme du riz en Indochine.* n.p., 1934.

Dredging the Rach-gia to Ha-Tien Canal, c. 1930.
(Credit: Centre des Archives d'Outre-mer).

construction of small channels, dug by hand, at the expense of private individuals or the provincial budgets. Absence of coordination between the provincial undertakings engendered certain disadvantages, as different gauges between two sections often caused bottlenecks and silting.

For the whole of the West, the results of the drainage works were impressive. From 1886 to 1930, they permitted the drainage of 1,425,000 hectares of land, at the cost of around 52 million piasters. The expenses were offset by the sale of land at public auction and the revenue derived from the export of rice. The increased value of land in the colony from 1879 to 1930 was estimated to be 235 million piasters.[3] Some provinces benefited more, or later, than others. For instance, the president of the Arrondissement Council of Ha-tien, speaking in 1905 of the dredging of the important Vinh Te Canal, declared that "We only have plans, and for thirty years the canal has remained impassable in the dry season, during four or five months each year."[4] In 1908, a dredger was promised; in 1917, it still had not arrived. Perhaps this deficiency was the particular fate of the province of Ha-tien, which was something like the "poor relative" of the West. Nonetheless, the design of the network of canals reveals an inequality of development between provinces.

As the canals were dug, roads were constructed on the excavated material. To this day in the West the principal roads follow the canals. Dense in the vicinity of the lower delta and the principal population centers of Can-tho, Long-xuyen, Soc-trang, and Bac-lieu, they are scattered or nearly nonexistent in the extreme south. The hydrographic configuration requires many bridges and culverts, some of iron, others of concrete, most of wood. Unless these were rebuilt after each wet season, ferries would be the only means of crossing the canals.

The *monographie* of the province of Long-xuyen affirms that automobile transport assumed importance only after 1916.[5] The road from Long-xuyen to Can-tho, passable for vehicles and one of the first with concrete bridges, dated from 1912. Some people viewed the roads as objects of prestige, luxuries reserved for the use of the *conseillers coloniaux*, the administrators, and prominent personages conducting inspection tours at the expense of the taxpayers. Most saw them as useless, or even evil, because they blocked the drainage of floodwater from the Bassac to the Gulf of Siam. Regardless of public animosity, however, roads quickly became unalterable and indispensable. Waterways became devoted principally to the transport of freight, and roads to the traffic of travelers.

The railways experienced no such success. A rail line constructed between 1881 and 1885 linked Saigon to My-tho, and there was talk of extending it to Can-tho, Soc-trang, and Bac-lieu. Pouyanne, the engineer who directed the Public Works, had advocated in 1908 an extension of the rails to break the power of the boatmens' monopoly on rice transport. The railway line had been financed originally by raising the export duty on rice. For the My-tho to Can-tho project, it would have been necessary to reconstruct all the bridges between Tan-hiep and Can-tho, to improve access ramps for the work, and to set up a ferry on the Mekong, projects that would have cost some 19 million francs. The calculated prices of transport by rail and water favored the latter: $2.72 per ton as opposed to $3.31.[6] The Colonial Council also rejected a tram project proposed by the Compagnie Française des Tramways in 1929 since the nature of the alluvial soil would require costly reinforcing work.[7] Thus, the West never got its railroad.

Migration to the West

As for the agricultural richness of the country, it could be great and give rise to considerable commerce if population were not lacking.[8]

This observation by Rear Admiral Lagrandière, made as early as the beginning of the conquest of Cochinchina, remained valid in the West for several decades. As settlement had been recent, very dispersed, and mobile, it was not possible to obtain an exact population figure. Fiscal and military obligations compelled the Vietnamese villages to keep a register of names but these did not represent the whole population. Autonomy within the villages allowed the *notables* (village elders) to indulge in a process of internal compensation between the registered and the nonregistered, and between the living and the dead, in order to lighten the tax burden. Nor did the absence of periodic revisions favor rigorous enumeration. After the conquest, the French administration frequently reminded its provincial officials of the need to check, in as strict a manner as possible, the declarations of registered persons.

Nonetheless, in 1886 the census was only an approximate enumeration, and those that followed were of the same character. Figures were highly variable. According to *L'Annuaire de Cochinchine* of 1908, for example, the population of the West numbered 863,987. According to the archives, it numbered 951,131 (and this excluding the Chinese!).[9] In 1921, distribution of a questionnaire to each family in the countryside improved the statistics. However, we must consider that these newer data furnish us only with an order of magnitude.[10] We do know that the population of the Transbassac, or Mien Tay, regularly increased due to new settlements. But what proportion of the increase resulted from natural growth and what proportion from immigration? The statistics are silent in the matter of births and deaths, though both rates seem to be high, and the excess of births considerable, if one extrapolates from the general trends in Asian delta populations. The administrator of Rach-gia spoke of a "remarkable local birth rate" in his report of 1914. In addition, internal migration was incessant, as the eastern and central provinces of Cochinchina witnessed the departure of tenant farmers and wage earners pushed by the need to find a means of making money or attracted by the prospect of becoming landowners.[11] As occupation and development increased in the older provinces of the West, inhabitants left them for the undeveloped provinces furthest east: Rach-gia, Bac-lieu, and Ca-mau. Undoubtedly, this is the reason for a decrease in the population recorded in Can-tho, Long-xuyen, and Soc-trang provinces between 1901 and 1910. Rach-gia, on the other hand, experienced an increase of 36,177 inhabitants.[12]

Consultation of lists of agricultural *engagés* (indentured laborers) kept in the province of Rach-gia permits one to determine the origins of most. The settler Do Huu Phuong, for example, employed 24 workers in 1913. Six were born within the province, 7 were from Can-tho, 5 from Long-xuyen, 3 from Vinh-long, 1 from Soc-trang, 1 from Chau-doc, and 1 from My-tho. In 1915, M. Fautier, a settler at Vinh Loi, employed 2 workers out of 151 from within the province. All the others came from elsewhere, the majority from Soc-trang, Can-tho, Long-xuyen, Sa-dec, My-tho, Vinh-long, and Tra-vinh. Similar findings are corroborated in the records of settlers in Rach-gia and Bac-lieu in 1919.[13] Other records show that from July 1928 to June 1929, 5,123 Vietnamese entered Bac-lieu Province and 2,149 left it, a further indication of the mobility of the population. Agricultural work engendered seasonal displacements from the rest of Cochinchina to the West and from the "old" provinces to the pioneer front. A seasonal laborer frequently remained in Mien Tay without settling in one spot, usually pursuing, and often for a long time, his quest for virgin land.

Did demographic evolution consolidate or reduce the ethnic diversity of the inhabitants of the West? Considering the three most numerous groups, ethnic composition over time is illustrated in Table 1. It will be noticed that the size of the two principal population groups, the Vietnamese and the Khmers, increased at nearly the same rate. But the Vietnamese reinforced their initial lead and remained in the majority. Analysis of the ethnic composition of specific provinces is more instructive. In 1886, at Soc-trang, for instance, the number of Khmers was nearly equal to the number of Vietnamese (20,161 and 23,327, respectively). At Rach-gia there were 8,850 Vietnamese, as opposed to 10,350 Cambodians, but as early as the end of the nineteenth century the Vietnamese surpassed their neighbors. In 1901, there were 25,892 Vietnamese as opposed to 21,225 Cambodians at Rach-gia, as well as 87,749 Vietnamese and 48,689 Khmers at Soc-trang.[14] Thus, the gap was accentuated between the two communities. Without resorting to the doubtful lyricism of one author who was convinced that "the future is for the Annamite spermatazoon, more virile and more enduring, more hardy, more ardent,"[15] we can conclude that the settlement of the West was principally due to the demographic dynamism of the Vietnamese.

Inequality of distribution is another feature of the demography of Mien Tay. In Table 2, the opposition between the "old" provinces of Can-tho, Long-xuyen, Soc-trang, and Chau-doc and the "frontier" provinces of Bac-lieu and Rach-gia is emphasized. Within the provinces, the contrast is especially clear in Bac-lieu where the lowest density occurs in the district of Ca-mau. Generally, the canals, the *rach*, and the immediate environs of the villages and towns attracted and retained people while the large swampy lowlands and the zones of large estates had sparser populations. The province of

TABLE 1: Ethnic Composition of Western Cochinchina

	1886	1908	1928
Total population	390,803	952,214	1,450,064
Vietnamese	307,052	655,135	1,131,456
Khmers (Cambodians)	68,706	150,770	224,452
Chinese	12,675	17,802	43,778

Sources: *L'Annuaire de Cochinchine* and *L'Annuaire Général de l'Indochine* for each year cited.

TABLE 2: Population Density of Mien Tay (persons per sq. kilometer)

Province	Mean	Maximum	Minimum
Can-tho	159	325	59
Long-xuyen	75	278	27
Soc-trang	72	234	39
Chau-doc	71	168	23
Rach-gia	43	68	24
Bac-lieu	25	234	9
Ha-tien	11	60	5

Source: Henry and Devismes, *Documents de démographie.*

Ha-tien, once renowned for its prosperity, was by this time reduced to a backwardness from which it never recovered.

The problem of the availability of labor was linked to the relative demographic weakness of the West and to the variable densities of settlement. Labor was scarce for a long time in Mien Tay, and the farther one penetrated into the southwest the more the scarcity increased. Climatic accidents, the abuses of employers, and worker mobility contributed to an unstable and poorly developed labor market. Tenant farmers as well as day laborers frequently fled, taking with them salary advances or even the harvest. They concealed themselves easily and were able to change identity thanks to a surplus of registration cards sold by the *notables*. Often obliging landowners took in the fugitives, if only to maintain them in a condition close to bondage and profit from their labor.

If we can believe the account of an administrator of Bac-lieu, the administration was well aware of the *notables'* deception.

> I remind you that it is expressly forbidden for settlers and planters to employ on their property individuals devoid of identity papers or in an irregular situation vis-à-vis the military authority. In spite of this express condition stated again by the memorandum of 1917, there have been many contraventions brought to light through the years.[16]

The workers, treated as bonded laborers, possessed no recourse other than the ability to escape. In response, some colonists recruited their work force in the east. In 1899, M. Guery arrived in the province of Can-tho, where he obtained a concession of five thousand hectares. He was accompanied by two hundred coolies from Hanh Thong Thay, near Saigon, where he already possessed a plantation. Hardly had they arrived before the coolies either succumbed to disease—thirteen died from cholera—or fled with the money advanced to them. One escaped with an advance of thirty or forty piasters and the wife of another coolie "who did not want to work any longer because, he said, he wanted to recover his wife."[17] Finally, all the men were dismissed without being obliged to repay their advances, a total of 4,000 piasters. Other colonists suffered similar disappointments.

The government made feeble attempts to improve relations between the colonists and their workers. In 1907, an Official Service of Colonization was created in the chief town of Can-tho Province to recruit labor, look after contracts, and settle disputes. Though the service was soon discontinued, nothing in the records reveals the reason for its failure, a fact that confirms to some extent the artificial and insignificant character of these administrative agencies.

In the first years following conquest, the French administration was preoccupied with the task of developing a sufficient labor force to build roads, bridges, and canals. Recourse was had to the *corvée* as it was employed traditionally in Vietnam. *Corvée* rapidly became "the most unpopular and heaviest tax."[18] It was abolished in 1881, perhaps due as much to its unpopularity as to the administration's fear that the gathering together of large groups of laborers would create conditions favorable to political agitation.[19] Over the next twenty years the government experimented with a variety of forced-labor schemes. A decree of October 1897 required that villagers work thirty days per year. For some this was obligatory; for others the obligation could be fulfilled with a cash payment. Another decree promulgated only nine months later abrogated the required service and established a single monetary tax intended to replace both the poll tax and the *corvée*. In 1901, the tax was abolished and labor was again requisitioned, a move apparently prompted by the expansion of large public works projects and the persistent lack of labor. The administration demanded that the village *notables* assist in the recruitment of workers. Labor was remunerated, in contrast to the *corvée* system, but the wage was fixed at a meager 25 centimes per day. Workers also had to remain on the job until the completion of the project. In 1904, Alfred Schreiner, writing in the *Courrier Saigonnais*, explained how this new method of recruitment functioned.

> We saw at Soc-trang, a few years ago, an ignoble thing. In order to complete a road or a canal, the administration, which could no longer find laborers—they were in the middle of their work in the paddy fields—encircled the market and the neighboring roads each day with the militia men who, always valiant, made their haul of all the villagers who came to the market for one reason or another and sent them to the construction site.[20]

In the 1930s, the administration substituted penal labor for required service. Officially, labor requisition was abolished in Cochinchina by a decree of 11 May 1933.

The colonial government also experimented with labor recruited from outside Vietnam. A session of the Chamber of Agriculture of Cochinchina in 1901 passed a resolution that all measures should be taken "to expedite the immigration of labor into Cochinchina." In 1906, a number of Javanese workers were imported with some success (45 percent of the first group and 85 percent of the second renewed their contracts) and the practice was continued. After World War I, however, the Dutch placed restrictions on the emigration of Javanese workers. At the same time, the French began to realize that Javanese workers cost more than Vietnamese laborers since their religious requirements posed problems in feeding them.[21] Thereafter their numbers remained limited to a few dozen employed on the isle of Phu Quoc.

In 1907, the governor of Cochinchina, Bonhoure, ordered M. Outrey, inspector of the civil services for the provinces of the West, to investigate means of attracting Tonkinese laborers. The project was submitted to the Consultative Chamber of Tonkin, although it was not pursued. The rare experiments with Tonkinese labor that did occur were not encouraging, and the disappointments were sufficient for the *Tribune Indochinoise* in 1927 to counsel Vietnamese landowners not to employ "Tonkinese recalcitrants."[22] In fact, the French had a marked preference for Chinese workers whose productivity and docility, the latter resulting from the risk of expulsion, were much appreciated. But they could not be obtained in sufficient numbers to solve the labor problem.

As these failures became evident, the colonial administration began to take measures to encourage the growth of a local labor force. In 1886, Governor Rousseau took a decision, detailed much later by the decree of 13 April 1909, concerning Annamite or Chinese *engagés* working on European farms. This decision regulated for the first time the recruitment of labor in Cochinchina. It exempted the *engagés* from all types of taxes and *corvées*. The *sojourn*, or identity card, was replaced by the card of the agricultural *engagé*. Pink in color, annual (and then quinquennial after 1921), this card released laborers from the requirement of communal service. The *engagiste* (employer) paid $1 for each card, much less than the village poll tax, which then could be as much as $6. As the relative benefit to the villagers was considerable, it certainly facilitated their recruitment by the French colonists. Furthermore, during these years the term *engagé* was applied to all workers, whatever their form of contract or mode of remuneration.

The *engagé* often seemed privileged in the eyes of others. In reality he paid dearly for his exemption from taxes. He could not move about freely unless his pink card was stamped each month by the *engagiste* (failing this he could be incarcerated). Many employers did not hesitate to exploit the situation. Some, having one hundred *engagés* would ask for only fifty cards, making themselves a profit while retaining half their workers as virtual prisoners. Others refused to give cards to *engagés* desirous of leaving a concession, so great was the fear of losing a coolie. The administration more or less tolerated these practices, considering that the colonists in this way possessed a guarantee.[23] In other cases, managers of concessions rented *engagé* cards to individuals who had not paid their taxes or freed themselves from required service.

Despite such hindrances, the number of *engagés* who fled were many, and they usually took their advances with them. Although the colonists complained bitterly, and called for penal sanctions, apprehended *engagés* were customarily treated as "natives lacking their poll tax cards for the current year." As for punishment for leaving with their advances, it was determined that "only the court is competent [to decide]."[24] In the remote and still unorganized provinces of the West, recourse to the law courts was too long and costly a process for the colonist to undertake.

As the years passed, the system of *engagés* became an awkward anomaly. Large, non-European landowners did not derive equal advantages from it, and the administration lost tax revenue when the number of tenant-farming contracts with European colonists increased. In 1927, the governor of Cochinchina asked the Colonial Council to rule that the term *engagé* would only apply to a salaried worker, thus excluding the *ta dien*, or tenants, who constituted the majority of the rural labor force of the West.

Land Legislation in Theory and Practice

In old Vietnam the customs in matters of granting land to settlers were simple: the *Gia-Dinh Thanh Thong-Chi* related in 1780 that

> The new settlers were allowed freedom of travel and to work the land where it was most convenient for them. The people thus had complete freedom to clear what seemed good for them and to set up their dwellings and new rice lands, by founding their villages at the spot chosen by themselves. . . . [Once] the plots of land were chosen, it was sufficient to express the desire of it to the mandarin to become a landowner. The land was not measured off when it was granted. One only took notice of whether it was of a good or bad sort.[25]

In the following century the emperors Gia Long and Minh Mang revised the system of land proclamations to account for changes that had already occurred, to augment their fiscal and military resources, and to initiate their work of imperial restoration. The principles, however, remained the same until the arrival of the French. It was work accomplished and payment of the land tax that justified land ownership. Although the emperor retained ultimate ownership of the soil, the imperial government only intervened in cases of nonpayment of taxes or of escheat.

Land ownership was recorded in the *dia bo* (land register) in which the area and limits of each plot were specified. The information was often incorrect due to lack of precision and the *notables*' practice of recording less than the actual area in order to reduce the amount of land tax due. The *dia bo* was not revised regularly nor was it often checked by the state. In Nam Bo the land was vast, and in matters of trade, loans, and land ownership the villages were left to regulate themselves. In these cases, village custom took precedence over imperial law.

As soon as the French began to occupy the eastern provinces of "Lower Cochinchina," the admiral-governors were confronted with land questions.

After the taking of Saigon in 1859, Admiral Bonnard applied the principles of French law, in which the state acquires by right of conquest not only sovereignty but ownership of all land not occupied by the indigenous population. Thus, when Bonnard took the place of the emperor of Annam, he also succeeded to ultimate ownership of the soil. The principle of accession to immovable property also was proclaimed for all: the French, other foreigners, and natives alike. In order to halt the considerable flow of emigration toward the as yet unconquered provinces, Admiral Lagrandière issued a decree, on 22 June 1863, that gave old landowners two months in which to lay claim to their abandoned property, under pain of confiscation. When it took the place of traditional authority, the French administration invented, to its own benefit, a policy of land concessions. The policy had two aims. Politically it was intended to settle the majority of the population on the land, and thereby create a secure social order based on small proprietors. Fiscally it was meant to expand agriculture as a means of swelling the tax base. As France desired that the colony should "pay for itself," the administration was intent upon raising enough tax revenue to balance the budget.

The development of land legislation can be divided into three periods. From 1864 to 1882, the domanial lands were either sold or given away as rewards for services rendered to the state. After 1882, the administration (by a decree of 22 August 1882) granted land according to a simple procedure. The administrator of a province (for areas of less than twenty hectares) or the Colonial Council (for areas greater than twenty hectares) decided how much land would be given to whom. In the absence of precise measurements, maps, and titles, however, the system was often arbitrary. The expense and perils of registering land also tended to discourage a claimant from having his concession recorded in the *dia bo*. While the concessions policy favored settlement up to 1914, it also encouraged speculation. Entire grants, sometimes immense, remained unimproved because the claimants either lacked the financial means to exploit them or had abandoned them for other reasons. These areas were often taken over by squatters whose intrusion caused many disputes. The administration tried to encourage development of the land by enacting a variety of laws. One protected the first occupants against land-grabbing (decree of 15 October 1890) while another allowed the concessionaire two years of tax-free status (decree of 4 January 1894).

The third phase began when Governor General A. Sarraut abrogated all previous provisions with the decree of 27 December 1913. Preference was given now to the sale of large plots to the highest bidder. Domanial lands of an area less than or equal to fifty hectares still were to be granted gratuitously but plots exceeding fifty hectares would be sold at public auction.[26] This new policy sparked numerous protests. In 1917, for example, the Syndicat Agricole expressed the preference that gratuitous concessions should not be limited to fifty hectares.[27] M. Le Bret, administrator for Long-xuyen Province, declared in a welcoming address to Governor Sarraut in 1918 that

> If the small landowner is to be encouraged, the large landowner must not be disregarded; he alone is capable of audacious initiatives. . . . That is why from all sides you are asked to return to the old system of gratuitous concessions of large expanses.[28]

Discontent with the new policy must have had some effect, since the 1913 decree was modified several times. Decrees of 26 November 1918 and 19 December 1926 allowed the administration of Cochinchina to grant free of charge areas of less than three hundred hectares.

The decisions taken between 1913 and 1928 swung back and forth between the administration's desire to maintain social stability (by encouraging small landowners) and the colonists' interest in obtaining gratuitous concessions of unlimited size. The authorities by no means wished to abolish large concessions but the numerous problems of determining their policies led to the desire to restrict them. In a decree of 11 November 1918, the government established a program meant to encourage colonization in each country of the Indochinese Union. The administration would clearly delineate areas open to colonization and areas to be reserved for the indigenous population. At the same time, as demonstrated in the administrative memorandums of Blanchard de la Brosse (dated 31 January and 13 July 1927), the government continued its attempt to encourage small settlers.

The liberality of this new policy favored the largest French concessionaires, a circumstance that requires some explanation. In the first three decades of French domination there were many advocates of settling French citizens en masse in the Cochinchinese West. Some even envisioned Mien Tay as an exclusive zone of French settlement. In a brochure entitled "Call to Colonization," P. d'Enjoy contended that the territories of the West would "yield an unlimited field to our investigations." [29] M. Paris, presiding over the Cochinchinese Chamber of Agriculture, was just as explicit in his inaugural speech.[30] In his opinion Cochinchina was destined to become a French settlement colony since the Annamite excelled at neither rice cultivation nor cash cropping.

European colonization had its adversaries, however, and these were not lacking persuasive arguments. "The true settler is the Annamite," declared A. Schreiner. The French concessionaires were destined to be, in his opinion, absentee functionaries or missionaries. Their needs for labor would be met either by the imposition of a *corvée* or an increase in wage rates.[31] Others noted that French colonists were slow to pay their taxes. In Long-xuyen Province alone, only twelve out of fifty French landowners were resident in 1929. Since their precise addresses were not known, the local administration complained that often it was necessary to search them out and make them pay. Nor did the Vietnamese look favorably upon the arrival of French settlers. Even when the colonists did not take possession of land already cultivated, they were considered intruders who disturbed such village customs as allowing water buffalo to graze freely and gathering wood on undeveloped land. Concessions granted to colonists usually were taken from the village's pool of undeveloped land, and, though it might be uncultivated at the time, excess land was needed to absorb growth in the village population. Thus, the colonists in effect were stealing from the village's future. An illustrative incident occurred in 1902 in the province of Can-tho. A surveyor, M. Sammarcelli, had obtained in 1896 a concession of three hundred hectares that he was unable to occupy himself (see appendix 2). On 19 August 1902, the lieutenant governor informed Sammarcelli that seventy-four hectares of his concession had been cultivated by villagers. The latter had occupied the land for three years and registered it on the village *dien bo*. The Cochinchinese Chamber of Agriculture was indignant at the "license that the village has taken."[32] This incident highlights not only the antagonism between French colonists and their Vietnamese neighbors but also the differing points of view with regard to custom and legislation. For the Vietnamese it was labor that conferred ownership. M. Paris, however fervent a partisan of French settlement, acknowledged the responsibilities of the colonists in conflicts with the Vietnamese, be they neighbors or laborers.

> The administration must ensure that the colonists behave equitably
> toward the natives who work for them. Some of them have a very pro-
> nounced tendency to believe that their race suffices to give them authority
> over the natives; they maltreat the latter, fulfill their obligations badly, or
> indeed take the law into their own hands. . . . The Annamites have been
> done violence and roughly handled so often by certain colonists that they
> are frightened when one asks them for any *corvée* whatsoever.[33]

Diverse phrases expressed the opinion of the villagers. When a colonist was known for violence, he received the sobriquet *thang cop* (tiger). When he forced changes in custom, he was called *pha lang* (that which upsets the village). The Vietnamese opposed, as best they could, the incursions of the French. Sometimes, in order to cause the request for a concession to be rejected, the villagers would simulate occupation of the land. Laborers imported by a colonist often slipped away with their advances, finding refuge in villages where the complicity of the *notables* allowed them to change their identities. Later, in the 1920s, the interests of certain land societies in the West aroused the opposition of the Vietnamese. Even the *Tribune Indochinoise*, the voice of the large landowners, raised a vigorous protest when the Société Indochinoise du Commerce et de la Finance, located in Paris, attempted to acquire thirty thousand hectares in the province of Rach-gia.[34]

In the end, the settling of Europeans in the West was gradual. Although the granting of concessions dated from about the year 1890, only the founding in 1897 of the Chamber of Agriculture of Cochinchina provided official recognition of their existence. This body, which was in fact an assembly of the French rice growers of the West, gave a boost to colonization. At the beginning of the twentieth century, rubber-tree plantations in Cochinchina mobilized European capital and energy. And, at the end of World War I, rice culture experienced a revival of interest among the French, a trend that continued until the economic depression of the 1930s.

The French concessionaires were recruited from diverse professional backgrounds and their numbers varied according to province. Civil servants were numerous. The electoral list for the Chamber of Agriculture of Cochinchina for 1901 included sixty-eight concessionaires for the West. Of these, thirty-seven were civil servants. For the rest, there were thirteen clergymen, four lawyers, two surveyors, two "managers," two employees of the Messageries Fluviales, one pensioner, one wholesaler, one contractor, one business agent, and only four settler-planters. The list for 1913 carries the names of eighty-two active civil servants, six pensioners, twenty-four clergymen, and five civil surveyors.[35] In 1907, the *Courrier Saigonnais* published the official figures by province (table 3).[36]

Numerous employees of the administration dreamed of possessing an estate, sometimes to operate themselves or to save for their retirement, more frequently for the rent they might derive from it. Concessions policy, especially in its early phase, was particularly favorable to the intense desire of certain Frenchmen to become landowners. As early as 1894, the question of

TABLE 3: Civil Servant and Non–Civil Servant Concessionaires in Western Cochinchina, 1907

Province	Non-civil servants	Civil servants	Number of missionaries included in non-civil servants
Can-tho	25	13	0
Rach-gia	23	9	11
Chau-doc	11	4	8
Long-xuyen	21	6	0
Soc-trang	6	3	0
Bac-lieu	7	1	4
Ha-tien	3	0	0

Source: *Courrier Saigonnais,* 27 April 1907. No source was provided in the newspaper for these data.

whether to grant land to civil servants was debated in the Colonial Council.[36] Subsequently the matter was taken up by Lieutenant Governor Rodier in a letter to the minister of the colonies. Rodier declared himself in support of reducing the size of concessions to civil servants. They were already favored, he believed, by a regular salary and the prestige of office. If they wanted to own land they could easily borrow money and recruit labor.[37] In spite of the resistance of the Colonial Council, Rodier limited such concessions to three hundred hectares. At the assembly of the Comité du Syndicat of the European plantation owners of Cochinchina in 1900, M. Paris deplored the decision of an administrative department not to allow its employees to engage in agriculture, viewing it as an obstacle to the colonization movement.

> The sentence for the civil servant [is] to stagnate at the café during his leisure, when he is prevented from being usefully occupied. It is the ruin of the civil servants who, previously trusting in the words and the encouragements given, risked themselves in agricultural undertakings.[38]

Apparently his fears were exaggerated, for the measures taken were not retroactive and a number of memoranda show that they were not strictly applied.[39]

TABLE 4: Number and Area of Farms in Mien Tay, 1929
(by province and type of settlement)

Province	European settlement		Asian settlement	
	No. of farms	Area (in ha.)	No. of farms	Area (in ha.)
Bac-lieu	440	21,171	47,783	350,000
Can-tho	261	unknown	39,728	195,236
Chau-doc	183	6,917	21,356	97,853
Ha-tien	8	5,185	5,374	9,036
Long-xuyen	244	29,601	35,053	177,326
Rach-gia	969	61,203	34,843	342,030
Soc-trang	442	22,928	33,241	190,720
Total	2,547	147,005	217,378	1,362,201

Source: *Bulletin de l'Agence Economique*, 1928.

The acquisition of numerous properties by Catholic missions provoked a reaction from the anticlerical French faction in Cochinchina, and from the Vietnamese, who mistrusted their encroachments. Although in principle the Société des Missions Étrangères of Paris had the right to possess real estate, until 1939 that right was not officially extended to the apostolic vicariate of Phnom Penh to which the majority of the provinces of the Transbassac belonged.[40] For this reason the early concessions were granted officially in the names of priests and prelates. Many missionaries possessed extensive tracts. In Long-xuyen Province alone they controlled half of the twelve thousand hectares of rice land owned by the French.[41] According to the authors of one petition, the missionaries also pressured their converts to leave their properties to the Church.[42]

What was the extent of French colonization? The majority of sources, most notably the documents of the Colonial Council, tempt one to overestimate the importance of concessions, for it was a matter of continual dispute. The actual figures indicate that concessions to Europeans were of relatively minor significance. In 1926, for example, of 430,141 hectares requested in concession, only 74,547 were requested by Europeans. Robequain advances the figure of 100,000 hectares for 1931.[43] But, even though the total amount of land owned by the French was small, it consisted of some of the largest rice tracts in Indochina and the individual concessionaires were powerful men. In 1918, in Bac-lieu Province, there were 55 French farms comprising 26,947 hectares, of which 14,767 hectares were under cultivation, utilizing the services of 5,300 *engagés*. In 1919, in Long-xuyen Province, 2,100 *engagés* were employed by the French on 13,228 hectares.[44] On the eve of the depression in 1929 the *Bulletin de l'Agence Economique* published statistics that show a mean of 117 hectares per European farm and 6 hectares per native farm (table 4).[45]

Measuring the Land

If any land policy was to be successful, a cadastral survey and a reliable land register would be crucial. The French authorities considered both the *dia bo* (land register) and the *dien bo* (village rice-land register) to be incomplete and inaccurate but initially they were unable to replace the system. From the 1880s onward, a desire not to upset indigenous customs combined with the numerous requests for concessions and incessant land-grabbing forced the administration to operate according to the *dia bo*.[46] It recognized that the land already registered in the *dien bo* authorized cultivation by villagers. Officials attempted to ensure that these cultivators would retain possession of land they had already cleared.

When a claimant received a concession, he had two years in which to survey and register it at his own expense. This procedure was only possible, however, in the neighborhood of towns and near Saigon. In the interior the scarcity of agents appointed to this task prevented most concessions from being measured. For small claimants the cost of a cadastral survey was high, all the more so since their parcels usually were scattered. According to Boudillon, who was charged with presenting a plan for land reform in 1924, the high cost of surveying hindered land measurement, and by 1911 most provinces were not even close to having been surveyed completely. In Soc-trang only five villages had managed to measure its plots. In Can-tho it was seven villages and in Ha-tien only two. Boudillon cites no instances of surveying in Bac-lieu, Rach-gia, or Long-xuyen. In 1927, in the *arrondissement* of Ca-mau, there still were 300,000 unmeasured hectares and Governor Blanchard de la Brosse estimated that the survey would take six or more years to complete.[47] Out of sixty villages in the province of Rach-gia, only fifteen or twenty had their land registered in the *dia bo*.[48]

The work of surveying village plots was allocated to private firms that carried out their duties unsystematically and sluggishly. Soc-trang Province was surveyed in 1916, Can-tho in 1929, Bac-lieu in 1929, and the southwest part of Rach-gia in 1927–30. The administration created boundary commissions,[49] each composed of a surveyor, his assistant, and three village *notables*. It used general triangulation to survey individual plots, recording the names of the occupants, their land titles, the amount held, and the current state of cultivation. Reports were examined by an administrative commission composed of the boundary commission itself, presided over by the deputy of the chief administrator of the province. The work sometimes lasted three years. Many situations proved to be indecipherable because the *dia bo* had not been examined for such a long time. Commissions would convene in the communal house of each village, not even visiting the plots, a practice that only reinforced the power of the *notables*. Sometimes the commissions sat without the knowledge of the cultivators because the *notables* did not give the survey the necessary publicity. Many peasants, either illiterate or living at some distance from the communal house, were unaware of their right to attend.[50]

It was always possible to resort to French law in order to gain ownership of a piece of land. Unfortunately, the requisite administrative procedures and travel were to ordinary rice growers irksome encumbrances involving the loss of too much time. If they attempted to work through an intermediary, they risked being swindled. In this domain, French law served the designs of those who were knowledgeable or cunning. In the most remote zones, on the frontier of the provinces of Rach-gia, Ca-mau, and Bac-lieu, and in provinces in which the thrust of Vietnamese migration had more or less disorganized the Khmer communities, possession of the soil became the subject of fierce rivalries.

The absence of impartial registers led to chronic delays in the settlement of land matters. Even by the 1920s, the administration had not succeeded in concluding its business. The *conseiller colonial* Le Quang Liem recalled that in Rach-gia in 1925, "when I had taken up my office there as administrative delegate I found several thousand requests for concessions pending."[51] In response the administration abandoned much of its responsibility to the *notables* who registered the land in the *dia bo* in any manner they pleased. In 1917, the *Courrier de l'Ouest* reproduced a letter from the agricultural society of the southwest to the administrator of Bac-lieu and the director of the cadastral survey requesting restoration of the provincial *dia bo*, especially that of the village of Hoa Binh. In copying the titles of concession onto the land register the boundaries had been deliberately changed. Thus, "a parcel of one hectare becomes a parcel of around twenty-five hectares."[52] Widespread incompetence and corruption resulted in boundary disputes, legal proceedings, and sometimes even in bloody clashes. A. Schreiner, who was a land surveyor in the West, recorded his observations.

> I write these lines this evening, November 11, 1894, at the village of
> Phu Duc (district of Soc-trang) where I am working. This locality is
> cultivated on its entire expanse: not an inch of usable land is not plant-
> ed with rice. . . . In fact, these people have no property title other than
> the registration on the *bo* and that is erroneous in most of the cases; the
> areas are too small. Also, since it is impossible for the men to foresee the
> provisions of the administration concerning the excess, above all
> because the rumor is widespread that land is being sold, they remain in
> cautious reserve, doing absolutely nothing, and rather than run the risk
> of working for a neighbor, they prefer to run the risk of losing the har-
> vest; absurd calculation but it is the manifest result of our legislation or
> better to say of our lack of legislation.[53]

He cites a flagrant case of the precariousness of land ownership.

> The third of November 1891, Tran Keo, a Cambodian living in the vil-
> lage of Phu Duc (Soc-trang) obtains a receipt against deposit of a
> request for a concession of 8 hectares. Cultivation takes place soon after.
> In 1894, the lack of water and the monsoon cause the harvest to fail.
> The occupant, short of rice and money, incapable of repaying the
> advances which had been made to him on the security of his harvest,
> pressed perhaps by older creditors, sells his parcel. When his transaction
> is presented at the office of the *inspection* it is declared invalid, the
> receipt of the request for concession is torn up and the clearer of the
> land—crossed off the register of requests—is simply shown the door
> (February 4, 1895). So with one stroke of the pen the surplus value of
> the soil from three years of work is confiscated, and everything that he
> has incorporated in the rice land is taken from him.[54]

Under the system introduced by the French, peasants retained only
that which was Vietnamese, traditional, and familiar to them. One can
imagine that a simple authorization of cultivation or a receipt for the
request of a concession clothed in official markings took on, in their eyes,
the value of permanent titles. Many settlers were ignorant of the domanial
legislation and cultivated land alongside the canals and rivers only to discover later that it had been auctioned off by the administration. The digging of
canals increased the value of riverside land. In order to profit from this, the

administration prohibited concession of the land, auctioning it instead in lots of fifty to one hundred hectares. In most cases, the buyers would then enter into conflict with the first occupants, who had developed the land. These disputes sometimes lasted for two or three years.

The administration, aware of the weaknesses of the system, made a number of efforts to reform it. In 1901, the higher authorities of Cochinchina reminded officials that they must be present at inquiries into disputes between Europeans or between Europeans and natives. Two years later, in a move designed to obviate reliance on the discretion of the *notables*, the administration directed the provincial commissions (composed of the chief of the province or his assistant, and three indigenous *notables*, including the chief of the canton) to examine requests for concessions by first determining the true status of the land in question. Before publicly announcing a request, the commission was to summon the claimant and the neighboring owners to resolve potential disputes beforehand.[55]

The rights of the first occupants were recognized formally by a decree (article 35 of the decree of 11 November 1924) that required the recipient of a concession to compensate them. Doubtless the first settlers cared more for the soil than for foreign juridical forms and would have preferred retaining the land to receiving a pecuniary indemnity. Cases of settlers' land being conceded to someone else and of settlers cultivating unclaimed concessions were frequent. Some of the most flagrant cases became very well known. In one, M. Vassal, a surveyor working in the border area between Bac-lieu and Rach-gia, carved out a superb estate of eight hundred hectares of rice land originally cleared by fifteen Cambodians. He then conceded ownership to one Minh Huong. When the dispute came before the Colonial Council it was settled in favor of the latter. The version of this story, published by the *Voix Annamite*, was never refuted.[56]

The Cochinchinese press reported another incident on 17 June 1927. On the occasion of the nomination of a new administrator for the province of Rach-gia, more than one hundred people had brought charges against Ha My Bao, chief of the canton of Thanh Bien, for land-grabbing and abuses of power. This man of mixed Chinese-Cambodian parentage had ordered a canal dug by small cultivators and then refused to pay them for the work. Next he tricked them out of the newly valuable land by sending confidential agents to the Cambodian and Vietnamese peasants declaring that their parcels must be restored to the government. Promising to defend their cause, the messengers confiscated the peasants' provisional titles of occupation, and the cultivators found themselves dispossessed. Although the results of an inquiry into the charges were never made public, apart from the fact that there was never a denial of the facts of the dispossessions, the information reported by the press implies that a fierce struggle between two bands of land-grabbers was underway. On one side was the faction composed of Le Quang Liem (the *conseiller colonial*) and the *huyen* Huy and their henchmen; on the other was that of Ha My Bao and his acolytes.[57]

Revolts of the Dispossessed

The years 1927 and 1928 witnessed an economic "boom" in the Cochinchinese West. They also saw bloody agrarian revolts erupt in two villages, Ninh Thanh Loi (in Rach-gia Province) and Phong Thanh (in Bac-lieu). The uprisings reveal much about village-level conflicts over land ownership.

On 6 May 1927, a band of Cambodians led by a Chinese-Cambodian, the *huong chu* (village vice-chairman) of Ninh Thanh Loi, seized the communal house, killed the father of the *xa truong*, and burned the tax register. In the three days preceding this act, the Khmers had been conducting religious ceremonies with the aid of a sorcerer. The sorcerer, who had demonstrated his supernatural powers by healing sick children, announced that the Celestial Emperor had designated the *huong chu's* brother-in-law as a new general and king. After the attack on the communal house, the administrator of the province ordered troops under the command of a French gendarme named Turcot to suppress the revolt. Although this force was driven back, and had to await reinforcements from Can-tho, the rebellion was finally overcome. The authorities initially interpreted the uprising as a paroxysm of Khmer religious fanaticism directed against the French. But when it was learned that one M. Emery, the overseer of a neighboring estate, had spoken with the rebels and had not been assaulted, this thesis seemed less plausible. During the subsequent legal proceedings in Can-tho, the provincial administrator, the gendarme, and a police inspector contended that it was actually a political rebellion.[58] According to the former administrator of Rach-gia, M. Lalaurette, who was sent by the governor to investigate, Khmer monks insisted that the uprising was not anti-French. Rather they complained of "the Khmers' decline and the lack of guarantees of their land ownership." Lalaurette's conclusion regarding the revolt—that it was an agrarian conflict overlaid with ethnic resentment—is probably accurate. In response to a question about the *huong chu's* properties, he stated that "The matter is critical because the delineation of lands in Rach-gia has not yet been achieved."[59]

Thus, the primary action of the rebels, the destruction of the village archives, can been seen as a protest against the actual land repartition. It is significant that the offending *huong chu*, who officially owned eighty hectares, strung a boundary line with a magic cotton thread around a full three hundred hectares. Testimony during the trial also revealed that a Vietnamese canton chief (*cai tong*) had bought land from Khmers who were settled on it with the right of "*premiers occupants.*" Another mandarin acknowledged that Khmers had borrowed money at a 200-percent rate of interest, adding that during a six-year period usury had dispossessed the Khmers of 1,500 of the 4,000 hectares they owned.[60]

The memory of this affair had not yet dimmed when a pitched battle broke out in Bac-lieu. On 16 February 1928, militiamen under the command of a gendarme named Fournier presented themselves at the property of Le Van Toai and his brothers in order to seize the harvest. The cultivators, who had been keeping watch on the threshing floor, fiercely opposed the seizure. In the ensuing battle the gendarme and three peasants were killed and two peasants were wounded. Most newspapers devoted only a few lines to the incident, portraying it as either an affair of banditry or a harvest quarrel. But the *Tribune Indochinoise* rushed a reporter, Le Trung Nghia, to the village. He concluded that the fight had been the climax of a decade-long dispute over land.

According to the published account, the Le Van Toai family had been established for twenty years in the *délégation* of Gia Rai. When the original settler died in 1908, he bequeathed to his children the 3 or 4 hectares he had managed to clear. Within two years, the eldest, Le Van Toai, and two brothers had cleared 20 hectares, which they were granted as a permanent concession. In 1912, they registered 72 hectares and 95 ares, and their ownership was officially confirmed by the administration in subsequent years. At one point proceedings were brought by a neighbor, and the Toai family's land was reduced to 68 hectares, 45 ares. Toai accepted the decision and the family was given property title number 303, dated 7 August 1916, which confirmed the reduction. Although the taxes were paid regularly, in 1917 a Chinese neighbor named Ma Ngan was granted Toai's plot, undoubtedly with the complicity of the *notables*. The boundary commission, without tracing the origins of occupancy, ordered the family to cede the land to the Chinese neighbor in March 1919. After four petitions submitted by Toai and his brothers, the government of Cochinchina reversed itself two months later, restoring the property to the family. Nonetheless, on 5 February 1920, Toai learned from the *notables* that the plot had been registered in the name of Ma

Ngan. When he consulted the *dia bo* at Phong Thanh, Toai was amazed to see that that his name had been erased and replaced by that of the Chinese settler. Although he continued to protest, Ma Ngan eventually obtained permanent title to the coveted land on 20 February 1926 by means of an administrative act. The act authorized a private sale, which was registered at Can-tho City on 11 May. The bailiff presented Toai and his brothers with an eviction order on 28 June but the family ignored it. Unable to evict them or force the payment of rent, despite some recourse to physical pressure, Ma Ngan ceded his rights to a Vietnamese landowner in October 1927. The new owner initiated proceedings to seize the harvest. That was when the fight broke out.[61]

Although this reconstruction of the affair by a journalist may be faulty, it is consistent with what we know of similar complaints, of allusions in speeches and reports, of the contents of legislative documents, and of the regulations of a cold and anonymous bureaucracy. The episode caused an uproar, and the subsequent trial, in which the Toai brothers were accused of murdering the gendarme, was followed avidly by the population of the Cochinchinese West. The magistrates displayed objectivity, the lawyers pleaded ardently on behalf of the accused, and all parties seemed sincere in their search for the true causes of the tragedy. After paying homage to the dead gendarme, Fournier, Advocate General Moreau declared that

> This affair, coming after that of Ninh Thanh Loi, testifies to a tendency that indicates a great change. It shows how tragic the land question is in the Cochinchinese West. It reminds the authorities of the necessity to take equitable measures which will prevent the repetition of these tragic occurrences. And this, gentlemen, is perhaps more serious than the death of gendarme Fournier. This is why the court should not be astonished if before grappling with the facts of 16 February, I go back to their remote causes. Without being a determinist, one must search for the relations of cause to effect. We are gathered in this room to render justice. Good justice must proceed as follows: in the first place to know, that is, to search for all that relates to the crime, then to evaluate, then to sanction.[62]

The brothers were acquitted, and public opinion declared itself satisfied with the verdict.

These and similar agrarian conflicts led to a decree promulgated on 4 October 1928 prohibiting the occupation or cultivation of domanial land without a provisional title of concession, unless specially authorized by the chief of the local administration. The *notables* would be allowed to include on the land tax register only those possessing property titles or permanent titles of concession. Occupants without authorization would be liable to eviction. The decree reiterated the prohibition against free occupation of canal borders and assured provisional maintenance on the land register of all the occupants inscribed there, with or without title. Nonetheless, although the pressure of circumstance forced the administration to concern itself with some agrarian questions, its efforts at reform failed to counteract the effects of its long-standing laissez-faire policies.

Land Distribution

In comparing systems of land ownership in the two major Vietnamese deltas, P. Gourou established that in 1930 there were 255,000 landowners out of a total rural population of 4 million in Cochinchina, and 965,000 landowners among Tonkin's 6.5 million rural inhabitants. There was a mean of 9 hectares per landowner in Cochinchina compared to 1.2 hectares in Tonkin. Gourou estimated that in Cochinchina 12.5 percent of the cultivated area was comprised of holdings under 5 hectares, 42.5 percent consisted of holdings between 5 and 50 hectares, and 45 percent was accounted for by holdings exceeding 50 hectares. In the interior of Cochinchina, in the provinces of the center and the west, the large estates of more than 50 hectares were owned by 2.5 percent of the landowners but comprised 45 percent of cultivated rice land. Large estates are sometimes difficult to identify since they might be scattered over several villages and frequently were registered in the names of several members of the same family or in the names of figureheads.[63]

In 1929–30, the inspector general for agriculture, Y. Henry, conducted an extended inquiry, the results of which are indispensable to our knowledge of the agrarian regime of French Indochina. Henry stressed the inadequacy of the provincial *monographies*, which failed to adopt a uniform procedure for determining the amount of land owned by different holders. After an extensive examination he concluded that the number of small holdings was fewer than that given in the official figures. A striking finding was the degree to which large-scale holdings predominated in Mien Tay. In Bac-lieu, 9.6 percent of the landowners were classified as "large" (holding more than 50 hectares) but they possessed 65.5 percent of the rice land. Small landowners (with less than 5 hectares) accounted for 38.3 percent of the total but held only 3.3 percent of the land. In Bac-lieu's canton of Long Thuy, the percentage of large landowners reached 29.3 percent and held 84.4 percent of the land. In Thanh Bien Canton (in Rach-gia Province) large landowners formed 19 percent of the total. In Bac-lieu, small owners took on importance only in the vicinity of the *giongs*, and in Rach-gia the distribution of small holdings was concentrated in areas inhabited by Cambodians. In the same provinces, the middle-sized owners (from 5 to 50 hectares) constituted 52.1 percent of the landowners and held 31.2 percent of the cultivated land.[64]

In the province of Long-xuyen, Henry found 559 large landowners, out of a total of 11,478, possessing 113,755 hectares and 70 ares. The rest, holding less than 50 hectares, possessed in total only 79,743 hectares. The mean size of a holding was 7 hectares, 30 ares.[65] Small owners predominated only in the provinces closest to the Mekong where the land was of relatively older settlement (as in Can-tho), little developed (as in Ha-tien), or containing significant numbers of Khmers (as in Chau-doc and Soc-trang). Soc-trang had 61 percent small landowners and Chau-doc 78.4 percent. In Ha-tien Province in 1929, apart from the European concessions, no owner possessed as much as 10 hectares. In the canton of Hon Chong, 239 people owned 962 hectares (or 4 hectares each on average), while in the canton of Giang Thanh the average was 3.5 hectares.[66]

In this massive colonization process, and the maze of land disputes that arose from it, what became of Vietnamese village property? Family-held private property and communal land had always coexisted in the Vietnamese village. The latter was of two types. The first was comprised of the *cong dien* and *cong tho,* which were inalienable, the second by the *bon thon dien* and the *bon thon tho,* which were alienable. The *cong dien* were communal rice lands and the *cong tho* were forests, gardens, fallow land, and ponds. They were accumulated through state or private donations or through recovery of abandoned properties by the village. The *notables* would redistribute them periodically to deserving members of the village.[67] *Bon thon dien* and *bon thon tho* were similar lands acquired by the village with its own resources. These properties could be alienated with the approval of the higher authority. In practice the division between alienable and inalienable properties was not observed, perhaps because of the absence of clear boundaries between them.

By the time French authority was established, communal village lands and their intended purposes had already met with great damage. In particular, the *notables* who determined the distributions tended to indulge in embezzlement and nepotism. Amid the uncertainty that accompanied the transfer of authority from the Vietnamese to the French, the *notables* alienated numerous communal properties. As early as 1880, one administrator sounded a cry of alarm.

It often happens today that, by ignorance or otherwise, all the communal lands are registered under the title of *bon thon dien*. This abuse must be checked, for it could lead to the alienation of lands which were allocated to the villages in the public interest.[68]

The trend was important enough to provoke a reaction from the French administration. A decree of January 1893 made the rental of communal lands contingent upon the signature of the provincial administrator and the approval of the lieutenant governor. It also made alienation of the *bon thon dien* and *bon thon tho* (even with the right of repurchase) subject to authorization by the lieutenant governor. But, although the decree was designed to slow the dispersal of communal lands, the administration was also following a policy that promoted their alienation. The leasing of communal lands was viewed by the French as an important source of revenue for the villages and tracts of *cong dien* and *cong tho* were rented at public auction every three years. There may have been other motivations for this practice as well, for the former system of periodically redistributing communal lands did not prevent land-grabbing to the profit of a particular clan. Redistribution may have been less prevalent in the West where the inhabitants were more mobile and consequently less attached to the village nucleus.[69] Nonetheless, gratuitous distribution already benefited the *notables*. Costly rentals put communal lands out of the direct reach of the poor. The adjudicators were often the larger landowners who then sublet the land to tenants.

When the administration proposed in 1917 to grant to the villages of Can-tho Province *cong dien* of five hundred, six hundred, and one thousand hectares, the Colonial Council reduced the area to two hundred hectares, arguing that it must not hinder the settlement process by the allotment of excessive *cong dien* and that it was useless to increase the revenues of villages that were sufficiently prosperous already.[70] In 1925, having concluded that the villages, in order to contribute to the general welfare, must possess sufficient resources to do so, the local assembly endorsed the administration's proposal to endow each village with a quota of *cong dien* equal to one-twentieth of its area. The decision gave rise to an attempt to record the actual amount of *cong dien*. Table 5 indicates to what extent it had been reduced.[71]

TABLE 5: Amount of *Cong Dien* in Villages of Can-tho and Rach-gia Provinces, 1927 (in hectares)

Village	Total area	Prescribed amount of *Cong Dien*	Actual amount of *Cong Dien*
Can-tho Province:			
My Thuan	5232	262	73
Truong Thanh Son	2386	119	7
Loan Tan	1957	98	18
An Phu Tan	2732	136	12
Thanh Loi	4204	210	105
Dinh Mon	2393	120	10
Hoa My	5500	275	103
Song My	4508	225	114
Binh Ninh	1814	91	25
Tan Binh	6375	319	80
Tan Ngai	2045	102	45
Rach-gia Province:			
Cu Hoa	823	41	16
Mong Tho	1558	78	45
Lac Binh	2598	120	17
Ban Thach	1730	86	7
Ngoc Thanh	1873	94	51

Source: Colonial Council, 4th session, 3 August 1927, *Procès-verbaux du Conseil Colonial* (CAOM).

Some older villages no longer preserved the *cong dien* at all. In a meeting of the Colonial Council in 1927, the governor of Cochinchina pointed to the case of the village of Vi Thuy in the canton of Giang Ninh, in which all the land had been allocated to private ownership except for a few small parcels the total area of which did not exceed 60 hectares. Even these small tracts had been cleared, registered, and alloted to the occupants. The Council concluded that "it has not been possible for the commission to reserve more than 42 hectares 25 ares of land to be allocated as *cong dien* for this village, which has a total area of 9,374 hectares 30 ares 6 ca."[72]

Other collective properties suffered a similar fate. Private donations of land intended for a shrine or to provide revenue for the support of a cult and

TABLE 6: Modes of Farming in Mien Tay, by Province, 1929

Province	Landowners farming directly	Landowners renting out their land
Chau-doc	26,358	2,979
Bac-lieu	6,910	4,112
Long-xuyen	8,540	6,227
Can-tho	9,606	5,881
Soc-trang	12,478	6,851
Rach-gia	14,015	3,707

Source: Henry, *L'économie agricole*, 158–63.

its priests often were diverted from their original purpose. In the provinces of Ben-tre, My-tho, Vinh-long, Sa-dec, and Can-tho the administration, on the evidence of information furnished by the *notables*, transformed the cult properties connected with Buddhist pagodas into *cong dien*, which were rented to augment village budgets. The bonzes were forced to submit tenders under the names of figureheads in order to become adjudicators. This deviation from the initial objective of cult properties provoked discontent among the Buddhists of the region.[73] A June 1930 memorandum from the governor of Cochinchina to the provincial administrators complained that much revenue from cult properties was being partially diverted and asked officials to see that regulations regarding these properties were enforced.[74]

Modes of Farming

As Table 6 demonstrates, with the exception of the provinces of Rach-gia and Chau-doc, indirect (or tenant) farming was commonplace. Even these figures, derived from Henry's study, are misleading, for in them mixed farming (some land in direct cultivation, some rented out) was placed in the category of direct farming. Moreover, managers in Mien Tay could not employ gangs of agricultural workers, leaving them no alternative but to rent land to *ta dien*. In general this was a practice of the absentee landlords but resident landowners also employed it.

In Vietnamese the term *ta dien* used by itself designates a tenant farmer. Some authors have described the agricultural tenant of Mien Tay as a sharecropper since each tenant paid his rent with a portion of the harvest. But the characteristic feature of the sharecropping (*metayage*) system, the division of profits and risks as a function of variations in the harvest, was absent from the *ta dien* contract. The sharecropping system, strictly defined, was found only in Chau-doc Province where the landowners received two-thirds of the harvest.[75] The *ta dien's* rent was not calculated as a percentage of the harvest, and this practice prevailed in 99 percent of the cases.

At the end of the dry season the *ta dien* traditionally entered into agreements with landowners, their managers, or their overseers. The owner furnished the land, which usually was divided into lots of ten hectares. To this he added livestock, advances of rice and paddy for use as food and seed, and a sum of money. These advances were the most common form of credit. In return, the *ta dien* supplied his tools and his labor, and he paid a part of his harvest as rent. The most common situation was one in which an owner of a large estate would rent his land to a "farmer general," or land broker,

> at a rate less than the direct tenant farming rate practiced in the region; the farmer general recruits the *ta dien*, sets them up and draws up a contract with them in order to fix the rent for the land. His profit is the difference between the rent that he charges and that which he pays to the landowner. But the farmer general profits especially from the interest on the advances that he grants to the *ta dien* in the course of the campaign. He operates, for this, either with his own capital, or with funds that he borrows from the landowner at an interest rate less than that he will require of the *ta dien*. . . . Half of the properties of more than 300 hectares in Bac-lieu would be farmed by this method.[76]

The incidence of tenant farming varied according to province and particularly with regard to type of rice land. Proximity to a town or access to transport tended to increase the rent. For the development of virgin land, two principal methods were adopted in the extreme west (in Bac-lieu, Ca-mau, and Rach-gia). In the first, and the most rapid, the clearing of the land was the responsibility of the landowner. The *ta dien* would perform the labor of cutting, burning, and digging ditches and canals for a cash payment of around 60 piasters per hectare. One *ta dien* could clear from twenty to thirty *cong* (two to three hectares) per year. He was paid in accordance with the advancement of the work but he often was required to pay rent as soon as the first year. Rents ranged from five to ten *gia* (forty liters) of rice or paddy per hectare.

TABLE 7: Tenant Rents, in *Gia* of Rice,
According to Quality of Land (per hectare)

Province	First class	Second class	Third class
Chau-doc*	20	12	10
Long-xuyen	20	10	5
Rach-gia	30	20	10
Soc-trang	25–30	15–20	8–10
Bac-lieu	25	15	8
Ha-tien**	3 piasters and 3 *gia*	2 piasters and 2 *gia*	

*For Cambodian cantons the figures are, respectively, 16, 10 and 8 *gia*.
**Rent in Ha-Tien was stipulated partly in piasters.

Source: Garros, *Usages de la Cochinchine*, 188–89.

In the second method, land clearing was the responsibility of the *ta dien*. The landowner's expenses took the form of advances to the tenant. In practice these advances were made without security, at least during the early years, and the total cost would nearly match the sum expended under the first method. The rent was set initially at a rate of five *gia* of rice or paddy per hectare, increasing progressively until it reached twenty or thirty *gia* at the end of seven or eight years. Advances by the owner at the onset of clearing were mandatory but interest rates were high. If the amount of the advance was the equivalent of five to ten piasters and ten *gia* of paddy, then each piaster would be repaid with three *gia*, and one *gia* of paddy would be repaid with two.[77] Around 1925, G. Garros compiled figures on rents charged to tenant farmers in Mien Tay. His findings are reproduced as table 7.

Tenant contracts sometimes stipulated procedures for dividing the harvest. In this case, the harvest and the threshing could not be completed before the landowner was notified so that he could verify the amount and quality of the crop. The landowner had first claim on the proceeds, for the rent had to be paid and the advances cleared before any rice was allotted to the *ta dien*. Surplus paddy would accrue to the tenant only with the consent of the landowner. When the harvest was insufficient to defray the *ta dien*'s obligations, it was left to the discretion of the owner whether to allow his tenant a subsistence. Under French regulations, the second and tenth months of the lunar calendar were those of payment of rent but in reality the landowner could demand it as soon as the harvest was underway. Sometimes the owner would arrive to take the rent in the fields. At other times, less frequently it seems, he would have his portion delivered to his house. In the latter case, transport costs were the responsibility of the *ta dien*. These practices recognized the landlord's veritable right to ownership of the harvest, a custom that French legislation revalidated.

Most contracts were renewed annually but in Bac-lieu they extended for a period of six to nine harvests. There was a single copy of each contract and the lessor kept it. The obligations of the landowner and those of the *ta dien* were inscribed either on the same side or front and back. If he could write, the *ta dien* put his signature (his *thu ky*) to it, sometimes in Chinese characters. Most often the tenant was illiterate, in which case he would use the *diem chi*, a print of the first two fingers of the left hand. The agreement was written on unofficial paper, without certification, and its legal status often became a matter of some contestation in the courts.[78]

When the harvest was over and the rent paid, if the landowner remained in possession of the contract, its renewal was tacit. It was conclusively established if the landowner let the tenant begin sowing. If the *ta dien* conducted his business with a manager, he was required to pay him a fee in order to obtain the renewal. Notices to quit the property were executed without the use of special forms: the landlord would simply summon the farmer to appear before the *notables*, and there he would express his grievances. A deficient harvest was considered an acceptable reason to break a contract, though this was often a pretext masking other motives. If the *ta dien* refused to leave, the landlord could take legal action. His case against the *ta dien* would not rest on documentary evidence but on the memories and sincerity (or bad faith) of the *notables* who would attest whether notice to quit had been given.[79]

In this domain, as in others, custom was the master. The French administration had never sought to intervene in the micromanagement of agriculture. Governor General Pasquier declared in 1931 that "We live under the regime of the freedom of conventions." In 1933, Inspecteur du Travail Bary declared that the existence of formulas consecrated by custom made the wielding of public power difficult. The landowners themselves, although they regularly insisted that the government punish workers who had absconded with their advances, were not keen to see the administration intercede in the execution of work contracts.

CHAPTER 3

The Monoculture of Rice

EXCEPT FOR A FEW well-defined regions, the arable land of Mien Tay was almost entirely devoted to rice cultivation. Clearing and development became continuous as peasant immigration from the eastern and central parts of the region increased. Statistical data reveal a sharp rise in population beginning around 1880 in conjunction with a rapid expansion of cultivated rice land (see figure 2). An examination of the course of the increase in rice production shows that from 1868 to 1879 progress was slow. Then, after a marked rise in cultivation in 1880, the curve ascends irregularly. From 1903 to 1930, it is very pronounced, though it is interrupted by a brief dip in 1907 and a longer one between 1917 and 1925. As the data are drawn from all of Nam Bo, it is not possible to determine exactly the magnitude of the increase in the West. It is safe to say, however, that Mien Tay accounted for the bulk of the growth.

The rapid expansion of rice land would not have been possible without the existence of a new and unifying element, free trade. One of the first proclamations of French Admiral Rigault de Genouilly granted the freedom to export rice. This action was motivated by the liberalism of the French Second Empire, the desire to stimulate economic development in the new colony, and the need to satisfy French exporters and Chinese interest groups. As Governor Le Myre de Vilers later wrote,

> As soon as we had taken possession of Saigon, we decreed commercial freedom of importation and exportation. Unquestionably public wealth increased notably. The cultivator, certain of selling his rice at a remunerative price on the markets of Singapore, Hong Kong, and Java, doubled and tripled his cultivated land; he speculates in grain just like a European or American farmer.[1]

The opening of the colony to foreign commerce stimulated the Vietnamese economy while creating a system dependent upon the monoculture of rice. Although the dangers of monoculture were perceived early on by the leaders of the colony, their warnings had little effect, particularly in Mien Tay. Following the economic downturn of 1907, the governor of Cochinchina noted that

> The colony went through an agricultural depression, which demonstrated one more time the dangers to which a country under the exclusive reign of monoculture is subjected. Whereas the population of the east has cane sugar, peanuts, etc., . . . which bring it appreciable resources, the population of the west, reduced in its sole revenue, was sorely afflicted.[2]

Mien Tay can be divided into three distinct zones according to the type of hydraulic regime in effect there (see map). The first, located north of the Rach Soi–Bassac Canal, is an area of floating-rice cultivation. Due to the low level of the land, it is impossible to drain off the stagnant standing water except in an area extending a few kilometers on either side of the Mekong River and within a few hundred meters of the canals. Every year when the river swells and floods the region, rice is grown in the standing water rather than on land. The second zone is located south of a line stretching between Rach-gia and Bac-lieu. Here the land is subject to tidal inundation. The third zone lies between the other two and is affected by both the sea and the rising and falling of the Mekong. In this zone the river washes away the toxic elements left by the tides and deposits a rich silt on the river banks. Rice is grown on land in this region, although the soil far from the river retains alum and a successful harvest depends on rain.

In its program of reconditioning existing canals and digging new ones, the French administration concerned itself principally with opening Mien Tay to settlement and increasing the production of export rice. Transportation was given a higher priority than flood control. Though several studies of the terrain were undertaken, and earlier ones consulted, a good working knowledge of the hydraulic regime of Mien Tay was never achieved. As late as 1947, one engineer concluded an article with the statement that the colonial government had never formulated an effective water policy. In 1913, another engineer, A. Normandin, submitted a long report, already stressing that "the questions of agricultural hydraulics have been up to this day virtually neglected in Cochinchina if one disregards certain waterways

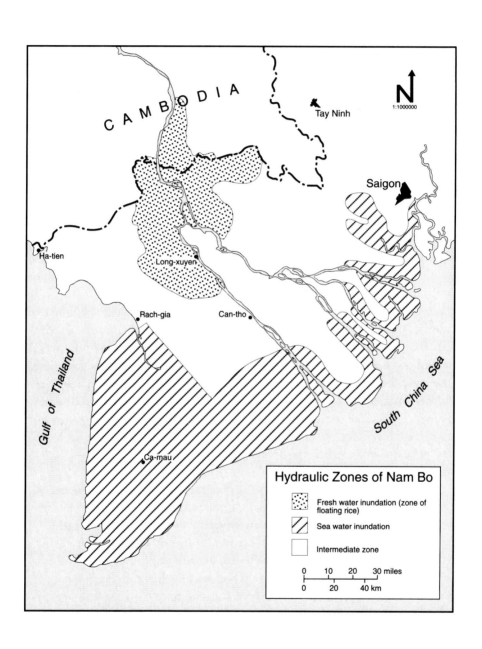

N
1:1000000

CAMBODIA

Tay Ninh

Saigon

Ha-tien

Long-xuyen

Rach-gia

Can-tho

Gulf of Thailand

Ca-mau

South China Sea

Hydraulic Zones of Nam Bo

Fresh water inundation (zone of floating rice)

Sea water inundation

Intermediate zone

0   10   20   30 miles
0   20   40 km

intended for navigation which have at the same time benefited agriculture."[3] Public works designed by the French actually aggravated the ill effects of the different hydrographic regimes. In the zone of floating rice, roads built perpendicular to the flow of floodwaters toward the Gulf of Siam blocked the waters' escape. In the intermediate zone, canals dug parallel to the Mekong impeded drainage. In certain places, the water became stagnant and toxic. In others, or during certain years, floods were catastrophic. In the tidal zone, newly constructed waterways leading to the sea induced the rapid desiccation of the soil following the wet season, which in turn caused alum to rise to the surface. In all seasons, these waterways permitted the passage of salt water into the interior.[4]

The lack of sufficient personnel to monitor the situation was not the sole cause of these problems. Prior to 1937, the administration had only its own budgetary resources with which to carry out the hydrographic program, and it gave preference to works that could be amortized rapidly through the sale of domanial lands. Although the new canals served to leach the alum soils, this effect was secondary and of limited scope.

Thus, in matters of hydraulic preparation for agriculture, the initiative was left to the cultivators themselves, working as groups or individuals without coordination of effort. Drainage and irrigation projects were not carried out in a systematic manner, and they tended to reproduce at the local level the same problems experienced in the national sphere. Sometimes the larger farms, well diked, diverted floodwaters into the fields of smaller landowners. Nonetheless, some local hydraulic schemes implemented by farmers or villages were ingenious. In 1910, an inspector of agriculture described an installation he had observed on the property of a settler named Gressier.

> In order to be able to drain this or that part and to regularize the maturation of the rice, the owner did no more than put in order the existing *rach,* damming them with embankments sixty meters in width and higher than the high waters. Moreover, he dug other canals, not following straight lines but along the line of greatest slope, indicated on the terrain itself by the water after the wet season when the drying out occurs. . . . He had made provision for irrigation: profiting from a rectilinear canal made by the previous owner, he firmly diked this canal so that he could, by stemming the water in the canal with a mechanical system, cause it to overflow onto all the rice land. So that he would be able to raise the water at any time . . . [he had installed] a steam engine

of forty horsepower with a ship's boiler, which could be stoked with wood . . . (two centrifugal pumps in case of inundation could serve to drain the water and ward off disaster).[5]

Though innovative, such systems could be operated only if the landowner were resident on the land, possessed the intelligence and experience needed to cope with problems as they arose, and had the right machinery at his disposal. They were beyond the reach of small landowners and *ta dien* who had no such resources.

Lacking the ability to master the waters, the average peasant of Mien Tay was reduced to reliance on the hazards of nature—rains, floods, and tides. He could hardly count on regular harvests, and was accustomed to saying that "the paddy harvest is only certain when it has entered the granary."

Methods of cultivation and the calendar of agricultural work varied according to the hydraulic regime, type of soil, and the time elapsed since the initial development of the land. In zones of older occupation (such as the provinces of Long-xuyen and Can-tho) and on newer but well-established rice lands (those located along the canals and near the *giongs*) peasants used the swing-plough (the *cai cay*, of which the ploughshare was not always made of iron) and the harrow (*cai bua*) to prepare the soil. Many fashioned these rudimentary tools themselves, though prices were moderate in the years preceding the depression of the 1930s. A metal ploughshare cost twenty to thirty centimes, a plough between four and five piasters, and a grooved roller (a tree trunk grooved with longitudinal ridges) seven or eight piasters.[6]

In the zones of more recent settlement, the methods of cultivation were much simpler. Peasants only had to clear the weeds and sow directly, without ploughing. In 1897, several members of the Chamber of Agriculture disputed the statement of L. H. Jammes that "in the provinces of the West, three-quarters of the land receives the crop without any preparation."[7] In 1909, however, at an agricultural competition organized by the Chamber of Agriculture of Nam Bo to stimulate improvements in the native plough, all the prizes but one went to provinces in the eastern and central regions. The administration attributed this to the fact that in Can-tho rice land was not ploughed, that in Chau-doc and Ha-tien rice culture was minimal, that in Long-xuyen peasants did not use the plough, and that in Rach-gia few Khmers used it either.[8] This last observation was connected to another: at the end of the nineteenth century, in the province of An-giang where Vietnamese and Khmers lived together, the latter used the plough but the former did not.[9] Other observers noted in passing that the Cambodian plough had been

Figure 2

Area of Rice Cultivation in Cochinchina, 1879-1924 (in hectares)

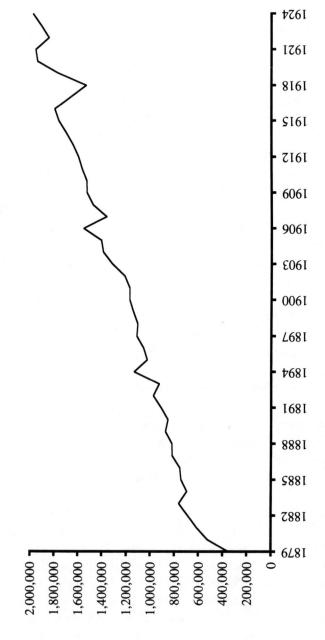

Source: A. Poyanne. *Les Travaux Publics de l'Indochine*. Hanoi, 1926.

borrowed by the Vietnamese,[10] though apparently this occurred prior to the arrival of the Vietnamese in the West.[11]

The three most important agricultural tasks were sowing, transplanting, and harvesting. They took place at different times according to the variety of rice planted. In the West many of these were early-maturing varieties used to bridge the gap between other harvests. Direct sowing was employed on new rice land and for the early varieties. In the inundated expanses of Chau-doc Province and in the northern part of Long-xuyen, floating rice was broadcast sown. But generally rice was transplanted after having been sown in seed beds. In Can-tho and northern Soc-trang, seedlings were transplanted twice, a practice that made them vigorous enough to resist asphyxiation by nitrogenous substances. Unlike traditional practice in the rest of Nam Bo, here the transplanters pushed the plants into the watery soil while spacing them farther apart.

Throughout the West the harvest took place in January, February, and March for the full-season rices, and in December for the early varieties. Threshing generally was done by hand, though occasionally by the feet of water buffaloes. The peasants made use of a simple device common throughout Vietnam: a basket (*cai bo*) mounted on a sled (*cai co*). The husked paddy was gathered in heaps and dried. Women winnowed it on a windy day.[12] When these operations were performed in the fields rather than on the threshing floor, the rice was transported to the landowner on a sled pulled by water buffaloes or by the men themselves.

In the course of relations between *ta dien* and landowners, the gathering of the harvest was crucial. The landowner's share—not only the rent but the repayment of advances and frequently the clearing of previous debts—was set aside first. This might also be a time of conflict. G. Garros, who, in his capacity as a defense counsel was engaged in numerous disputes, refers to frequent brawls.

> The period of settlement of harvests . . . usually brings an increase in imprisonments on suspicion of inflicting bruises and injuries. And, since in each village a landowner is head of a family and a proprietor for numerous tenants, the struggle is generalized and sometimes takes on the proportions of a combat of hundreds. Possession of the land, the collection of the paddy it produces, these are the acts which arouse this race of ploughmen and transplanters the most.[13]

After the landowners and tenants settled the division of the harvest, the paddy was stored in makeshift sheds or sturdier granaries owned either by the large landowners or Chinese merchants. In the granaries the paddy was stored on an elevated floor to avoid the damp. Large, hollow, bamboo poles ensured proper ventilation. The capacity of these private granaries could reach seventy thousand *gia* of rice.[14] It was more common, however, for the harvest of a few hectares to be stored in an open shed, sometimes securely in mats rolled to form cylinders open at the top, and sometimes badly in closed wooden bins. At worst, the grain was left on the banks of a *rach* or on a strip of flat ground where it was vulnerable to the weather, insects, and rodents.

Work such as constant surveillance of the seed beds and paddy fields, and their protection from crabs, rats, birds, and disease, required a large work force. Women played a major role, especially in transplanting, harvesting, and sluicing. Children were mobilized for surveillance and in the struggle against the enemies of the harvest, and often the period of greatest work in the fields coincided with high rates of absence from school.[15] Work under the full sun was arduous, so the harvesters would begin at three or four in the morning, working on average ten hours a day. The transplanters pursued their tasks in the mud, leeches clinging to their skin. The reflection of the sun on the sheet of water in the paddy fields also was responsible for the frequent incidence of ophthalmic illness.

Labor, always scarce, was altogether insufficient during the harvest. This was also a time of inmigration. As the rice matured in different places at different times, Mien Tay benefited from the import of labor from the eastern and central provinces of Nam Bo. Small landowners and *ta dien* of Vinh-long, Sa-dec, Tra-vinh, My-tho, Long An, and Go Cong would embark for the West in their sampans, and the *rach* and the canals would spring to life with a floating crowd. These labor gangs were headed by chiefs who organized the groups and negotiated salaries with an employer or his recruiting agent. The contract was always verbal, and payment was generally in kind, sometimes accompanied by a small sum of money. Only rarely were workers paid entirely in cash. These seasonal laborers were compensated by the day or by the piece. Wages varied greatly according to the type of work and the place where it was carried out. On the eve of the Great Depression, on the large estates of Soc-trang, Bac-lieu, and Rach-gia, workers were paid by the piece, without food. Harvesters, on the other hand, received one sheaf out of each ten or eleven harvested. Occasionally they demanded payment in cash (at Bac-lieu and Soc-trang they received $.70 with food or $.80 without) but as a general rule payment in kind was preferred. In good years a harvester could make $1.10 to $1.50 per day without food.[16]

Unlike the *ta dien*, the labor of seasonal workers was subject to the laws of supply and demand. This was the only sector of the agricultural economy in which one could speak of a labor market. In prosperous years, when the harvest was good and work was plentiful, many peasants preferred to wander about working as day laborers rather than settling down as tenant farmers. French authorities saw a potential for rebellion in the movements of itinerant laborers, and the landowners suspected the work gangs of harboring seditious elements, but their need for labor was pressing and they were forced to tolerate the situation.

Payment of the poll tax was due during the harvest period, and each year the checking of tax cards gave rise to a merciless hunt for those in default. Gendarmes herded them into the chief towns by the dozens, detaining them despite repeated protests from the landowners that this hindered the circulation of the migrant work force. In 1927, the Colonial Council secured permission for itinerant workers to pay the poll tax at the chief town of whatever province they were in at the time, eliminating the need for them to return to the villages in which they were registered. This measure did not remove all the difficulties, though, for it was still neccesary to travel to the chief town, which sometimes was far from the place of work, and to wait there for a card that was not always ready. Often a worker was forced to go back once or even twice.

In the off-season, which followed the harvest, the peasants occupied themselves with diverse work on their farms or on those of their landlords. They cleaned the canals and the ponds and strengthened embankments along the edges of the paddy fields. Some large landowners would initiate special activities. The settler Gressier, for example, built a brick works, which was operated when the *ta dien* were free of work in the fields. Leisure time was devoted to fishing, hunting, collecting insects, and repairing straw huts.[17]

The West had little dry cultivation—only maize, which was important in Chau-doc. Despite the encouragement of the administration, introduction of a castor-oil plant and efforts to promote mulberry cultivation in Longxuyen were not successful.

Attempts at Improvement: Seeds and Machines

Though rice culture was sovereign in the West, it suffered from several disadvantages, which gave rise to attempts at improvement. As a relatively recent exporter of paddy and rice, Nam Bo, of which the principal producing area was Mien Tay, faced stiff competition from Burma and Thailand, both of which held strong positions in the foreign market. Customers in European, and even Asian, markets were demanding a high-quality product, and this stimulated government efforts to improve the crop.

Attempts at improvement had been made before. As early as 1868, the Comité Agricole et Industriel de Cochinchine had concerned itself with the quality of rice, as had the administration. In 1876, indigenous agricultural shows had been organized upon its recommendation, and regional and national shows were held periodically from 1896 to 1904. Though these gave rise to some interesting observations, their results were judged to be less than satisfactory, and in 1905 they were discontinued. In 1910, the correspondence of the chief administrator of Bac-lieu Province reveals that an agricultural show to be held in Saigon was cancelled because it was believed that distance would keep most cultivators from attending. The administrator was of the opinion that preliminary shows held in Bac-lieu had not been successful,[18] a conclusion reinforced by the *notables* of the cantons and villages.

In 1908, the Colonial Council took up the question of improving rice cultivation. Along with numerous settlers, it suspected that the defectiveness of the paddy and rice was the result of poor seed selection. In cooperation with a program set up by Morange, an agricultural expert, and following a memorandum of Governor General A. Sarraut dated 4 April 1913, a rice-culture research station was created in Can-tho. Its principal functions were selection of seed and its distribution to growers. This was the beginning of a concerted effort that proceeded in three principal directions: research into improvement of the yields through better seed and the introduction of fertilizers; experimentation with new tools and machines; and attempts at mechanization.

Vietnamese rice growers were not ignorant of the use of organic fertilizers and manure crops. The important role played by the gatherers of night soil and dung was well known. In the deltas of the north, both Dumont and Gourou noted the use of the azolla, an aquatic plant, to improve the soil.[19] In Mien Tay, however, where perhaps the corpus of traditional agricultural practices was not preserved adequately and where a scattered population was the rule, peasants farmed less carefully. They burned stubble but did not bury it. Animal manure was recovered inefficiently, if at all, and in any case was lacking in many places due to the shortage of livestock. The youth of the soil did not encourage attempts at improvement, and even on older or more developed farms fertilizer generally was not used. Should one attribute this simply to the force of habit? During an agricultural campaign of 1929–30, the administration launched a vast project, experimenting with chemical fertilizers on rice land. The trials were accompanied by lectures and the distribution of pamphlets in Vietnamese. Commercial houses sent representatives. Though a few cultivators bought chemical fertilizers, indiscriminate use and the resulting disappointments were detrimental to the cause. A credit of $500,000 was placed at the disposal of the SICAMS in 1930–31 to be used to encourage the purchase of fertilizer but in 1930 only $12,000 was expended. Although by this time the worldwide economic depression had begun to affect Nam Bo, without it would fertilizers have had more success? The greatest disadvantage was unquestionably the price, high enough that chemical fertilizers remained beyond the reach of the rice growers.

Exporters of rice did not complain of an insufficiency of production. Rather their criticism focused upon the poor quality of seed. Seed improvement required a spirit of inquiry that was not lacking among Vietnamese rice growers. The introduction of the Hue-ky variety of rice is revealing. In this instance, a cultivator, having received a chest of glassware from America, noticed in the packing straw some well-preserved grains of rice. When he sowed them they proved to be very productive.[20] The introduction of floating rice in Chau-doc Province in the 1920s also should be credited to a Vietnamese, despite the fact that French tradition attributes it to a missionary. In reality, the obstacles to seed improvement had more to do with the prevailing commercial and marketing structures than with the initiative of the cultivators.

Although the agricultural authorities of Nam Bo promoted the use of mechanical sorters and distributed tons of seeds, except in a few cases the results did not justify the effort and expense entailed. A few settlers such as Gressier did take a vital interest in this work but most were cultivators who used the seeds themselves and sold their paddy without the services of intermediaries. This is the important point. Why should the majority of rice producers, with no control over redistribution, take the trouble to improve the quality of their seed only to see Chinese middlemen mix all the grain together? This is why the agricultural shows promoting new seed varieties were useless. While a few owners practiced selection with the intention of entering the shows and winning prizes, the results were without practical meaning.

Soon the sorted seeds were mixed with the ordinary ones again. By acting this way was the rice grower yielding to an inconsistency inherent in the pre-logical mentality so dear to colonial psychologists? More likely it was empiricism that inclined him toward prudence. The farmer mixed his seeds according to a maxim, closely related to the land, which advised a wise man not to put all his eggs in one basket.

In the domain of agricultural equipment, two improvements were sought: the first involved improving native implements while the second called for the introduction of European and American tools. Several early attempts were made to improve indigenous tools, principally the plough. In 1901, on the suggestion of a settler named Josselme, the Chamber of Agriculture organized an exhibition of native ploughs, which was repeated in 1909. The lack of participation by Mien Tay cultivators in these shows has already been noted. Improved hydraulic equipment would have been more useful to the farmers of the West and the only effective innovation we know of is an invention of R. Henry, who gave his name to a lifting wheel. It is a good example of improvement in the details of an implement, not spectacular but useful and inexpensive. But, although attempts at popularization were made, and it would seem that its diffusion would have had some economic significance, the Henry lifting wheel makes no further appearance in the documentary record. One cannot help but wonder whether it stimulated more improvements of a similar nature.

French settlers introduced the first foreign agricultural machines, principally ploughs, harvester-threshers or harvester–sheaf binders, and mechanical rice threshers. As early as 1899, the Chamber of Agriculture was taking notice.[21] Certain settlers were devoting themselves to the first experiments. Paternelle, a settler at Rach-gia, had the commercial house Amouroux, of Toulouse, send him a horse-driven mill and a thresher. From the same establishment he later ordered a centrifugal pump for irrigation.[22] Another settler, Barbier, emphasized the advantage of a horse-driven thresher, which did not leave 5 percent of the grain in the sheafs, as did threshing by hand. He complained, however, that maximum effciency could not be attained due to lack of experience on the part of the coolies.[23] The Vietnamese, too, took a lively interest in these novelties. At one demonstration of a reaper-binder and a reaper pulled by mules there was "a great meeting of the population. Numerous rich Annamites were interested. But the trials, and even the permanent use of implements for ploughing and harvesting, have not yet dispensed with animal power, that is, with water buffaloes."[24]

It was the beginning of the colonization of Mien Tay. Progressively, with the formation of the great estates, a scarcity of labor became more evident and the need for draft animals increased. In the clayey, compact soil, water buffaloes were employed in preference to oxen. Garros, however, asserted that in the provinces of Can-tho, Rach-gia, and Long-xuyen water buffaloes were rarely used by *ta dien* because they cost too much. Initially imported from Cambodia by the Malayans of Chau-doc, the livestock were often decimated by epizootics. Mortality was such that landowners were forced to replenish one-third of their herd every year and the large landowners purchased from one to five hundred animals annually.[25] The adoption of sanitary regulations, which mandated inspections and vaccinations for animals coming from Cambodia, wearied the cattle and prolonged the trip. The Malayans found in this an excuse to increase their prices. Smuggling was faster but involved increased risk, and so the price of contraband animals soared as well. In 1894, one water buffalo sold for $50. By 1905, the price had doubled to $100. The landowners rented buffaloes to the *ta dien* but the price was high. Garros put forward the figure of 60 to 70 *gia* of paddy per year.[26] Moreover, the working capacity of a good water buffalo was only four or five hours per day. Thus, it was not long before the large landowners began to look toward mechanization.

Invoking Italian and American precedents, the advocates of mechanized agriculture found ardent spokesmen in Ernest Outrey, a colonial administrator who was then deputy for Cochinchina in the French Parliament, and in de Magen, the inspector of agriculture. The latter advocated complete mechanization. There were objections, however. In April 1914, in the Chamber of Agriculture, some speakers warned that machines would require strictly level terrain and could not be adapted to marshy ground. Moreover, gasoline was expensive. In spite of the reservations, however, the administration established subsidies for mechanized agriculture, taking care to favor French tractors. The subsidies for French machines amounted to a quarter of their cost. Subsidies were only an eighth for foreign tractors, although these were best suited for working on rice land. They also were cheaper; an American Ford could be had for only eighteen hundred piasters, while a French Renault cost three thousand.[27]

The first trials of tractors took place with Ford and Caterpillar models on the testing field of the Can-tho agricultural station and on the estates of the settlers Gressier and Jourdan in 1921. These implements proved to be too heavy. Experiments continued over several years, conducted by official departments and privately. It was established that the tractors deteriorated rapidly, in spite of the efforts of the settlers to adjust them to the terrain.[28]

By 1926, it was concluded that the most efficient means of tillage was still that of animals. The withdrawal of the mechanization credits followed a declaration by the governor of Nam Bo that the tractor experiment had failed.[29]

Tractors did not disappear entirely. Some large landowners had already acquired them or others did so later. In 1929, at Rach-gia, Nicholas Le Phat An is known to have possessed nine tractors. At Chau-doc five landowners, and at Bac-lieu four, were engaged in mechanized agriculture. The *monographie* of 1927 for Long-xuyen Province listed twenty-four tractors owned by eleven landowners, nine of whom had Vietnamese names.[30] In many cases the tractors became a symbol of modernity, and for some, perhaps, a mark of prestige. But eventually the enthusiasm passed and illusions disappeared. Landowners came to use the machines judiciously, employing them and other machines only for the heavy work of clearing, leveling, and ploughing large areas. For other work they left the *ta dien* to their traditional ways. The fewest tractors and mechanical implements were found in the West.

On the eve of the Great Depression, the sometimes considerable efforts to improve seed selection, both private and official, had not resulted in any notable progress. Fertilizers were never used, and the complete mechanization that some had dreamed of had not been realized. The most popular explanation for this at the time was psychological. The Vietnamese and Cambodian peasants were attached to their traditions, it ran. They were routinized, if not simply lazy.

In fact, on many occasions the peasants showed great curiosity about the agricultural experiments. M. Sambuc, a settler at Thoi Lai (in Can-tho), declared that "the Annamites, who like all machines, were perfectly suited to furnishing teams of workmen, drivers, and mechanics capable of running even complicated agricultural equipment."[31] Young apprentices were quick to grasp the feel of the machines.

> Only yesterday, I saw the director of the Can-tho school give a practical lesson in agriculture. A reaper, a reaper-binder, and our thresher put at the disposal of the department of agriculture, had been transported by the department to Can-tho for trials in that province. The teacher, M. LaPlanche, who had been forewarned, had previously explained the workings of these machines to his students, and yesterday as the experiments took place two kilometers from the chief town, he escorted them there and gave them further instruction on the spot, where two machines were working. Moreover, the demonstrations gave good results, principally that of the reaper.[32]

The head of the Service Agricole de l'Institut Scientifique of Saigon emphasized that

> The Annamite is remarkably gifted as a mechanic. On January 30–31, when I gave a mechanized agriculture demonstration with a Caterpillar, a Bajac plough, a Ford tractor, a Norwegian harrow, and a scarifier, it may be said that these implements, driven by Annamites who had only five or six days of training, functioned very well.[33]

There is sufficient agreement in the testimony to suggest that belonging to an unmechanized and prescientific sociocultural milieu was not a major obstacle to adoption of new technologies. However, people steeped in such a milieu were at the mercy of nature. They could not permit themselves to dabble in experiments that might turn out to be disastrous.

Other factors were more decisive in hindering the improvement of agriculture in the West. Implements were expensive. In 1927, a French plough with a large ploughshare sold for 16 piasters, while an imported plough with two ploughshares, after deducting the official subsidy, cost at least 320 piasters.[34] The use of machines such as tractors was feasible only when the farmer could control the admission and withdrawal of water, permitting the leveling of the soil. On large concessions, mechanization could have been beneficial but the system of renting land to *ta dien*, which saw an estate divided into small parcels, made it impractical in Mien Tay.

Marketing Structures: The Chinese Monopoly

Improvement in the quality of rice was not going to lead to increased productivity as long as agriculture was subordinated to the prevailing commercial organization. The dominant Chinese buyers of paddy and rice never paid particular attention to seed selection, and the mixing of the different grades of paddy deflected the growers from the search for better quality. The large European export firms used Chinese intermediaries to make their purchases. Except for the medals and token prizes bestowed at the agricultural shows, the efforts of the rice growers never secured a stable and assured remuneration. Agricultural improvements involve not only much capital, for a return that is hardly immediate, but they also require technical training and experience, and solid analysis of the results. This is particularly true in the training of a labor force, in the organization and use of hydraulic systems, in the selection of seeds, and in the use of fertilizers. It all comes down to education and experimentation, which require the constant presence of the landowner or a technically qualified representative. It also presupposes the renunciation of immediate profits and tolerance of setbacks. These conditions were difficult to reconcile with the agrarian pattern of Mien Tay where the large absentee or speculating landowner, more of a moneylender than an entrepreneur, could not play the roles of educator or innovator. Only landowners who resided on their estates, or the companies that employed capable managers, were able to improve production by introducing new techniques, concerning themselves with hydraulic improvements, and attending to the milling and sale of the crop.

The primitiveness of rice cultivation in Mien Tay, then, is only indirectly attributable to psychological or financial causes. In the final analysis, the agrarian and economic structures were responsible for the dual character of rice cultivation: extensive and speculative monoculture. No sooner did the harvest end than the marketable surplus of rice left the hands not only of the producers but in many cases of the landowners as well. This was a result of a commercial structure of which the Chinese were the masters.

The Chinese monopoly was established prior to the arrival of the French in Nam Bo. According to an early report by Rear Admiral Lagrandière,

> Commerce and agriculture are much more closely linked in the colony than in any other country. . . . The Chinese has the immense advantage over the European of knowing the natives, who have been accustomed for a long time to make all their transactions with him. These Asiatics have agents in the interior markets. There are about one hundred Chinese established in each *huyen* [subprefecture], generally in communication with the commercial houses of Saigon and even of China.[35]

For a long time the center of manufacturing and commerce was situated exclusively at Cholon, where there was a rice exchange. A network of large canals converging there drained all the paddy of Nam Bo. After milling, or even before, the grain was exported. Except for one Franco-German company, which disappeared in 1914, all the mill owners were Chinese.[36]

The possession of flotillas of junks and knowledge of prices on foreign markets, principally in Hong Kong, gave the Chinese a noticeable advantage. They maintained representatives in the rice-growing provinces; at the chief town of Bac-lieu in 1929 there were twenty-five of them. Before the harvest, Chinese brokers sent out buyers who scouted the countryside appraising the

TABLE 8: Rice Brokers and Warehouses in Mien Tay,
by Province, 1930 (in tons)

Province	Number of Brokers	Capacity of Warehouses
Rach-gia	22	8,180
Bac-lieu	18	6,760
Soc-trang	24	7,240
Can-tho	24	14,360
Long-xuyen	unknown	14,040
Chau-doc	5	2,280

Source: Henry, L'économie agricole, 350–51.

crop and making small and middle-sized purchases. A broker attended only
the most important transactions, those involving ten thousand *gia* or more.
Agreements with the owners of the crops were rarely concluded in writing.
Owners pledged their grain against cash loans advanced with interest. This
interest could be cancelled but only when the harvest was sold at a price fixed
in advance by the broker. The web of commerce and credit was so all-encom-
passing that it was nearly impossible for a rice grower to dispense with the
Chinese intermediary. In an attempt to rectify the fixing of prices, which
worked to the disadvantage of uninformed producers, the French administration adopted the practice of telegraphing market quotations to the chief
towns, and making their posting mandatory, but the Chinese evaded this
regulation in various ways. Often they persuaded the postal clerk to post the
prices after the principal markets had closed, or they prevailed upon him to
falsify the figures. In 1934, Governor Pagès had to dispatch a memorandum
to administrators, reminding them that posting prices was obligatory.[37] The
Chinese spread tendentious and fanciful rumors: the war that would end the
world was at hand, the Japanese were on the point of arriving, the harvest
was so abundant that prices would be disastrous. Gambling was also an efficient means of placing peasants at the mercy of merchants who masqueraded
as managers of gambling dens. Once the transactions were completed, the
small quantities having been measured in *gia* and the larger quantities by
weight, the Chinese collected the crop in granaries situated along the waterways. The capacity of these granaries could vary from ten thousand to one
hundred thousand piculs.[38] Numbers of brokers and the capacity of their
warehouses in 1930 are presented in table 8.

From every corner of Mien Tay, sampans, and later junks, transported the paddy to collecting centers at the principal provincial markets. Apart from Can-tho City, the most important was at Bai Xau (in Soc-trang Province), which gave its name to a well-known variety of rice. Transport conditions were primitive judging by the repeated complaints of mixed grain, the lack of protection from rain, dampening of the grain to increase its weight, and the lack of its separation from cargo such as charcoal.[39] In the collection centers large junks transshipped the paddy and moved it on to Cholon. Transactions were settled not by tranfers of large sums of money but by a system of accounts. In the provinces the retail or wholesale grocers, whether agents of the Cholon brokers or dependent upon them in some way, furnished the mill owners with the money needed to purchase rice from the farmers. The mill owners later repaid the grocers. The increasing importance of this business required the infusion of more and more capital, which was obtained either from banks or from the large European export companies. The banks granted loans with paddy pledged as security, the amount of the loan corresponding to 70 percent of the value of the stored grain. Other loans were made with property as security, or sometimes on personal credit if the Chinese borrower was well known. The European export firms advanced grocers, on the contract of delivery of rice, sums of less than 50 percent of the rice's value. By discounting their notes, the banks greatly facilitated these advances.

Advances became the rule, so much so that when a Chinese had enough funds at his disposal that he did not need more, the exporters paid him interest on the uncollected advances.[40] The wholesalers–mill owners sometimes had considerable capital at their disposal but they usually remained on the margin for 20 to 70 percent. As the practice of advances encouraged speculation, the commercial system was fragile. Many failures occurred in 1910–12, and more in 1928–29. In the latter period it was by means of the commercial links of the "rice-culture chain" that the Great Depression was propagated.

There were attempts to dispense with the Chinese. Some large landowners, rather than delivering the harvest immediately, were able to store their paddy and wait for higher prices. But the margin for waiting was small because the storage silos (more commonly sheds) could not keep grain over a long period without deterioration. Nor did location and distance favor Mien Tay in this process, for the rice growers of the central provinces of Nam Bo also possessed stocks that had to be disposed of, and the Chinese could afford to wait until the producers of the West cried for mercy.

By the end of World War I, steam huskers were common in the West. Previously all the marketable paddy had been milled at Cholon and rice

TABLE 9: Steam Rice Huskers Operating in Mien Tay, 1931

Province	Number	Daily Output (in tons)
Chau-doc	10	28.5
Can-tho	28	193.5
Soc-trang	15	138.5
Bac-lieu	21	101.5
Rach-gia	33	184.0

Note: This information differs markedly, however, from that given by Estebe in *Le problème du riz*.

Source: Henry, *L'économie agricole*, 351.

intended for local consumption was husked by hand. By the 1930s, several dozen huskers were operating (see Table 9). In the provinces, the numbers ranged from a few in Chau-doc to about twenty in Can-tho. The most important, those producing grain for export, were situated at Rach-gia City, at Khanh Lang (Bai Xau), at Lap Vo (in Long-xuyen), and at Phu Loc (north of Bac-lieu). Equipped with motors of fourteen to thirty horsepower and installed under sheds, they required two or three men, processing paddy on demand, whose productivity ranged from three hundred to eight hundred kilograms of paddy per hour per person.

The machines belonged mainly to the Chinese. In 1923, for example, apropos of a dispute with the administration, we learn that fifteen owners operating huskers in Bac-lieu were Chinese, most of them Teochiu, as were their employees.[41] Thus, even after the milling of paddy had become partially decentralized, it remained under their control. The French were unable to gain a foothold in the wholesaling of rice. Lagrandière suggested that this was not just due to the precedence of the Chinese but because the colonizers had been discredited by the activities of "a few unreliable [French] adventurers."[42] Although this reputation had been made during the period of conquest, time did not bring a change in attitude. The large European firms found it no easier to enter into regional commerce than they had at Cholon. If the position of the Chinese merchants remained impregnable, it was also due to the fact that they were much more than wholesalers. Acting as banker, trader, transporter, and mill owner, the Chinese intermediary was polyvalent. Moreover, solidarity permitted the Chinese to rid themselves of intruders.[43] For these reasons the isolated initiatives of the administration failed to dislodge the Chinese from their powerful positions. A partial admission of this was made by the lieutenant governor to the Colonial Council in 1907.

> The measures enacted in order to put the native cultivators on guard against the speculation of the Chinese intermediaries gave good results. Nevertheless, natives obliged to find money to meet their debts sometimes were constrained to accept the conditions of the Chinese agents.[44]

Only a few exceptional landowners were able to overcome the dominance of the Chinese. One, the settler Gressier, dispensed with them by establishing his estate at Phu Loc and transporting his rice to Cholon in his own fleet of junks.[45]

The administration was no more capable of amending the entrenched commercial structure than were the export companies. In this domain, as in so many others, the status quo was maintained. Thus, on the eve of the Great Depression in 1929, the rice culture of Mien Tay was dependent upon the exterior geographically, financially, and economically. The rice growers worked only with foreign capital, and in most cases they did not control prices, which were fixed either at Cholon or in foreign markets. Both transport and commerce were in foreign hands. Mien Tay had never been an integral part of a national, or even a peninsular, market.[46] The French only exacerbated this long-standing situation since the colonial economy was tied to markets outside Vietnam.

Although a regional market survived (run by Indian, Chinese, and Malay merchants), this did not prevent its regional dimensions from being "closely interdependent, closely united by a powerful 'operator': economic subordination vis-à-vis the Occident."[47] In the 1920s, Mien Tay possessed a colonial economy in which the traditional sector of rice culture had been integrated into the world capitalist economy. The decision-making centers, like the outlets, were located outside of the colony. Thus, it was subject to a considerable levy, operated jointly by interest groups of the colonial power (principally the banks), foreign minorities, and a few privileged nationals most of whom were Chinese, Indians, or large landowners.

Subordination made the economy very vulnerable to natural fluctuations and crises, both economic and political. The climate and the rudimentary hydrographic infrastructure combined to reduce or destroy many harvests.

This resulted in local recessions, such as the one that accompanied the typhoon of 1904. The price of rice fluctuated with the dictates of supply and demand, fiscal exigencies, and currency exchange rates.[48] Thus, the "peripheral" character of the Mien Tay economy predisposed it toward disaster when faced with a disturbance of which the epicenter was situated outside the colony.

Credit: A Pyramid of Dependencies

French policy on land concessions and agricultural labor favored the concentration of land ownership and the formation of large rural estates. Another contributing factor was usury. In the precolonial period, family and local consumption was the principle aim of agricultural and craft production. Even under these conditions some credit was needed in the form of personal loans for consumption, tools, textiles, cult objects such as joss sticks, and firecrackers to celebrate the New Year. Marriages, funerals, and elevation to the office of *notable* in a village were occasions for expenditure and thus for borrowing. On a grander scale, credit to finance the clearing of land reached a considerable volume, though it may have been almost exclusively in kind. Advances to *ta dien* and other agricultural workers were primarily in the form of paddy for consumption, seed, tools, and occasionally the loan of a water buffalo. All these were repayable with a portion of the harvest. Advances made by Chinese merchants also were secured by the harvest to come. When a landowner borrowed from another landowner, he practiced the *dien mai*, the securing of a loan with the title to land, which the French sometimes compared to the *vente à réméré* or the *vente avec rachat*.[49]

Dien mai was the principal means of procuring credit in the precolonial period. Under this system the borrower would deposit his property title with the lender though he remained in physical possession of the land. In a provisional sense the borrower was selling the land. If he did not repay the sum due within the term specified by the agreement, the lender would be registered in the *dia bo* as the new owner. If no time limit for repayment was recorded in the contract, the right to regain title was limited to thirty years by a 1839 edict of the emperor Minh Mang. This system did not totally dispossess the "seller" since it authorized him to continue to reside on the land as a tenant of the creditor. Under French law, on the other hand, the *dien mai* became in practice a form of security. Default or bad faith on the part of the debtor authorized the creditor to evict him and sell the land to recoup his investment. The *dien mai* did preserve one of its original features, however, as the creditor could not become the lawful owner of the property. As a form of credit, *dien mai* was suited to the traditional village in which everyone knew everyone else and a measure of social equilibrium prevailed. It also took into account the aversion of the Vietnamese peasant to leaving the land and the tombs of his ancestors.[50] Besides the land and the harvest, personal possessions or children could serve as the principal collateral. To repay a debt, parents sometimes placed a child in the home of the creditor, furnishing its labor to him, and if they were lucky they might secure an apprenticeship for the child.

The French conquest modified these credit patterns. The construction of canals and roads progressively accelerated trade, and new consumption requirements emerged. The formation of large rural estates especially increased the demand for credit. Nonetheless, the new demands were not accompanied by new forms of credit until after World War I. Traditionally, the principal lenders were Vietnamese landowners and Chinese merchants. The practice was widespread; as soon as a man had at his disposal a surplus in kind or in cash, almost invariably he would lend it to his fellows, though large loans could be furnished only by the middle-sized or large landowners. Most commonly the latter advanced rice, seed, tools, and even money to their *ta dien*. When they lent to other landowners, their aim was usually to enlarge their own estates.

Often, the large as well as the small and middle-sized Vietnamese landowners took recourse in the services of the Chinese moneylender. This was a merchant with an excellent information network at his command, well acquainted with the needs and the resources of his clients. He lent wisely and flexibly, always accepting payment in kind, and he came to play an essential role in the rice trade. Though a lender, he made his profit in the market. The moderate rate of interest he charged was compensated by the low price of rice and the high profits to be made in selling it.[51]

Unlike the Chinese, the Indians (or *chettys*) practiced moneylending exclusively. They seem to have entered the business later than the Chinese, for it is only in 1907 that the *L'Annuaire de Cochinchine* lists two prominent Indians, Karoupanachetty and Ramassamychetty, operating in the province of Long-xuyen. The same year, a report of the administrator of Rach-gia Province mentions that Lam Van My, secretary to the inspector of Can-tho, was a debtor of Souna Pana Kouna Mana Sidambaramchetty in the amount of $2,500.[52] In 1930, ten *chettys* were listed as doing business in Can-tho City alone.

The success of the *chettys* derived from their lending methods. Formalities were kept to a minimum. The *chetty* did not demand physical collateral but only two guarantees affixed to a simple written statement of private debt. This advantage to the borrower was only apparent, however, for under the French Civil Code the *chetty* could appeal to the mortgage law that would bestow upon him the pledged land.[53] Sometimes in cases of default the *chettys* would consolidate several notes of debt by means of a notarial act that permitted them to take possession of land pledged as security. But the *chetty* preferred to use personal pressure, for which he seemingly developed a devastating technique. In turn insinuating, insulting, and menacing, rarely did he fail to convince his recalcitrant client to pay up.[54] It seems that gradually, as new forms of credit appeared, the *chettys* became lenders of last resort.

The Indian lenders preferred to deal in rural properties. Over the course of the first decades of the 1900s, they expanded their holdings by acquiring land their borrowers had pledged as security.[55] By 1937, they had come to possess 22,204 hectares of rice land in Mien Tay distributed as follows: in the province of Bac-lieu, 5,191 hectares; in Rach-gia, 2,592; in Soc-trang, 5,367; in Can-tho, 5,573; and in Long-xuyen, 3,481.[56]

P. D'Enjoy described the *chettys* as moneylenders "of a ferocious greed."

> They fall into the company of ten to fifteen friends in order to rent a
> room where they install their safes on which they sleep during the
> night. Their food is wretched, they live only for hoarding, and in the
> Orient, with its sensual morals, the contrast of these ascetics, made
> chaste by avarice, with the polygamous peoples, is of a peculiar effect.
> The Indians, with close-cropped hair and long robes of white muslin,
> fleece our scatter-brained subjects. And the French money thus drained
> passes via India into the hands of the English.[57]

Although this description is forced and its contrasts facile, including even an allusion to perfidious Albion, the text expresses well the prevailing sentiments concerning the *chettys* and it exhibits the principal grievance against them— that their profits did not benefit the colony. The Indians had their defenders, however, and sometimes found support in unexpected places. In 1916, by virtue of a 1914 decree concerning usury, two *chettys* were ordered to be expelled from the colony. Ernest Outrey, the deputy for Cochinchina, wrote a letter to G. Doumergue, minister for the colonies, in which he defended the *chettys* on the basis of their utility.

In summary, I consider that the primitive organization of the Indian bankers, in spite of all their defects, is still a benefit and as long as a new organization has not replaced it, it is important to maintain it, in the enlightened self-interest of the Colony.[58]

The *chettys* do not deserve all the scorn that has been heaped upon them. The amplification of their scandalous reputation in articles and books should not cause us to forget that they did not possess a monopoly on usury. Other moneylenders demanded high rates of interest, although these varied according to personal conventions, the social situation, and the degree of solvency of the borrower. For a loan on the order of a thousand piasters, the approved interest rate amounted to 2 to 3 percent per month. The smaller the loan the more the rates increased, up to 5 to 10 percent for one hundred piasters in the short term. In all probability this was no better than the rates charged by the *chettys*.[59]

The most common type of credit in the countryside, and the one considered most oppressive, was the *bac lua vay*, the money-paddy loan. Under this system, a peasant borrowing a sum of money was required to repay it in the form of paddy at the price prevailing on the day of the loan. Since the price of paddy followed a generally ascending curve prior to the Great Depression, the system functioned to the disadvantage of the borrower.[60]

To combat what was depicted as a plague upon the cultivators, decrees against usury were issued regularly. But their numbers were usually in inverse relationship to their practical effect, and the legislation was remarkable for its uselessness. One magistrate, M. Leonardi, who heard cases concerning usury, voiced his disillusionment. Although he was citing examples from Saigon, his observations are valid for the West as well.

In a judicial area such as that of the Saigon court, wherein acts of usury are established at each hearing, no convictions for habitual usury offenses have occurred for several years, though the number of cases judged surpassed 2,400 in 1925.[61]

Early on it was recognized that the true remedy would be the creation of abundant, cheap, agricultural and land credit. An early initiative was the attempt to create a credit system based solely on the peasants pledging their harvest as security. Loans on harvests were granted by the Banque de l'Indochine. The administrators, whose signatures served as a guarantee, acted as intermediaries. The moderate interest amounted to 8 percent per year. The granting of the loans, in fact, was essentially an operation of the Treasury; the bank, which did not disburse the money directly, showed little enthusiasm for this kind of lending.[62] As an administrator of Bac-lieu reminded a delegate in 1912, these loans were earmarked especially "for small landowners in need."[63]

A summary drawn up by the administrator of Ha-tien Province for the years 1880–81 describes the lending of fairly modest sums. Three villages had borrowed less than $500, and one $3,130. Individual loans ranged from $20 to $200.[64] Ha-tien was not typical, however, as it had been settled relatively recently, was the least developed province of the West, and had the largest proportion of small landowners. Summaries for the provinces in which large landowners predominated present a different picture. In 1911, loans contracted at Rach-gia amounted to $1,000 to $3,000 for landowners holding 110 to 683 hectares. In 1907–8, 196 requests involved less than $100; 53 between $100 and $500; 2 between $500 and $1,000; and 15 were for $1,000 or more. Also in 1907, the 5 defaulting debtors whose property was sold at public auction had borrowed $57, $60, $60, $80, and $95, respectively.[65]

On the whole, though, it appears that debts incurred through the loan-on-harvest program were collected regularly and without major difficulty. Contrary to an opinion sometimes expressed, the Banque de l'Indochine granted delays in repayment in response to nearly all requests. In only one season was the government of Cochinchina forced to compensate the bank for unpaid loans (totaling $43,000).[66] This occurred during the 1906–7 season when the West had not yet recovered from the typhoon and flooding of 1904. Even then, M. Tholance, chief of the second bureau of the Cochinchinese government, remarked that the rebate of 2 percent brought benefits to the bank that more than compensated for its losses.[67]

The peasants did not borrow money themselves but worked through the *notables* of the village in which the land was located. The *notables* saw this as an added burden on them, for sometimes the borrowers did not reside in the village in which the land was situated. Since the village was held responsible for the sums due the bank, "the *notables* are [the guarantors] by their personal property."[68] There was much confusion, and, as an administrator remarked in a memorandum of 1886,

Most of the inhabitants and *notables* were ignorant of the decree of April 2, 1876, and of the formalities to be observed for borrowing. On the other hand, where there were requests, the *notables* were believed to be solely responsible for the repayment of the loans, and consequently demanded of their borrowers large commissions, which rendered the institution sterile, though in reality they were only responsible for the sincerity of their declarations.[69]

The stipulation that the government's loans on harvest must be repaid by a fixed date regardless of when the loan was granted reduced the scheme's attractiveness.[70] One administrator reported that "The obligation to repay by the sixteenth of May no matter what the date of the loan constitutes an inconvenience for the cultivator. Consequently, he prefers to resort to the *chetty*, despite the scandalous rates."[71] The dependence of the scheme on public financing also caused some inconvenience to the government, as in 1912 when a financial crisis obliged the administration to cancel all loans.[72] The decree of September 1927, which finally abolished the system of loans on harvests, seems to have only confirmed a decline in its use over several years.

The emergence of a sound agricultural credit system was long delayed by the absence of reliable security. The harvest was easily subject to destruction or deterioration since bonded warehouses did not exist. Land titles were unreliable, if they existed at all. Obviously, this situation did not appeal to the banks. Although the early leaders of the colony tried to address the problem of credit, they always stumbled over the absence of a cadastral survey and thus the lack of solid security for loans.

The short-lived Banque de Cochinchine attempted to address the problem of security by offering around 1908 to issue bonded warehouse warrants for harvests. The rice growers, having received credit from the Banque de l'Indochine, would deliver their crops to these warehouses. But the Saigon Chamber of Commerce condemned the proposal as ineffective and unprofitable. Although the Banque de Cochinchine made a few mortgage loans, after one or two years of disastrous operation it closed down. It appears that the administration and the Banque de l'Indochine did not encourage its development.[73]

At about the same time, in April 1907, Lieutenant Governor Rodier proposed the creation in each province of an indigenous self-help society. His plan involved creating a system of agricultural credit and collective assurance within the framework of the village. The general plan was approved by the Colonial Council but it was never carried out. Although Rodier left the colony in July 1907, he had found a sympathetic audience: in the province of Can-tho where "the sums lent by the *chettys* to the natives were estimated at a million piasters,"[74] a group of Vietnamese (some of whom were naturalized French citizens), led by the president of the *Société de l'Enseignement Mutuel de Cochinchine*, conceived the creation of a cooperative society that would grant agricultural credit. Its statutes were elaborated in anticipation of Rodier's return. In the same period, Me. Loye, a French magistrate at Soc-trang, led an ardent campaign in favor of the promotion of mutual agricultural credit.

These plans led to a decree of November 1912, which called for creation of native agricultural societies and funds in the form of Sociétés Indigènes de Crédit Agricole Mutuel (or SICAMs). The first such organization was founded at My-tho. Although World War I interrupted their development, as early as 1918 additional SICAMs were established at Soc-trang and Long-xuyen, and in 1919 at Bac-lieu and Can-tho. In 1924, the province of Rach-gia, in 1927 Chau-doc, and in 1930 Ha-tien instituted similar organizations. In all except the last two cases, a fund for credit was created along with the agricultural society.

By a decree of 28 January 1928, the SICAMs were given charters that specified their organizational structure and functions. A Central Commission for all of Cochinchina supervised the management of provincial funds. Each SICAM was managed by a Vietnamese Council of Administration presided over by the chief administrator of the province. Financing was assured by the subscriptions of the members, the profits from operations, and particularly by the Banque de l'Indochine, which rediscounted the SICAMs' notes at an interest rate of 6 percent.

The SICAMs dealt in agricultural loans exclusively, principally those of short and middle term. The borrower could pledge a personal guarantee for loans of less than $500, and real property security, in the form of a warrant, for larger loans. The initial rate of interest of 12 percent per year was gradually lowered to 10 percent. The loans were almost always granted without fees for commissions, appraisals, or the preparation of documents.

In the spirit of their initiators, the SICAMs came to play several roles. In the first place, they served as regulators of the price of credit. The availability of reasonable rates of interest caused a decrease in, if not the disappearance of, usurious rates through the process of competition. To accomplish this they worked to ensure that their loans would reach small cultivators as well as the large landowners. The SICAMs also functioned as schools of management for agriculturalists whom it familiarized with modern forms of credit. Lastly, the SICAMs were able to draw into circulation private savings that previously had been hoarded in the form of jewelry and gold ingots destined for the moneylenders.[75]

In 1927, the Société Française de Crédit Agricole Mutuel came into being. It performed operations analogous to those of the SICAMs but in the much smaller circle of the French settlers. These clients were predominantly rice growers. In 1931, when a total of $214,133 was loaned, $184,733 was dispensed as short-term notes to rice growers. Between 1927 and 1931, the number of full members did not exceed 159 and nominal capital was $26,050.[76]

The Banque de l'Indochine was itself concerned with rice cultivation in the West. The establishment, in August 1930, of offices at Can-tho City is revealing. In his inaugural speech the director of the Saigon office, M. Gannay, stated that the aims of this branch would not be to grant long-term rural loans but "to facilitate commercial operations, seasonal loans, and advances on rice stocks, linked to the preparation of crops and to the fluctuations of the harvests," in other words, to create a market for paddy and to combat usury.[77]

In the wake of these projects, the West found itself with an actual surplus of credit, and lending institutions went so far as to solicit the business of landowners, usually offering them rates of 16 percent per annum while easing the conditions of guarantee. This led to abuses, which came to the attention of the administration when the onset of the Great Depression prompted an examination of the situations of debtors. M. de Feyssal, an official entrusted with such an inquiry, reported on several cases, including one in which a farmer appeared on paper to be the proprietor of 290 hectares of rice land. In reality he was the owner of a large tract covered with water in extreme southern Cochinchina. Here he fished and bred tortoises for their shells, growing on the rare parcels of land that emerged from the water only enough rice to feed his nine children. The investigator inquired how he had succeeded in borrowing $15,000 from the Banque de l'Indochine? "I was offered $20,000," he replied, and added that he had borrowed an additional $11,000 from various compatriots.[78] The offers of credit from several sources doubtless caused interest rates to fall. It was noted that the relatively moderate rate of 18 percent per year, previously rare, was common on the eve of the depression. Another official wrote that "The influence of the SICAM appeared preponderant with regard to the general land situation; the rates for loans between natives were lowered from 24 percent per year (around 1920) to 16 percent per year in 1929.[79]

But did this beneficial situation affect a large proportion of the users of credit? Had the obstacles that had hindered the generalization of the loans on harvests and the foundation of an effective agricultural system and land

TABLE 10: SICAM Membership for Selected Provinces and Years

Province	Number of Members		
	1922	1929	1931
Can-tho	257	—	1,390 landowners out of 37,978
Soc-trang	170	—	—
Chau-doc	—	119	—
Long-xuyen	—	992	—
Ha-tien	—	223	—

Sources: *Monographie de Long-xuyen* (1937), ANVN; *Monographie de Chau-doc* (1937), ANVN; *Report to the Colonial Council* (1922).

credit finally been removed? Probably not. Membership in the SICAMs, and the borrowing of money from them, were feasible only for large and middle-sized landowners. Le Quang Liem, who served as president of the SICAM of Rach-gia from 1926 to 1931, justified the dominance of the large landowners.

> The directors of the SICAM are nearly always drawn from the ranks of the most important rice growers who belong to it. As large landowners they all need to contract loans in order to prepare their lands, make advances to their tenants, finance their rice-growing activities, and sometimes to expand their estates. . . . In the provinces the large and middle-sized landowners know and visit one another. It is, moreover, thanks to this thorough knowledge of the men and their properties within the regions where they live that the directors can evaluate better than anyone else the worthiness of the requests for loans submitted to them.[80]

Actual numbers of SICAM members, known as *sicamants*, remained low (see Table 10).[81] The administrator of Ha-tien explained in 1937 that SICAMs had not "developed much because the small landowners do not present genuine security."[82] His judgment is confirmed by the 1927 compilation of the number of small loans dispersed through the SICAMs reproduced as Table 11. During the same year loans totaling less than $1,000 amounted to only $762,797 out of an operating budget of $7,485,000.[83]

TABLE 11: SICAM Credit for Small Loans Allotted and
Used in 1927, by Province

Province	Credit allotted	Credit Used
Can-tho	unlimited	$176,612
Chau-doc	$20,000	5,400
Long-xuyen	110,000	102,000
Rach-gia	80,000	38,000
Soc-trang	80,000	30,960
Bac-lieu	60,000	58,550

Source: Records of Loans Secured on Harvests, Ha-tien, 1880–81 (ANVN).

Contrary to the initial views of its promoters and the administration, the SICAMs often functioned only as a means by which large landowners could obtain funds. These, in turn, were used primarily to make private loans or invested in nonagricultural, commercial and industrial operations. Management of the SICAMs was often imprudent, and some directors operated the societies as profit-making organizations. Direct loans commonly were granted in amounts exceeding the value of the borrower's liquid assets, and often it was stipulated that all or part of the interest must be deposited in advance.[84] A clear distinction between short- and long-term loans was not always established, and, as precise notions of time were lacking in Vietnamese society, repayment tended to be sporadic. Finally, there was no conception of joint risk; the gravest fault of these societies was the absence of a sense of mutual aid and a lack of the cooperative spirit. In short, instead of draining their savings, the SICAMs simply furnished the large landowners with a supplementary means of practicing usury or provided them with financing for nonagricultural investments.

Credit dominated the economy of the West. It created a pyramid of dependencies: for the tenant farmer or the artisan vis-à-vis the landowner or the Chinese merchant; and for the landowners, even the largest, vis-à-vis the banks, the *chettys*, or the Chinese. The edifice was crowned by the Banque de l'Indochine.

An abundance of capital in the years 1925–27 encouraged land speculation and aggravated the chronic indebtedness of Mien Tay where the average ratio of encumbered to freely held land was by that time 18 percent. In Bac-lieu Province it was higher still, 27 percent, and in Can-tho it was 31 percent.[85] Even these percentages are misleading, however, as a large proportion of land pledges or sales with the right of repurchase was not recorded. Loans from one native to another also were ignored, as were loans secured with personal guarantees and harvests. Private debt was considerable, and its extent was impossible to calculate. In spite of the efforts to lower it, the rate of interest remained usurious. The SICAMs aided the larger landowners but left the peasants and tenants dependent upon the old forms of credit. It has been estimated that for this same time period capital obtained at first hand, at rates varying from 10 to 24 percent for the duration of an agricultural season, effectively cost the cultivators 50 to 150 percent. For a season lasting eight months, the rate was never less than 40 percent. The depression of the 1930s dramatically revealed the precariousness of agrarian indebtedness in Mien Tay.[86]

Means of Subsistence in the Villages: Fish, Salt, and Forests

Besides being Nam Bo's largest export crop, rice was the primary food of the population. But rice is not eaten alone, and the alimentary trilogy of Vietnam is rice, fish, and *nuoc mam* (fish sauce). As the latter two usually are processed with salt, the salt industry is also crucial. The French government recognized this when it included salt in the *trois bêtes de somme*, or three beasts of burden—the monopolies on alcohol, salt, and opium—created at the time of the budget reorganization of 1898.[87] The forest was another essential in the villagers' lives. It provided not only building materials and indispensable foodstuffs but items such as bird feathers, snake skins, and tortoise shells, all in demand by the imperial court and the nobility for consumption and trading. Honey, wax, and charcoal were collected as well, and water palm from the forest was the main source of building material. The fate of all three of these resources (fish, salt, and the forest) under the influence of rice monoculture is worth investigating.

After rice, fishing was the most important economic activity of the West.[88] In the province of Ha-tien fishing was actually the principal occupation. Both *L'Etat de la Cochinchine en 1891* and the *Monographie de Ha-tien* of 1937 reported that nearly all the inhabitants participated in fishing, at least in a seasonal manner. In the canton of Hon-chong 80 percent, and at Phu Quoc 90 percent, of all economic activity was devoted to it. A 1923 report stated that fishing along Bac-lieu's four hundred kilometers of coastline employed some three hundred inhabitants.[89] These were supplemented by seasonal fishermen who participated during lulls in the rice-growing season.

Fishing was not practiced on the high seas. Vietnamese fishermen seldom ventured more than four thousand meters from the coast of the Gulf of Siam or the South China Sea.[90] Fishing also was widespread along the *rach*, in the canals, and in ponds. In the provinces of Chau-doc and Long-xuyen it generated important primary income but everywhere it was a complementary resource in the absence of secondary crops. The paddy fields themselves were used as breeding grounds. Families would fish from January to May, benefiting from the progressive drying of the small waterways and marshes. They worked cooperatively and divided the catch. Fishing implements were simple: large standing nets, bow nets, and square dipping nets were made of bamboo and rattan; in the ponds the fish were caught by hand.

Before the arrival of the French, the right to fish was granted as a privilege to the founders of villages in the region of Ca-mau.[91] During the colonial period many villages leased their fishing grounds to large Vietnamese or Chinese landowners. In Chau-doc Province in 1936, the majority of village revenues came from three-year leases of fisheries (24,000 piasters annually).[92] In 1881, lessees maintained teams of three to nine men under the direction of a foreman. The latter received a fifth of the catch and the lessee took the rest. The fishermen were paid fifty centimes per day plus food. Later, in Chau-doc and elsewhere, similar agreements were in effect. Individuals could fish after paying a fee. Lessees sometimes raised fees arbitrarily, however, and closed the *rach* and canals with weirs even when they were essential to water traffic.

A small commercial fishing industry did exist. Junks brought in large catches of fish and shrimp from the sea. The catch was dried, salted, and exported, sometimes to Saigon but more often to Hainan, Hong Kong, and Singapore by way of the ports of Ha-tien and Ca-mau. A related industry, the principal one at Phu Quoc and in Ha-tien, was the production of *nuoc mam* and *mam ruoc* (salted shrimp paste). At Phu Quoc the annual production of *nuoc mam* was estimated at 1.3 million liters; in Ha-tien the figure was 15,000 liters.[93]

Both fishing and the processing of the catch were affected by economic conditions. The minutes of the Provincial Council of Ha-tien in 1922 refer to a third year of depression in the fishing sector without setting forth the causes. It recorded a drop of a third in licensee-tax revenues, and stated that of the 560 tanks used in the making of *nuoc mam* only 75 were being utilized. In the winter months the profit could be nothing.[94] In addition, the fishermen were often cash poor. The Chinese merchants intervened here as elsewhere, forming moneylending companies for the duration of a season if the return seemed promising, and the interest on sums borrowed by the fishermen sometimes absorbed an entire year's income. Another problem was the price of salt. In 1913, fishermen in Rach-gia threw back into the sea a large quantity of fish because high prices rendered salting impossible. Production of *nuoc mam* in Ha-tien also was limited, despite the fact that fish were abundant.[95]

There were no real attempts by the administration to modernize fishing in Mien Tay. In accordance with French policy, the government took care to maintain only what already existed. In 1887, M. Jouffroy d'Abbans, residing in Paris, requested from the minister of the navy and the colonies authorization to establish salt-water fisheries in Nam Bo in order to supply Saigon and Cholon with fresh fish. The governor of Cochinchina demurred, explaining that if a monopoly were set up,

> The economic conditions of a population of 2 million inhabitants would in this way be profoundly disturbed and the budget would by the same stroke lose a revenue of 180,000 francs that would no longer be paid by the abandoned establishments.[96]

In 1920 and 1923, responses to government inquiries concerning fishing pointed to a number of features: the artisanal and empirical character of the industry, which was largely seasonal; the material and financial destitution of those who devoted themselves to it; and the economic and social dependencies that resulted from it. A 1922 decree of the governor general attempted to encourage more mechanization.

> With the object of developing maritime fishing in Nam Bo, there is established by the following conditions a system of premiums, which will benefit vessels of the trawler type, of more than two hundred tons unloaded, mechanically propelled by steam, internal combustion engine, or any other engine, used for the indicated industry.[97]

However, the stipulations of the decree prohibited its application to the Cochinchinese West, and on the eve of the depression substantial uncertainty still weighed upon a resource vital to the population.[98]

The salt industry, too, was rendered unstable by the colonial economy. The administration kept for itself the exclusive and lucrative right to buy and sell salt, obtaining thirty centimes from the consumption tax and twenty from the warehouse surtax per picul.[99] By virtue of this system, operations in the salt pans were placed under the authority of the director of customs and excise who determined the opening and closing dates for production. The customs men could inspect the pans night or day and the entire product was delivered to the administration, at the latest on the third day following collection and manufacture. This system did not prevent fraud, despite draconian application, and it was unpopular with both producers and consumers. The retail price also reflected a consumption tax: $2.25 per one hundred kilos after 1906.[100] To this was added a sum proportional to the general expenses of the warehouses and retail stores.

Bac-lieu possessed the most important salt pans of the West. There four landowners dominated an area that varied from 500 to 885 hectares between 1915 and 1928. Average annual production reached twenty thousand tons in 1929, and was as high as forty thousand tons in some years. The salt was greyish in color but it contained 94 percent sodium chloride, which made it suitable for salting fish and for use in the brine industry. The salt season, which extended from January to March or April, employed a sizable labor force. Twenty to 35 hectares of salt pan usually required the attention of forty to fifty workers, nearly all of them Chinese.[101] In 1931, the administration tested a variation of its monopoly system in Bac-lieu Province, authorizing the salt makers to dispose of all or part of their salt privately and replacing the consumption tax with a lump-sum payment.[102] These new arrangements were designed principally to relieve the administration of the expense of surveillance and storage during depression years. They did not ameliorate the problems of distribution or succeed in lowering the price.

The French administration's opening of the West to settlement resulted in constriction of another rural resource, the forest. Exploitation of the forest, as well as the progress of settlement, adversely affected the villagers' hunting and gathering activities. As rice land was cleared, the forest was delivered to fire and machete without restriction from 1862 to 1912. Numerous concessionaires sold off the forest products located on their tracts (initial profits from these activities were higher and more immediate than those deriving from cultivation) and thoughtless exploitation led to the gradual disappearance of the forest. Deforestation had serious consequences, for along with the trees went climatic tempering. Repeated droughts were attributed to the deforestation, and bees and birds migrated elsewhere, leading to a decline in honey gathering and hunting.

When the administration finally came to realize what riches were embodied in the forests of Mien Tay, it took measures to protect them. In 1912, it created a forestry service, which regulated the felling of trees in established reserves. Despite these efforts, the onslaught continued. Personnel were few, and corrupt forest rangers shut their eyes to illegal cutting while others failed to thwart the ruses of clandestine hewers. According to one observer, the forest was "strewn with corpses."[103]

The new wave of settlers and increasing consumption of charcoal were not the only reasons for this wholesale destruction. "Hunger for the forest" also resulted from the exhaustion of communal forests. In addition, the forest was an important source of revenue for the administration, which wavered between the attraction of fiscal yields and the principal of conservation. In 1931, it promulgated a decree establishing new forest reserves in which settlement, lumbering, and cultivation would be prohibited.[104] In 1915, a decree of the governor general of Indochina forbade the hunting and capture of marabous and egrets in all of Nam Bo, a move intended to halt the destruction of these species and put an end to quarrels among farmers over hunting territories.[105] The water palm, an essential building material, became scarce, and its price increased as the river banks became more and more populated. In 1913, one cultivator in Rach-gia Province planted some water palms. Initially the butt of jokes, five years later he was making a profit, and his example was soon followed by a great many families.[106]

The Pepper Industry of Ha-tien

Pepper cultivation was the only sizable commercial enterprise in the West outside of the rice economy. It was limited to the vicinity of the town of Ha-tien and the canton of Hon-chong where Cambodian, Vietnamese, and Chinese landowners had settled in the valleys. The Chinese were in the majority. In 1892, there were 1,000 Hainanese in Hon-chong; in 1925, they numbered 1,500. Two European settlers, Messrs. Blanc and Blanchy, and later a M. Mayer, acquired concessions that they entrusted to the Hainanese (in 1897, of Blanchy's 185 *engagés*, only 9 were Vietnamese). French settlers also planted pepper on the island of Phu Quoc.[107]

Pepper cultivation, which had begun early in the nineteenth century, made rapid headway during the first two colonial decades. In the five-year period from 1893 to 1898 land under pepper cultivation increased from 250 to 550 hectares.[108] Governor General Paul Doumer attributed the prosperity of the pepper plantations to a measure of 1892, the Meline Tariff, which removed half of the tax on Indochinese pepper and established quotas for its entry into metropolitan areas, which discouraged smuggling.[109] Nonetheless, pepper cultivation suffered several setbacks after 1900. The administrative report of Ha-tien for 1913 notes a continual drop in prices from 1900 to 1909. The *huyen* of Hon-chong wrote in 1909 that "I find Hon-chong today depopulated, with some pepper plantations abandoned or in bad repair."[110] A recovery in prices that occurred in 1910–12 was not accompanied by a resurgence of production and soon the growers were subjected to a new series of price fluctuations. The price per picul varied from a low of $14 during the 1916–22 period to a high of $105 in 1928.[111] Production declined throughout the period.

Fluctuations in prices and production derived from a variety of causes. The Hainanese had introduced expensive and time-consuming methods of cultivation that tended to impoverish the planters while benefitting the merchants and moneylenders.[112] The plants were grown on supports set in the ridges of earth formed by two furrows. They were fertilized with pulverized shrimp shells and only fruited after six to twenty-five years. The agronomist A. Chevalier wrote that even modern viticulture was simple in comparison.[113] A great number of supports were needed, tobacco juice to combat parasites had to be imported, and the amount of fertilizer had to be constantly increased. These requirements, plus labor, pushed the costs of production above the selling price. Small and middle-sized planters found themselves under the thumbs of their creditors and the suppliers of fertilizer, tobacco, and agricultural implements—namely, the Chinese merchants. Nearly always it was one of these creditors, or the principal one, who bought the harvest, the planter paying him off in kind. The official picul of 68 kilograms became 70 or 75 on these occasions, and if any pepper remained the planter was obliged to sell it to the merchant at a price fixed in advance, a sum always lower than the probable market price. The administration's reduction of the tax and establishment of the quota system did not benefit the producers given the web of dependency in which they were caught. Certificates of reduced tax slipped through their fingers, finding their way to the merchant-exporters, or more precisely to their compradors, who could have these certificates endorsed like negotiable bills.

Pepper cultivation also appears to have declined due to restrictions placed on the immigration of Chinese laborers and changes in France's import policy. In 1901, new entry procedures were applied to the Hainanese who were subjected to anthropometric measurements and had to pay $19 fee upon arrival. From then on they preferred to work in the neighboring Cambodian province of Kampot, where pepper cultivation was expanding. European settlers, protesting against the fee, obtained a postponement for *engagés*. But, since the pepper season began in June and lasted until May of the following year, the workers were obliged to pay the fee in January. The narrow definition of *engagé* also limited the scope of the deferment.[114] The Arrondissement Council of Ha-tien took notice of the exodus of three hundred Chinese to Kampot in 1906 and expressed alarm at the competition generated by the Cambodian plantations in 1909.[115] Pepper production, already in decline, received an additional blow in 1928 when the French government abolished the quotas and repealed a prohibition on foreign pepper. Cochinchinese pepper was then placed in an inferior position vis-à-vis the competition. By then, even duty-free status for colonial pepper, which was conferred later, could not revive it.

Shopkeepers and Peddlers

The settlement of the West under a commercialized rice economy spread trade throughout the region. The activities of small itinerant peddlers, operating principally out of sampans along the canals, were as important as the commerce of the towns. The itinerant merchant proclaimed his arrival and his specialty with a cry, a tambourine, or clappers. Often this sort of trading became a source of odd money for the women and children of farmers, fishermen, and artisans. With fruit, vegetables, sweets, or drinks packed into baskets and placed in a small boat or on either end of a pole, they frequented crossroads, ferries, and markets. Sometimes selling illicitly, these merchants were pursued by the contractors who controlled the markets. The latter, mostly *chettys*, were seldom indulgent, and sometimes they arbitrarily increased the rates for market space. In one instance, the contractor of the My Duc market raised his rates beyond the limits of his authority. Moreover,

> There is provided in the contract a single fee of 4 centimes ($.04) for a load of paddy, rice, or other merchandise having a certain price. But the fees are also imposed by the contractor for the sale of merchandise with a nearly insignificant value of 20 or 30 centimes ($.20–$.30) sold by the women and children of the countryside for the sole purpose of procuring daily nourishment.[116]

In 1910, the administrator L. de Matra referred to repeated abuses of the lessees of ferries and markets.[117] In 1927, the administrator of Bac-lieu abolished the leasing of the market in the chief town following a strike by merchants protesting the decision of the contractor to triple his fees because leasing costs had been increased.[118] The merchants in small boats suffered from analogous troubles in the form of licenses and mooring rights.

The merchants operating out of stalls were nearly always Chinese. Their shops were a sort of bazaar in which one haggled over prices. Merchandise was sold in small quantities: one seldom bought 100 grams of salt but only a *sou*'s worth. The merchants calculated exclusively with an abacus, and the absence of accounting was a source of difficulty for tax collectors. The shops, which were attached to the merchants' living quarters, remained open very late and the Sunday holiday was ignored.

The presence of small Chinese shopowners, even in the hamlets, was a feature that Nam Bo shared with Cambodia.[119] In other parts of the colony it was exceptional to encounter small Chinese merchants in the countryside. For the Chinese who practiced trading, business was a matter of barter. Merchandise was supplied in advance and repaid with paddy, rice, or items such as rush mats. In the latter case, the merchant would deliver all the goods the client desired on the condition that the latter would repay him with his entire production of mats.[120] The same system was applied to transactions in pepper.

A description of the commerce of the West would be incomplete if it did not mention the maritime trade carried out by junks between the Nam Bo ports of Rach-gia, Ha-tien, and especially Ca-mau, and the Southeast Asian ports of Singapore, Thailand, the Dutch East Indies, and southern China. These ancient flows of traffic provisioned the West with *touques* of lamp oil from Sumatra and incense, firecrackers, silk, and tea from China in exchange for rice, pepper, salt, shrimp, dried fish, *nuoc mam*, and charcoal. Were these commercial circuits in decline or did they flourish? The rare documents we possess provide figures for traffic out of Ca-mau in 1880 (see appendix 3), 1900, and 1903 but, as they stand alone, no comparison is possible.

In 1880, the choice arose between enlargement of the main canal and improvement of the port installations of Ha-tien, and the construction of a road and bridges between Saigon and My-tho. Although the first option would have stimulated commerce between Ha-tien and Bangkok, the second was chosen. In 1931, conditions at the port of Ca-mau were discussed before the Chamber of Agriculture of Cochinchina. According to the administration, the port had been closed to imports due to a high incidence of smuggling and insufficient customs personnel. M. Chêne, president of the Chamber of Agriculture, denounced this as a measure designed to suppress the considerable commerce in fuel, which had become essential to the local population following the introduction of kerosene lamps. According to Chêne, the large petroleum companies were seeking to quell this competition. In December 1931, the port was reopened to traffic.[121]

These examples highlight the two main areas of commerce: large-scale operations at the port of Saigon, which drained the greatest part of the production of the West; and regional maritime trade, a carryover from the past, which, though modest, was vital to the population. It may be that the growth of the former caused the latter to decline, or that a division of duties and spheres took place between them, resulting in a certain equilibrium (see appendix 3).

Artisans

The artisans of Nam Bo worked within a familial and restricted labor force. On average, three or four workers were employed at each manufacturing site, and these often were paid by the piece. All the links with the land were not broken: the quarrymen of Nui Sam (in Chau-doc), like the brick makers of Phu Huu (in Can-tho), cultivated parcels of rice land in keeping with the seasonal variations in activity.[122] Nearly everywhere, the work was manual, methods and equipment were traditional, and most of the product, whether bricks or textiles, was destined for local or regional markets. The most prominent feature inherited from the past was ethnic specialization. The Chinese predominated in the manufacture of handicrafts and their distribution. They were charcoal makers, sawyers, joiners, carpenters, jewelers, cobblers, brick makers, salt makers, and, of course, merchants. In the domain of trade they were joined by the Malayans, who dealt in cattle, and a few Indian fabric merchants. None of these activities encroached upon the others. The situation permitted the existence of monopolies, or in many cases quasi-monopolies. The latter could arise due to the scarcity of candidates for a profession. For example, in Ha-tien the provincial budget of 1910 provided subsidies of 300 piasters for the butcher and 180 for the baker (both Chinese). These sums were paid until 1917.[123] Even when the Chinese came from different provinces, they managed not to interfere with each other. In 1926, at Rach-gia, there were twelve butchers, two-thirds of whom were Cantonese, while the others were Hainanese and Teochiu. But, since the contractor was

Cantonese, he reserved the business for his fellows and paid compensation to the others. In this way the Cantonese controlled prices.[124]

The Vietnamese attempted to find their way into commerce. In 1918, Can-tho City had five Annamite houses of commerce, and in 1924 it registered fifteen. They also made an effort to improve their professional training. In 1924, the Imprimerie de l'Ouest published a brochure intended to explain commercial accounting methods.[125] Although the Vietnamese recognized that it would be difficult to overcome Chinese competition, they established a few large-scale concerns in the West. One French-backed trading company in Can-tho claimed operating capital of a million francs in 1922. Called Les Galeries de l'Ouest, its main asset was a department store with branches at Soc-trang and Bac-lieu.[126] Although the existence of the firm had social as well as economic significance, it disappeared in 1931 during the depression. In another example, a mechanized brick works was opened at Can-tho in August 1930 backed with Vietnamese, Chinese, and French capital.[127] Despite such efforts, however, prior to the depression there was no qualitative transformation of artisan activities and commerce in Mien Tay. These occupations were secondary compared to rice culture, upon the success or failure of which everyone depended.

CHAPTER 4

Mien Tay Society: Old and New Contradictions

IN THE LAST QUARTER of the nineteenth century, the precolonial society of the West possessed two main features: it was rural and it was "plural." Peasants resided in village communities that were as much social cells as work units. Although those of the Vietnamese were structured, they were quite amorphous among the Khmers. Rich and powerful people existed but their influence was limited by the scale and the aims of a rural subsistence economy. Their power was exercised mainly at the heart of the communities (through acquisition of land, the practice of usury and the holding of communal "honors"), and occasionally at a higher level when local *notables* entered the ranks of the literati-mandarins.

Because Mien Tay was a frontier, however, its people harbored individualistic tendencies. They were inclined to show less respect for recognized values and were more active in the quest for material goods. The apparent stability of a society built on Confucian principles in fact concealed latent impulses. The measures taken by Minh Mang with regard to the *cong dien*, for example, reveal the need to promote sociopolitical stability through the maintenance of agrarian equilibrium. The consultation of village assemblies by Admiral Ohier, too, reveals the existence of motivations and ambitions running counter to concerns for the moderation of wealth and the maintenance of social equilibrium.

The rural communities formed the core of a society of "estates" in which the Vietnamese accorded primacy to the literati and the Khmers revered the Buddhist clergy. Since both groups gave low status to merchants, that economic function was left to foreigners. This latter circumstance was the key factor in the West's "plural" society, for such a world is not created simply by the proximity of ethnic groups but by the sharing of economic tasks between them. Each group played a role in the socioeconomic structure, a social division of labor that was both solidly established and well articulated. The result was a close association between Vietnamese or Khmer peasants, fishermen, and woodcutters, on the one hand, and Chinese merchant-lenders and transporters on the other. The association was based on well-understood needs even though its benefits were not shared equally. As such, the socioeconomic structure of Mien Tay appeared homogeneous.

French conquest added another feature to this society, making it colonial. It is true that before the coming of the French colonialism had not been entirely absent. The Vietnamese themselves were relatively recent conquerors and a part of the indigenous population still remained. But the disruptions caused by the Vietnamese were not as profound as those caused by the French. Under the Vietnamese the economy had not changed and in matters of taxation and administration the emperor's laws and customs were compatible with an agricultural society. This was not the case with European colonization. While under the French the society remained essentially rural, its dimensions and many of its aims were altered. Supremacy was accorded to those who filled vital offices, regardless of whether they were French in origin, French by means of "naturalization," or simply in the service of the dominant power.

The old social hierarchy did not entirely disappear. Rather, among the Vietnamese, the prestige of the literati and mandarin was transferred to new social classes: the intelligentsia and the bureaucracy. Among the Khmers and others who were less developed socially, Buddhist monks, *achars*, and *hadjis* remained at the head of their communities. The internal equilibrium of these communities did disappear, however, for the redistribution of wealth resulted in a new arrangement of social classes. The new structure was particularly beneficial to middle-sized and large landowners, both Vietnamese and French. This was also the case for the moneylenders, wholesalers, and transporters who functioned as the hinge in the joint of the economy.

At the same time the peasantry became proletarianized. The formation of latifundia and the nature of the frontier, where property rights were poorly defined and law enforcement difficult, contributed to this situation. Other factors such as land speculation and the prevailing financial system resulted in the dispossession of settlers and small landowners. This latter process, the effects of which were permanent, worsened during economic downturns and was particularly severe during the Great Depression of the 1930s.

In 1880, French governor Le Myre de Vilers lucidly described the social and moral consequences of colonization.

This measure of "commercial freedom" brought a new factor to the organization of the Annamite community and society. Its effects, inconspicuous at the outset, are becoming manifest today and it appears that they must lead, in the not too distant future, to a complete modification of the relations of the landowners with the working class. As long as the old landowners were alive, they preserved the traditions of the fathers, but many are dead. Their sons and grandsons no longer practice their old patriarchal customs: they exercise their rights and neglect their obligations. If we do not take care, within ten years the majority of the Annamite population will be reduced to an agricultural proletariat. This is the worst of all fates, for the work of the land is not permanent and remunerative like work in the factory or the yard.[1]

From this time onward, the wealthy landowners gained access to the first ranks of society. The desire for enrichment, the acquisition of material goods, and (to a lesser degree) participation in commercial and industrial ventures were no longer belittled. Did this result in greater social mobility? Certainly the social hierarchy was less rigid than before, the "estates" declined in importance, and opportunities for enrichment were more numerous, but at the same time social differentiation was more accentuated. These phenomena were not peculiar to the West but prevailed throughout Vietnam.[2]

By allowing the *chettys* to establish themselves in the economy, by not erecting barriers to Chinese immigration, and most of all by utilizing to the full the services of Chinese intermediaries, the French maintained and even strengthened the "plural society," at least in the beginning. But they also accentuated ethnic inequality by taking no measures to protect the Khmers against eviction from their land. The proletarianization of this minority was ethnic and social at the same time. Later, around the time of the Great Depression, Chinese economic supremacy was contested when the Vietnamese began to participate in activities that heretofore had been the preserve of the immigrants. It may be said that the pauperization of the Khmers and the first timid attacks upon the Chinese monopolies set forces in motion that would lead to the demise of the "plural" society, setting the stage for national independence and efforts to effect the assimilation of the different communities by the Vietnamese state.

The Khmers

Although the Vietnamese comprised the majority of the population, they neither absorbed nor decimated the Khmer and Chinese communities. The endurance of these groups and the relationship between ethnicity and professional activity warrant attention: the minorities maintained a vertical cellular position in society.

The Khmers, or Cambodians, numbered about 224,000 in 1929 and around 250,000 in 1940. The smallness of this increase may be attributable to emigration to Cambodia, though reliable evidence is lacking.[3] Groups entering Vietnam settled, in decreasing order of importance, in the provinces of Rach-gia, Soc-trang, Chau-doc, Bac-lieu, and Can-tho. In Ha-tien and Long-xuyen their numbers were very limited.[4] The Khmers gathered in hamlets organized around a pagoda or Buddhist monastery. Many of these were located at the base of the *nui* or the *giong* where houses on pilings were surrounded by closed gardens that gave them a pleasant appearance. Pagodas and bonzes were numerous. The residents of each hamlet were represented by their own elders.[5] The further one traveled from these zones, the more individualized the Khmers became. They no longer gathered in their own villages but settled among the Vietnamese. The numbers of Khmers residing in villages in the province of Bac-lieu (recorded in 1899) offers an example (table 12).

In the 1940s, Administrator Fraisse noted that the Khmers of Long-xuyen were in the majority near the "mountains" but that their numbers dwindled proportionately as one moved further away. Frequently the outlying population was represented by foreign *notables* rather than its own, a situation that often worked to their detriment. In 1937, *notables* of Dinh An village (Rach-gia Province) accused their mayor of having "urged militiamen to surround the Cambodians in the midst of ploughing their land and tending their seed beds. In order to be exempted from the *corvée*, each Cambodian arrested had to pay the mayor a sum of $3 to $4."[6] The land situation among the Cambodians was precarious at best. Many fled to uninhabited zones in the provinces of Rach-gia and Bac-lieu where they made up an appreciable part of the floating population of the swampy or forested margins. Abandonment of Khmer customs sometimes occurred. Women were observed to wear their *sampots* (traditional skirts) only on feast days and instead of coiling their hair on their heads they cut it like a boy's. The men adopted Vietnamese language and customs. This transformation occurred just as rapidly on the large estates where Cambodians were engaged as *ta*

TABLE 12: Ethnic Composition of Villages in
Bac-lieu Province, 1899

Village	No. of Vietnamese	No. of Khmers
Khanh Hoa	252	210
Lac Hoa	404	180
Vinh Chau	420	580
Vinh Phuoc	133	466
Lai Hoa	121	445

Source: Bac-lieu, E.12 (ANVN).

dien. On the lowest level of society there were mixed marriages between Vietnamese and Khmers.[7]

Before the arrival of the French, the Khmers had maintained more hostile relations with the Vietnamese, punctuated by numerous revolts. After the conquest, such open animosity was replaced with degradation and forced tolerance. The Cambodian custom of facing the back of a dwelling toward the road was interpreted by the Vietnamese as sulking. It was tolerated but viewed with contempt. Administrators deplored the absence of cooperation between the two groups in the regulation of communal affairs. The archives of Rach-gia provide a few examples of this. At the village of Ban Thach, taxes were levied by a Vietnamese *huong su* whom "the Cambodians distrust entirely, no taxpayer wishing to pay him their taxes. Moreover, no Cambodian *notable* wants to stand alongside the *huong su* during the collection."[8] Concerning the election of a canton chief at Thanh Binh, another administrator cautioned that it would be imprudent to elect a Khmer to the post since "the Annamite population would be greatly offended by it and it would certainly produce conflicts that would render the situation untenable."[9] The Cambodians called the Vietnamese *yun* (barbarians of the north) and in turn were given the nickname *tho* (men from the earth). During one land litigation case, a Vietnamese referred to his opponent as "that Cambodian who is nothing." Another Vietnamese member of the Colonial Council described the Cambodians as "a rather backward people in our midst."[10]

The "Pax Gallica" of the French established a fragile equilibrium that was constantly under threat, mainly in the agrarian domain. While we do not possess information on income, the documents never mention Cambodians in the provinces known for their wealth.[11] Spoliation of land at the expense of Cambodians was frequent. At Ninh Thanh Loi, as elsewhere, explosions of anger only punctuated what was a slow but methodical process of eviction carried on by *notables* and concessionaires, both Vietnamese and French.[12] The Khmers were inclined to regard the Vietnamese as their principal exploiters, however, and the socioeconomic inequities strengthened ethnic tensions.

The subjugation of the Cambodians was cultural as well. In many villages and cantons, due to a lack of teachers, Cambodian children were forced to attend schools in which a Vietnamese teacher instructed them in *quoc ngu* and rudimentary French. Most Cambodian children were older than their classmates, less assiduous, and enjoyed little scholastic success. They commonly left school early and returned to work on the land.[13] With no chance for social promotion by means of education, the Khmers usually preferred pagoda schools where their children were given a basic knowledge of their national language and were inculcated with Buddhist values. Only in 1929 was a certificate for Cambodian at the elementary-school level created, which officially sanctioned studies conducted in Khmer. Not until that time did the recruitment and training of Cambodian teachers commence.[14]

The withdrawal of the Cambodians into themselves and their efforts to maintain their traditions may have been the defensive reflex of a minority but their vulnerability was aggravated by their own elite, the *achars* and bonzes, who, according to Malleret, were "unenlightened concerning the obligations and rigors of modern existence."[15] The archaic social structure reinforced the traits of a southern temperament prone to languidness, and Hinayana Buddhism certainly did not inject a spirit of competition or the will to overcome adversity. Administrators and the French and Vietnamese landowners valued Cambodian workers for their docility but regretted what they perceived to be a poor capacity for work and an absence of the will to surmount difficulties or keep abreast of innovations.[16] Nonetheless, there were gradations of wealth and class within the Khmer community of Nam Bo. In French documents this is not evident, but one Vietnamese author cites a few examples of Cambodian landowners who held five hundred to a thousand hectares. Most of these were *doc phu su* or *conseillers d'arrondissements*.[17]

For the French, the existence of a submissive minority proved beneficial in the maintenance of order. It also was in their interest to shield Cambodians from the rapaciousness of certain French, Chinese, and

Vietnamese. One author offered an unexpected justification for the protection of the Cambodians.

> Of Aryan origin, as our own, the Khmer race resides in our possessions in the Far East. This race is the one that seems best able to absorb the teachings of the Occident. All its sons, whether they inhabit Cambodia or Cochinchina, have a right to our active and affectionate solicitude.[18]

Nonetheless, local authorities did not grant preferential treatment to the Khmers, harboring a poor opinion of people who represented "a force of inertia to all endeavors of the administration."[19] One administrator stated flatly that "the Cambodians of Tra-tien are idlers."[20]

Suzanne Karpelès, a curator at the Royal Library in Phnom Penh, visited Nam Bo with a Khmer delegation from 19 January to 12 February 1928. The mission, which investigated the situation of the Khmers, found that the standing of Cambodian people and culture varied in different provinces and districts. In Tra-vinh Province, Karpelès wrote, Buddhist faith and the Khmer language had persisted but the language had begun "to deteriorate." In Bac-lieu, the language was "slightly deteriorated and Vietnamized"; in Soc-trang, Rach-gia, and Can-tho, it was "deteriorating"; and "in the district of Phung-hiep, the population is so Vietnamized that it did not comprehend the purpose of our visit." In Long-xuyen, there was a clear trend toward Vietnamization but in Chau-doc and Ha-tien, on the Cambodian border, the language was "still pure."[21]

The most common complaint voiced by the Khmers was that they could not contact the French authorities directly because all the middle-level functionaries were Vietnamese. According to Karpelès,

> We feel that all the monks are exasperated at being humiliated by the Annamites, and they are very disappointed not to have received any help from the administration. Khmer children are reluctant to attend the "Franco-Annamite" school where the more numerous Vietnamese schoolboys always humiliate them.[22]

The observations of Karpelès reveal not only the intricacy of Vietnamese and Khmer relations but also the concern of the most homogeneous Khmer groups with maintaining and cultivating their cultural identity. Her report concluded: "If hatred seems to be on the decrease, maybe it is because another feeling, rancor, is creeping into the Khmer community."[23]

In addition to cultural and historical conflicts, land-grabbing played a major role in the process of Khmer impoverishment, for it recalled old and bitter experiences. In 1925, the Colonial Council proposed the creation of two autonomous Cambodian villages in the provinces of Bac-lieu and Rach-gia. The land was to be granted to the villages with eighteen-year leases in order to discourage transfer of the land to Vietnamese or Chinese neighbors. Although the Assembly rejected the project because it would have violated common law,[24] in 1932 the proposal was revived. This time it was adopted due to the urgency of the situation: evictions had increased in the province of Rach-gia and in the village of Thanh Loi the Cambodian population had almost completely disappeared.

The Chams

If the Cambodians survived only after a fashion, the "Malays" seemed to be better off, forming a community that was numerically small but relatively prosperous.[25]

M. Ner, inquiring into the subject, discovered that the "Malays" were actually Chams, Muslims who had settled in Chau-doc Province to avoid reprisals after serving as mercenaries to the emperor of Annam in his expeditions against the Cambodians. Ranked with the other Asiatic subjects by the French, the Chams were granted the right to own land. They did not work it directly, placing it instead in the care of Cambodian or Vietnamese *ta dien*. Cham occupations tended to involve travel, which helped reinforce their religious links with foreign Islamic communities. They specialized in trading water buffaloes and pirogues, which they obtained in Cambodia. They also milled the paddy of their tenant farmers and neighbors, and loaded it into their sampans (which could hold between five and six hundred *gia*, or ten to twelve tons) along with tobacco, *sarongs*, and *sampots* made by their wives. They either transported this cargo to Saigon or practiced an itinerant trade in the provinces. The Chams were grouped in "two zones of vermiform agglomerations" stretched out along the banks of rivers and canals. These settlements did not form a continuous line but were juxtaposed or connected with Annamite or Khmer communities.

The distinctiveness and cohesion of the Chams stemmed from their Islamic faith. There were beautiful mosques at Chau Giang and Phum Soai, and in some villages Koranic schools surpassed the official ones. The Chams maintained regular relations with their coreligionists of Cambodia and Malaya and pilgrimages to Mecca were frequent. *Hadjis* and *gourous* who were capable of reading the Koran in Arabic and commenting on it enjoyed great authority.[26] Some Chams married "Islamisized" Vietnamese, and their children were accepted in the Muslim community, but male foreigners were not received even if they had converted to Islam. Ner also observed that Chams who lived among Cambodians, Chinese, or Vietnamese were less prosperous than those living in the homogeneous villages of Chau Giang and Phum Soai.

The Great Depression reduced the resources of the Chams by limiting their travels. By the eve of World War II they had taken up fishing and some had even turned to agriculture.

The Chinese

The Chinese were not a minority on the defensive, like the Cambodians, nor were they a residual minority, like the Chams. In Cochinchina, on the borders of two great civilizations, the Indian and the Chinese, the Chinese formed the vanguard of colonization in the eighteenth century. Of course, the establishment of the Chinese at Ha-tien and elsewhere was carried out on behalf and for the benefit of the emperor of Annam but the Chinese eventually achieved ascendancy not only at Ha-tien and Phu Quoc but also in Baclieu. In 1902, for example, after the arrest of members of the secret society Heaven and Earth, administrator Chabrier informed the lieutenant governor that "the registered Chinese number around four thousand, the Minh Huong form a third of the population, and nearly all Annamites who are natives of the province speak Chinese."[27] A couplet from a Vietnamese folk song paints this picture:

Bac-lieu is a rustic country.
The silurus fish are in the river, the Teochiu on the banks.[28]

The Minh Huong, or Sino-Vietnamese, also were numerous,[29] and few Vietnamese of Mien Tay today do not have at least one Chinese ancestor.

In imperial Vietnam, the Chinese were grouped in administrative associations (*bang*) that were distinct from the villages. The *bang truong* fulfilled the function of internal conciliator and external spokesman. He also drew up the register, collected the taxes, and turned them over to the local authorities.[30] The French employed an analogous system, that of the *congrégations*. Through these organizations the French were able to regulate the Chinese, for no immigrant could enter Indochina unless he were received by

TABLE 13: Voters in *Congrégation* Elections in
Rach-gia Province, 1911

Congrégation	No. of Members	No. Registered on License and Tax Lists	No. of Voters
Canton	305	72	15
Hainan	361	21	8
Teochiu	735	136	17
Hokkien	86	5	4

Source: Rach-gia, E.6, ANVN.

a *congrégation*. At the same time they provided an administrative and fiscal structure.[31]

Each *congrégation* had a headquarters located in the chief town of a province, and the governor of Cochinchina chose the chiefs and subchiefs of the *congrégations* from a list compiled by election. Franchise was limited. According to the amount of taxes they paid, members of the *congrégations* were placed in six categories, and only those belonging to the first three could participate in elections. As table 13 demonstrates, the number of voters could be small.

The *congrégation* was a convenient means by which the government could enclose and regulate a foreign group while remaining in communication with it. Viewed from the outside, these groups appeared cohesive enough but one must ask how the Chinese behaved toward one another. Did national or regional solidarity prevail over social divisions? Relying upon the report of a high civil servant of his acquaintance, Laffargue was convinced that oligarchic rule predominated within the *congrégations*.[32] It is also probable that many of the guarantees given by the chiefs of the *congrégations* had to be cemented by some service or other.

The responsibilities of the chiefs and subchiefs of the *congrégations*, principally relating to fiscal matters but also to others, were heavy. In 1902, for example, the administrator of Bac-lieu imposed a fine of $100 on the chief of the Teochiu *congrégation* because he had not controlled his members: some had joined the secret society Heaven and Earth. The collection of taxes was another task sufficiently arduous to have prompted fairly frequent flights from it. One such incident occurred in Ha-tien in 1904, when

TABLE 14: Numbers of Chinese Recorded
in Rach-gia Province, 1904–12

1 Jan	Increase	Decrease	Departed for China	Deceased	Dis-appeared
1904	6	50	7	5	33
1905	11	57			46
1907	15	89			51
1908	46	144			78
1912	38	124			122

Source: Rach-gia, E.6, ANVN.

the chief of the Hainan *congrégation* left a sum of $2,760.50 unpaid to the regional budget. This represented the *centièmes and prestations* of nearly five hundred of the members of his *congrégation*. I warned this chief that he would be prosecuted if he did not pay, and he fled.[33]

In 1910, the chiefs and subchiefs of the Hainan *congrégation* in the province of Rach-gia fled for the same reason.[34]

The position of the *bang truong* was rendered more difficult by the poverty, the extreme mobility, and the frequent changes of identity undertaken by many Chinese. Some changed identity two or three times and the administrative correspondence contains numerous telegrams sent from one province to another requesting searches and identifications. Nomadism was sometimes occupational but more often was undertaken to avoid fiscal obligations. Some Chinese managed to go two or three years without paying taxes.[35] In the course of the year there tended to be little movement but every January first, when the period for payment of taxes began, disappearances increased. Numbers of Chinese listed as residing in Rach-gia Province from 1904 to 1912 are revealing in this regard (table 14). The problem continued to plague administrators and the *congrégations*. As late as 1933, a letter from the *congrégation* chiefs to the administrator of Bac-lieu asked him to reconsider his decision to increase taxes, pointing out that "the Teochiu *congrégations* have had to disburse thousands of piasters in order to pay the taxes in place of the 300 or 400 missing annually."[36]

We lack the data that would permit us to ascertain the professional distribution of the Chinese, as the registers of the *congrégations* are silent on this subject, but the 1933 letter confirms what our knowledge of the economy of the West has already revealed—that the Chinese were not confined to the profession of trader-lender. It is evident, however, that the Chinese exercised effective control over the distribution of rice by virtue of which they came to be considered indispensable. In fact, the French colonizers clamored for increased importation of Chinese labor. One anonymous author wrote in praise of

> the facility and flexibility with which the Chinese lend themselves to all the measures which concern their settlement; they submit with a rare intelligence to French ideas and civilization. The assimilation of a genius as personal as is that of the Chinese race was a glory that was still lacking in the colonial annals of France.[37]

In 1908, the administrator of Bac-lieu left a portrait of one prominent Chinese. Duong Xuong arrived in Bac-lieu in 1895. He married a Vietnamese woman of "good" family, worked initially as a miller of paddy, and for twelve years ran a thriving grocery store. He did not smoke opium or misuse alcohol. The administrator described him as "one of the rare Chinese who dress European and do not wear the braid. . . . Very intelligent, very polite, very obliging, very conscientious, he enjoyed general esteem."[38] Eventually he became chief of the Canton *congrégation*.

As this case confirms, the Chinese were not imbued with notions of racial superiority, and most found wives among the Vietnamese or Khmers. Offspring from these marriages were known as the Minh Huong, or Sino-Vietnamese, and the *dau ga dit vit*, or Sino-Khmers.[39] Even in economic matters the Chinese did not practice exclusivism, sometimes entering into partnerships with Vietnamese or even with the French.[40] Conflicts between the Vietnamese and the Chinese were not racial but economic in character. Though cultural kinship probably reduced tensions somewhat, European observers relied on an erroneous interpretation of the term *khach chu*, adopting a literal translation of *chu* (uncle). *Khach chu* actually is a deformation of the word *khach tru* (immigrant), which was used to describe the Chinese in Vietnam.

Although the Vietnamese might fume at their inability to dispense with the Chinese, and they might envy an immigrant who arrived penniless but ended up with a house of his own, they did not despise the Chinese as they despised the Khmers. In an account of a strike in which Chinese sawyers had demonstrated great professional and ethnic solidarity, the *Tribune Indochinoise* cautioned that "Annamites should reflect long and hard on this Chinese lesson!"[41] In fact, the Chinese became models to the Vietnamese who concluded that if they were to rid themselves of Chinese economic dominance it would be necessary to acquire their business sense, imitate their frugality, and take inspiration from their spirit of solidarity.

The Indians

The Indians, known as *chettys*, did not appear to the Vietnamese in the same light as the Chinese, for they lacked the kinship relations that might have offset the indignities suffered by the Vietnamese as a result of the *chettys'* money-lending activities and economic exploitation. Indians were represented in other professions, however, with many serving as merchants and contractors. They also acquired land, sometimes by purchase, though more commonly through foreclosure. Few in number, they were grouped by the French in the Chinese *congrégations*. In November 1897, when fifteen Indians of Bac-lieu asked permission to form an autonomous *congrégation*, their petition was rejected.[42]

A representative story will indicate the reputation of Indian merchants among the Vietnamese. In it a poor village elder comes to Can-tho City and enters the shop of a merchant to buy a cane. He is charged $1.90, while a local inhabitant buys the same cane for 30 centimes.[43] Such practices, or the rumor of them, engendered prejudices that clung to all Indians.[44]

The French

The official meaning of the term *French* was broad in Cochinchina, being applied not only to those of French origin but to naturalized Vietnamese, to Eurasians, and to persons from the French colonial enclaves in India. Although the French were few in number, as colonizers they were able to assume an important role: they were the minority that filled the most important offices.

Records included in the 1911 census provide a limited picture of the origins and professions of French nationals living in the chief provincial towns of Mien Tay. At Bac-lieu, the clerk of the judicial department was a native of French India, and there were fifteen civil servants in the customs and excise of which nine were Corsicans. At Can-tho, the contractor of the

markets, a lawyer's clerk, and the clerk of the court were "Pondicherrians."
One of the two civil-service administrators and five of six customs officials
were Corsicans. At Ha-tien, a clerk of the civil service and two of the seven
customs officials were Corsican. At Long-xuyen, a clerk of the court, his colleague, the magistrate, the civil surveyor, and one of the six customs officials
were Corsicans.[45]

More complete documentation would probably show that most of the
French were civil servants, and that nearly all came from the most economically disadvantaged regions of France (Corsica and the southwest) or from
the country's overseas territories (the Antilles, Réunion, and the French colonial enclaves in India). In fact, these origins help explain much colonial
behavior. It was observed, among other things, that the "Pondicherrians" and
people from Réunion and the Antilles were "more French than the French"
in their treatment of the natives. Although the records say little about them,
French women, too, must have had an effect, their presence perhaps serving
as an obstacle to smooth relations with the indigenous inhabitants. Certainly
the presence of Vietnamese wives and concubines did not necessarily lead to
amity among the various communities.

Although our information is sketchy, we can construct a profile of the
typical French administrator and colonist. The civil service administrator
who directed the affairs of a province was in principle the most important
person in the European community. He was educated at the Ecole
Coloniale (founded in 1899) and his sojourn in a province often took place
at the beginning of a career still marked with enthusiasm and youth.[46] Most
took their jobs remarkably seriously. Not content merely to supervise the
development of the economy, hygiene, and education, they applied themselves to improving social conditions. The desire to do good sometimes con-
flicted with fiscal realities, however, and when natural disasters such as
floods and bad harvests gave rise to requests for exemption from taxes, the
administrative correspondence takes an almost pathetic turn. It reveals men
anxious to help the people under their jurisdiction, pleading their cause
with ardor, and struggling against a central administration that was only
concerned with revenue. The administrators also defended the indigenous
population against the depredations of certain Europeans who exploited the
Vietnamese and Cambodians. Concerning a request for land received from
a Frenchman in 1913, the administrator of Rach-gia Province wrote the
lieutenant governor that

it would be desirable to turn away this would-be civil surveyor who is more and more turning into a man of business, without any resource whatever. . . . His ambition, in my opinion, is simply to levy a rent on the natives already established on the land that he is requesting.[47]

Concerning the same person, a colleague in Tan An reckoned that "M. Belugeaud . . . has none . . . of the qualities needed to conduct, and make a success of, many of the affairs requiring an active and continuous collaboration with the natives."[48] On another occasion, when an officer of the customs and excise conducted himself in an irregular manner vis-à-vis his *engagés*, the same province chief (of Rach-gia) proposed the transfer of this functionary, stating that "It is without regret that I will regard the removal of an agent from the province whose relations with the indigenous population leave much to be desired."[49]

It sometimes happened that in cases of occupation of land without title an administrator proposed to settle the question in favor of the squatters. In 1901, for example, the Baron of Rothiacob obtained a concession of 1,537 hectares and 39 ares in the province of Rach-gia. As the baron never set foot on the soil of Cochinchina and made no effort to improve the land, squatters occupied his concession, putting it under cultivation in small plots. The provincial administrator, M. Parera, wrote the governor of Cochinchina that

Even though the latter [the natives] have made no proper request for concession, it is equitable that they should not be dispossessed of the rights they have acquired by their labor. If you share this view, I will invite the natives to put their situation in order as quickly as possible.[50]

With a few exceptions, the administrators were not well disposed toward the large concessionaires, although they took care to distinguish them from the *colons* who actually cultivated the land. In one case, in 1910, the chief of Can-tho Province opposed a resolution of the Colonial Council to allow the election of *colons* to the Provincial Council.

The *colon* . . . does not pay the poll tax, nor an additional centime, nor prestation. In a provincial budget such items furnish three-fifths of the total. At Can-tho, they amount to $185,000 out of a total of $300,000. . . . This favored treatment is extended to his indigenous personnel . . . [who,] though they neglect to pay the province . . . do not neglect to cause it expense.[51]

The most active administrators were hard working and undertook frequent tours. In the best cases, knowledge of the Vietnamese language enabled them to make direct contact with the population.[52] In other cases, direct contact was lacking, in part due to ignorance of the language, in part because theirs was a time-consuming job. The duties of the province chiefs became heavier as the provinces developed. Those with a sedentary temperament preferred to remain in the chief town. Administrators caught up in the routine of the bureaucracy usually surrendered quickly to the *apéritif,* bridge, and tennis.

The situation was aggravated by the presence of native intermediaries: secretary-interpreters, the *phu,* and the *huyen.* The theory that the *notables* were truly representative of their constituencies supported the idea that intermediaries were indispensable. As one administrator put it, "You are the intermediaries solely charged with making its [the population's] needs known to me."[53] In 1930, a *colon* complained that "the administrator was made a bureau chief who sees the province through the filter of his native collaborators. He sees it badly."[54] As the term of a head administrator was short (sometimes only two years), he could familiarize himself with neither the material problems nor the psychology of those under his authority.

The execution of the administrator's decisions, especially those concerning taxes, monopolies, and the police, was left to the native subordinates (the chiefs of cantons and *notables*) and to French gendarmes and customs officials. The latter were perceived as the agents of an oppressive force at the service of unpopular institutions. Their behavior could be brutal, sometimes by necessity but also due to ignorance of or contempt for the natives. The *Tribune Indochinoise,* hardly inclined to trumpet calls for revolt, regularly published the complaints of bourgeois Vietnamese whose dignity had been injured by a French gendarme—a slap in the face, a thump on the back, or simply a wounding word—for reasons as frivolous as the order of passage over a bridge or the right of way on an embankment.[55]

The majority of the French belonged to the tertiary sector, with the greater portion employed as functionaries, men concerned with the law, or missionaries. "True" settlers residing on the land and cultivating it were rare, especially among those of French origin.[56] Of those who tried the settler's life, lasting success undoubtedly came to men who not only gave proof of character but immersed themselves in the environment, marrying Vietnamese women, learning the local language, and determining to live on their estates even in the beginning when comforts were lacking. The complaints of the administrators about the *colons* had their counterpart in the antiadministrative spirit of the concessionaires. There existed a widespread custom of protest, and of claiming advantages of all kinds, including near immunity from government control. On the estates the *colons* adopted attitudes ranging from easy-going paternalism to quasi-tyranny toward their *ta dien* (in this respect, of course, they differed little from the Vietnamese landowners). Individualists, and much devoted to laissez-faire policies when profits were at stake, the concessionaires never failed to reproach the colonial administration for ignoring their interests.

Leaving the administration aside for the moment, for its regulatory and even its benevolent actions were inextricably linked to the process of domination and exploitation, what was the contribution of this European minority to life in the Cochinchinese West? In several places, the true settlers devoted themselves to experiments that stimulated change in agricultural practice. Certain lawyers contributed either to the creation of enterprises such as sugar refining and rum distilling (as at Can-tho) or to the founding of the SICAMs. On the whole, however, their influence was slight because the number of enterprising men was limited and the institution of tenant farming is not conducive to progress. As one administrator of Rach-gia observed, "the native is routine-minded through idleness and the colonist imitates him through prudence."[57]

The Vietnamese

The Vietnamese became the majority in the delta they conquered. In the course of their migration south along the peninsula they either drove out or partially assimilated the native Chams and Cambodians. The inevitable racial mixing resulted in a southern Vietnamese populace with original somatic and psychological features and a common speech like that of the north, yet different. Most of them became rice cultivators on the plains, grouped in families around the cult of familial ancestors and in villages around the cult of guardian spirits. Along with these beliefs, they practiced the rites of Buddhism and Taoism.

None of these religions, however, could rival the hold of Confucianism over that society. Confucianism governed the system of social relations extending from the family to the emperor, defining the interactions between children and parents (it did not contradict, but in fact reinforced, the cult of the ancestors), husband and wife, pupil and teacher, and subject and sovereign. It also reinforced the traditional social hierarchy—the *tu dan*—at the head of which were the literati (*si*), followed by the cultivators (*nong*), the artisans (*cong*), and the traders (*thuong*). In another tier—the *tu thu*—were the fishermen (*ngu*), woodcutters (*tieu*), ploughmen (*canh*), and herders (*muc*). For first-generation pioneers in the West, the family remained the fundamental social unit. Unable to retain their traditional places in the villages of their birth, they also grouped themselves into *don dien*. They did not disperse themselves across the countryside; settling new lands was a collective affair.

The strength of Confucianism assured the cohesion of the Vietnamese people, and it was probably one of the principal reasons why they were able to dominate the Chams and the Khmers.

> Study literature to fill yourself with the moral rules of life. Cultivate the land in order to reap from it the fruits that nourish your own people and your fellow men. Perform manual labor in order to develop your capacity and produce what you need. Intensify commerce in order to lower prices and maintain friendly relations with your compatriots and the inhabitants of neighboring countries.[58]

This exhortation, addressed to the pioneers by the mandarin Nguyen Tri Phuong, called for respect for a customary social order that corresponded with the values of Vietnamese civilization without the imperatives of a caste system.

Immovable wealth was held in greater esteem than was the possession of movable goods. The Vietnamese disapproved of the display of material wealth, for it was not considered seemly to flaunt one's fortune.

> It was improper for a modest merchant, though he might be immensely rich, to live like a great mandarin; everyone had to have a lifestyle consistent with his tradition.[59]

Thus, social norms and the concepts of wealth, its acquisition, and its use were closely linked. That the *Gia Dinh Thanh Thong Chi* remarked about the inhabitants of Ha-tien that "they are inclined to luxury and they have little conscience" was attributed to the Chinese influence on morals and customs and to the effects of practicing commerce. But it also reveals the germ of a social transformation in the West, one that began long before the French conquest.

All of these observations are encompassed in the work of the southern-born revolutionary and historian, Tran Van Giau, who noted that the bounties of nature favored the relative autonomy of the settlers and that the beginnings of individualism may be seen in the plans for the new villages. Unlike the villages of the north, in which dwellings were concentrated behind bamboo hedges, houses in the south were more scattered. And the southerners themselves were less inclined to submit to the bonds of either feudal power or Confucian ethics.[60]

Social Categories: Landowners and Ta Dien

In the essentially rural society of Mien Tay, the relationships of production generated two main social groups—the landowners and the *ta dien*. The landowners were divided into strata according to their wealth and their economic and social roles. The smaller landowners cultivated their fields themselves. If the area they possessed was insufficient for the subsistence of the family, they would attempt to work additional land as tenant farmers. Their situation was less established than that of cultivators in the "old" provinces of Cochinchina. In fact, the situation of small landowners in the West was nearly identical to that of the *ta dien*.[61] In normal times, most small and middle-sized landowners could preserve their independence but a bad harvest or an economic downturn could spell disaster. This was the case in 1931 when creditors proceeded with massive court-imposed liquidations of property.[62]

When a landowner managed to acquire a slightly larger estate he would rent it out in its entirety or in part. We have discussed the system of reciprocal obligation upon which rested the practice of indirect farming. This system required the landowner, or *dien chu*, to supply the means of production: soil, seed, livestock, sampans, and sometimes tools. To credit in kind was added credit in money, not only in the form of cash but in the redistribution of debt resulting from loans on harvests and loans from the SICAMs.

At the summit of the social hierarchy were the large landowners. The origins of this upper class date primarily from the French conquest, for when the conquerors wished to reward Vietnamese who had collaborated with them, they granted them vast concessions. From that time on, the existence of open-handed legislation, the practice of usury, and sometimes outright purchase permitted the large estates to expand. The largest landowners sprang from a relatively well-to-do agricultural class and from the ranks of urban mandarins who had collaborated with the French. These included secretary-interpreters and sometimes orderlies and riflemen. Few landowners of the highest rank cultivated their own land. A rich landowner might put in an appearance or supervise the principal activities of the estate but usually such

Leaders of the Agricultural Syndicate of Vinh-long, c. 1930
(Credit: Centre des Archives d'Outre-mer).

A ta-dien's thatched hut, province of Bac-lieu, 1930
(Credit: Centre des Archives d'Outre-mer).

A french colon's silo, workshop, and boat for
transporting paddy, province of Bac-lieu, 1930
(Credit: Centre des Archives d'Outre-mer).

work was delegated to a relative or a manager. A landowner nearly always appeared in person during the harvest, however, to estimate the value of the crop and supervise its collection. To get some idea of numbers, table 15 shows landowners subject to income tax in 1938, the year the tax was established.

Large landowners essentially functioned as lenders, as did the the middle-sized landowners with regard to the holdings they rented out. According to the number of their *ta dien* and the network of personal relations they wove about themselves, the *dien chu* also found themselves acting as "patrons" at the head of more or less extensive "clientèles," which were added to the "parentèles." The network of dependency that resulted from this system of reciprocal obligation helped institutionalize paternalism in Nam Bo. The system also suited the Confucian ethic, producing doctor-landowners who would treat patients and distribute medicine without charge and *dien chu* who might respond to a bad harvest by lowering rents or adopting the sons of his tenants.

Some of the wealthiest *dien chu* became philanthropists, like the European merchant-bankers of the Middle Ages or American business tycoons whose religious convictions compelled them to devote a portion of their fortunes to helping the poor. One such man was Tran Trinh Trach, a philanthropist celebrated for his charitable donations. Such solicitude was not incompatible with severity, or even harshness, however, in their treatment of the *ta dien*. Partly this was the result of the force of circumstance and partly it was the consequence of paternalism, which does not exclude corporal punishment. Bui Quang Chieu, one of the most prominent of the large landowners in Can-tho, described the typical *dien chu* as simply "a *ta dien* who has succeeded, just as the mandarin is only the son of a *nha que* who passed the literary examinations." He attends to his estate personally, advising his tenant farmers and contributing

> in a very large measure intellectually and materially to the progress of the collectivity of which he is the strongest support. Owner of the soil and principal beneficiary of public order, the *dien chu* is the vigilant and self-interested guardian of a regime with which he is not entirely satisfied.[63]

TABLE 15: **Landowners Subject to Income Tax
in 1938, by Province**

Region	Province	Landowners Subject to Tax
West	Bac-lieu	36
	Can-tho	53
	Chau-doc	19
	Ha-tien	1
	Long-xuyen	18
	Rach-gia	55
	Soc-trang	31
Other	Cholon	24
	Ben-tre	14
	Ba-ria	0
	Bien-hoa	0
	Capt. St. Jacques	1
	Gia-dinh	9
	Go-cong	23
	My-tho	19
	Sa-dec	12
	Tan-an	0
	Tay-ninh	0
	Thu-dau-mot	0
	Tra-vinh	50
	Vinh-long	45

Source: *Tribune Indochinoise*, 14 October 1938.

A few years later Chieu returned to the subject.

There are no water-tight partitions between the classes of Annamite
society. We all are born of the people, to whom we remain attached
with profound ramifications. Members of the elite, we must work slowly following our immutable principle: evolution not revolution. We are
not in a country in which there are wealthy people, people "rolling in

money," as they say. We are one of the rare countries in which there is no hereditary nobility. Nor are we in a country in which there are closed castes. All of us here emerged from the Third Estate. . . . All of our parents were poor, and in consequence we have close ties to the working class.[64]

Although these statements were shaped in part by political events, they express an ideology to which the landowners consistently adhered, or at least referred, with apparent conviction and sincerity. Beginning with the myth of a communal democracy in which an equal chance of ascending the social ladder is offered to all, it culminates in the organic solidarity of *dien chu* and *ta dien*.[65] This natural solidarity is reinforced by the fact that both classes are subjected to a colonial regime, suffering the same heavy taxation and abusive behavior. Moreover, both consider themselves to be exploited by Asian foreigners—the *chettys* and the Chinese.

Thus the ideology of social integration contained an implicit affirmation of national solidarity and of the exceptionality of a Vietnamese society in which, because there were no castes or classes, there was no social antagonism. Although personal and family rivalries and political expediency often pitted the large landowners against each other, they shared a fundamental conception of social relations.

Education

Wealth and social influence allowed, and sometimes inspired, the *dien chu* to seek higher education. If they could not afford to undertake the studies themselves, they educated their children. After World War I, it became customary for respected *dien chu* to send their children to colleges in Can-tho or My-tho, or to the Lycée Chasseloups-Laubat at Saigon, and then to the University of Hanoi or to institutions in France. Many boys and girls chose courses in law or medicine. Bui Quang Chieu's daughter Henriette Bui was the first Vietnamese woman graduated as a *docteur en médecine*. Agronomist studies also were in vogue; Bui Quang Chieu and Phan Khac Suu were both *ingenieurs agricoles*.

Every successful graduate was the pride of the bourgeoisie. Diplomas represented elevation to what was traditionally the most highly respected state of being, that of the literati, and such status served as an affirmation of Vietnamese abilities in the face of a dominant colonial minority. Well-educated Vietnamese acquired a solid background in French culture. The dissertations they delivered and the articles they wrote testify to real mastery of the French language and a thorough understanding of Cartesian reasoning, which placed them intellectually well above the average French inhabitant of the colony. Along with shared economic interests and similar social behavior, which linked the largest French and Vietnamese landowners, education allowed the most prominent of the latter to be admitted to society on a nearly equal footing with the *colons* of French origin. Thus, Bui Quang Chieu was described as follows.

> Bui Quang Chieu effectively represents, through his qualities of shrewdness and courtesy, the accomplished sort of our Cochinchinese. Furthermore, he is one of our own people—and this should not displease us—agricultural engineer, great landowner, and administrator of vast estates in the West. His interests are precisely the same as those of the rice grower who endures in the plains of Lower Cochinchina in spite of bitter toil.[66]

Although this statement undoubtedly has political overtones, the sentiments expressed were widespread. They responded to a constant of the French spirit, the desire to assimilate others. However, Bui Quang Chieu (and a few others) represent isolated cases. Generally the rich landowners, even if they had become French citizens, maintained only episodic relations of a professional nature with persons of French origin. In the official receptions, for example, one always found the two groups on opposite sides of the room. There was also a less sympathetic face to the offspring of the gentry, some of whom constituted a kind of "gilded youth," mocked by the Vietnamese as *cong tu bot* (literally, "flour mandarin's sons"). The sense of the term is that of arrogant upstarts enjoying an undeserved, leisurely way of life.

Material Wealth

Increased ownership of the land, which functioned as the material foundation of this social category, was the object of a constant quest. Landowners requested vast areas in concessions and pursued acquisition through usury and foreclosure. They gave land to their children and acquired more plots and *compartiments* in the urban areas. But they also concerned themselves with the acquisition of movable wealth. While this sometimes took the form of purchasing government bonds,[67] most *dien chu* exhibited a preference for hoarding jewels and ingots of precious metal.

Hoarding brought with it opportunities for thievery. On the night of 29 March 1917, for example, in the region of Ca-mau, bandits invaded the home of a wealthy landowner of An Trach village. They took from the safe 2,300 metallic piasters, 600 Mexican piasters, 2 one-hundred-dollar bills, 4 carved gold necklaces worth $600, 6 carved gold bracelets worth $200, 16 gold rings worth $600, 800 grams of gold dust, 23 pairs of earrings worth $150, and 15 silver ingots worth $225.[68] In another case, in the province of Long-xuyen in 1930, a band of fifteen thieves found its way into the home of a rich *notable* of Binh Phuoc Xuan village. They forced open the safe and ripped apart pillows, which, according to the statement of the victim, contained 20,000 piasters worth of silver and jewels.[69]

Landowners devoted much attention to their lifestyles and spent accordingly. As soon as he became well-off, a *dien chu* would have a brick house built and roofed with tiles—a tile roof being commonly cited as an indication of improving fortunes. Once he became rich, he would build a villa, which he would furnish in an eclectic fashion, half-French and half-Vietnamese. The *Tribune Indochinoise*, during a campaign intended to promote local handicrafts, deplored the preference of the Vietnamese bourgeoisie for furnishings and curios imported from Levitan (a large Paris department store) at the expense of the products of local artisans.

European foods were adopted as well, at least on grand occasions. To celebrate his promotion to the rank of officer in the Légion d'Honneur, Conseiller Colonial Tran Trinh Trach gave a banquet for 250 guests at his residence in Bac-lieu. The dinner, catered by the Hotel Continental of Saigon, consisted of *consommé aux paillettes d'or, vol-au-vent financière, poularde poelée aux ceps, petits pois à la française, gigot de mouton rôti, salade panachée, glace à la vanille, patisseries,* and *corbeille de fruit.*[70] An article published in the *Courrier de l'Ouest* in 1917 is revealing of the lifestyle of another large landowner. This one resided on the road leading from Can-tho to Long-xuyen, where one saw "pretty cottages built in the European manner" bordering a *rach.* "The principal room of the villa is of European architecture," the article continues, and during the reception there were served "the most exquisite wines of Bordeaux and Bourgogne, complementing the items of a select menu which honored the numerous guests, among whom we observed the European colony."[71] Rich landowners also purchased consumer durables such as automobiles and motor boats.[72] Tran Trinh Huy, a landowner of Bac-lieu, bought an airplane and had a landing strip prepared on his property.

Commerce and Industry

Most rich landowners of the West participated directly, or as financial backers, in extra-agricultural activities: rice mills, the transport and wholesaling of rice, retail stores, workshops for mechanical repairs, brick works, and road transport firms. In 1921, the French launched a campaign intended to encourage the Vietnamese to orient themselves toward commerce and industry, not so much in preference to agriculture as to divert them from aspirations to administrative office.

> Our young compatriots henceforth will concentrate their activities on the large field of free enterprise, of fertile endeavors. . . . We must aspire to first place in all branches of economic activity. It is in this direction that our compatriots must face and toward which parents must direct their children.[73]

In 1924, the theme reappeared in *L'Echo Annamite*.

> We must have the courage to recognize our mentality, which is too enamored of pompous titles and honorary decorations. It is a great defect of our social condition. . . . Let us be merchants or manufacturers, let us have our mills and our factories. Let us shake off our indolence. Let us join together.[74]

The most important initiative, greeted as outstanding even by the Vietnamese bourgeoisie, was the founding of the Société Annamite de Crédit in 1927. This first Vietnamese banking establishment was organized by a group mainly composed of large landowners. On the Board of Honor and Consultation sat Tran Trinh Trach, with the title of vice-president, and at the head of the Council of Administration and Management was Truong Tan Vi, honorary *doc phu su* of Chau-doc. Another vice-president was Dr. Tran Nhu Lan, a landowner in Rach-gia and a *conseiller colonial*. The *Tribune Indochinoise* cited the example of Ziep Van Giap, owner of four thousand hectares in Soc-trang and a former *conseiller colonial*, who subscribed a million francs to the enterprise.[75]

This class of rich landowners of the West gave birth to two new social categories, for a large number of liberal professionals and the embryo of an entrepreneurial bourgeoisie sprang from it. Their members retained an attachment to the ownership of land, which they both inherited and continued to acquire. Their extra-agricultural professions aggravated the problems of absenteeism. In 1936, the existence of these new social strata was clearly evident in the debate over creation of an income tax. The *Tribune Indochinoise* objected that such a levy would become a "super tax" because the lawyer or doctor who owned land would be forced to pay a license tax for an office, taxes on real estate in town and on his agricultural estates, and income tax on the revenue from all three.[76]

Matrimonial alliances tended to consolidate the upper stratum of society. For example, in 1923, Dr. Jean Le Quang Trinh, *conseiller colonial* and recipient of the Croix de Guerre, married Marie Nguyen Thi Dac. The bridegroom was the son of Auguste Le Quang Hien, officer of the Légion d'Honneur and retired *doc phu* member of the Government Council of Indochina and of the Privy Council of Cochinchina. The bride was the niece and ward of Nguyen Van Yen, honorary *huyen* and one of the largest landowners of Can-tho Province.[77]

Obituary notices provide further indications of elite relationships. In one, Cao Van Tinh, retired *tri phu* at Can-tho and holder of the Médaille d'Honneur first class, was announced to be deceased. The notification was presented by Nguyen Tan Thanh, manager of the Galeries de l'Ouest at My-tho; Tran Dac Nghia, director of L'Imprimerie de l'Ouest and of the *Courrier de l'Ouest* at Can-tho; M. Cao Van, captain of the First Regiment of Zouaves (Algerian riflemen of the colonial army) in Algiers and Knight of the Légion d'Honneur; Cao Ngoc Chan, a trader in Can-tho; and Cao Van Tho, former secretary of public works at Vinh-long.[78]

Administration

Possession of land and the patronage system invested the large landowners with an authority that allowed them to exercise wide social influence sanctioned by custom. It was from the ranks of the merely well-off landowners, however, those whose reputations did not go beyond the confines of the village or canton, that village *notables* and subchiefs and chiefs of cantons were recruited. These constituted the intermediate level of the administrative structure.

In the settlement zones, the practice of choosing *notables* from among the ranks of the well-off or rich cultivators could not be maintained. The settlers were destitute men. Villagers of Hung Thanh, for example, who were *engagés*, requested a postponement of the election of their *huong chu* (vice-president of the village council) until after the harvest. The results of the harvest would permit them to choose the most affluent among them.[79]

Despite the situation in the West, the French administration upheld traditional practices, and even extended them, in order to respond to the ambitions of the upper stratum of landowners. It allowed the large landowners to participate in administrative bodies such as the SICAMs and consultative bodies such as the Chamber of Agriculture and the Colonial Council. By the time a *dien chu* reached this summit he was often a *naturalisé* (a holder of French citizenship) or he had applied for it. For some, this reflected a sincere desire for assimilation; for others it was a means to another goal. The advantages of French citizenship help explain the behavior of some members of this bourgeoisie. As one critical observer of the colonial regime observed,

> In this train, we encounter the great Ninh. The great Ninh is a knight of the Légion d'Honneur. He is a former *conseiller colonial*. He is one of that type of badly Frenchified Annamites whose loyalty is not only to a burning acceptance of the French order but to a resounding fidelity to the governments, whichever they may be.[80]

The Decline of Patronage

The well-off and rich landowners were conscious of the places they occupied in society, each on his own level. They did not fail to affirm their importance and their roles, especially in periods of crisis. When alarming rumors began circulating in the region of Ca-mau in February 1938, three hundred *dien chu* met at Bac-lieu under the chairmanship of the *conseiller colonial* Huynh Ngoc Binh. After a long and stormy discussion, the participants came to an agreement. Henceforth they would require tenant farmers to sign contracts with their landlords and they would prosecute defaulting tenants in court. The assembly was reminded by a member that "the rural bourgeoisie has been the economic and social support of the Annamite peasant population."[81] And, on 12 March, five hundred members of the Syndicat Agricole of Rach-gia met at the chief town and adopted a resolution with the following principal passages.

> Considering that a lost opportunity in the form of land left fallow is more profitable than the loss of an advance occasioned by some recalcitrant *ta dien* without counting the loss of time and money in case of civil action. . . . Considering that the decree of October 6, 1936 . . . will inevitably lead to the tightening of credit for those who have no security at their disposal. . . . Considering that the said decree constitutes for

those who would default an incitement to bad faith even for loans other than money . . . [we resolve] not to overdo the advances to be granted . . . to eliminate the bad *ta dien* and to systematically refuse new tenant farmers of whose morality we are not certain.[82]

Thus did paternal declarations give way to a sharp defense of menaced positions.

The landed bourgeoisie also stiffened its attitude toward the colonial administration. At the time of the floods of 1937, for example, five hundred members of the *Syndicat Agricole* of Long-xuyen, meeting on 5 October, renounced their land rents and delayed repayment of advances they had made in money and in paddy to their tenant farmers. Was this magnanimity wholly disinterested? "Where are the estate-owning vampires?" asked the *Tribune Indochinoise.*[83] The resolution adopted at the meeting provides one answer.

The administration, which is the good mother to all, will it show itself less clement than the four hundred landowners of Long-xuyen toward the disaster victims of the rural population of this province by remaining deaf to the demands that are summarized hereafter.

1. Complete exemption from land taxes and taxes on oxen and water buffaloes for 1937–38.

2. With the surety of the landowner, advances of seeds by the administration or any credit society for the *ta dien* for the next agricultural campaign.

3. Postponement of payment of debts for one year.

4. A gratis extension of one year of the rent contracts of the *cong dien.* This to be in aid of the victim tenant farmers who undertake to pay the land taxes of the *cong dien* according to their category.[84]

The landowners thus petitioned the administration to replace them in the fulfillment of their obligations.

The *dien chu* also resisted the adoption of government measures deemed contrary to their interests. Thus, in 1934, Nguyen Phan Long criticized two plans designed to decrease the poll tax from 50 to 25 centimes in an open letter addressed to the governor of Cochinchina and signed "a bourgeois who is not afraid of being one." He emphasized that a decrease in the poll tax would constitute "an injustice to the owners who have been bled white," and complained that "the nonowners complain of being unable to pay a tax that is too heavy for them but they do not complain of seeing their employers or landlords pay the same sum as themselves."[85] This specious argument implies that the antagonism of the subject peoples toward the colonial mode of taxation overshadowed the inequalities of the Vietnamese social system.

Le Quang Liem, on the other hand, came out in favor of a progressive increase in the poll tax, although he opposed an income tax.[86] Bui Quang Chieu argued against the income tax as well.

> You tell me that I defend the rich. I defend those who must pay and the rich are among them. All the same, they constitute the support of the country. I will certainly appear fascist but after all I am not very Front Populaire. I think that at this time the income tax is inappropriate in light of the degree of development of our country.[87]

Resistance to the payment of taxes was observed among the large landowners who "induce the less wealthy taxpayers to act likewise."[88] In the canton of Giong Rieng (in Rach-gia), where the tax amounted to $12,000, more than half was owed by persons residing outside the *circonscription* and against whom the elders could take no action. These offenders were "those who could be termed rich taxpayers."[89] On the matter of tax relief, one administrator thought that the

> large landowners do not seem to me to merit any attention. The money they owe to the internal revenue, which they may wish to defraud it of, they set aside for making new clearings, as the attached statement of requests for concessions testifies.[90]

Pagès, the governor of Cochinchina, was in a good position to reply in a scathing manner to the *conseillers coloniaux* who rejected the plan for an income tax.

> Everything has been considered, except for those who are not there, the *dan*, the peasant in aid of whom the plan has been presented. You are social standpatters. You are supporters of inequality when it benefits you, supporters of the hierarchy when you are at its summit.[91]

In the triangular relationship prevailing among the landowners, the *ta dien*, and the administration, we find very consistent lines of conduct. Regardless of whether they were French or Vietnamese, the large landowners exhibited identical defensive reflexes, which sprang from their common class consciousness. The administration presented itself as an arbitrator of conflicts and, when needed, as the champion of the humble. The conduct of the third side is examined below.

Frontier Society

The "frontier" quality of the West generated a race of settlers who answered the call of the vast forested or marshy areas of Bac-lieu and Rach-gia, just as they had in different provinces in other times. They ventured there in spite of the obvious disadvantages. To leave a settled and familiar territory was to abandon oneself to an untamed wilderness, as a couplet suggests.

> The country of Can-tho, with handsome boys and pretty girls.
> The country of Rach-gia, with the screeches of gibbons and the singing of birds.[92]

The emigrant would be forced to confront real dangers and ancestral fears.

> In a sampan, the fear that crocodiles will snap off your foot.
> In the swamp, the dread of leeches.
> In the forest, the fear of spirits.[93]

Nevertheless they went, emigrating as families and cooperating in the building of straw huts, the clearing of land, harvesting, fishing, and hunting. Their only possessions were a sampan, a machete or an ax, a wire pot or net for fishing, a mosquito net and a few clothes, an earthen fireplace, and a pot for cooking rice. But they were rich in energy and endured because of the vigorous resistance characteristic of their race. The causes of their migration and nomadism are not always ascribable to infringements of morals or laws. The accounts agree in correcting the idea that the pioneer or the wanderer was invariably an unscrupulous individual with crimes on his conscience or a psychopath.

One can discern other reasons for this mobility, both positive and negative. Schreiner believed that most emigrants were drawn from the ranks of the unregistered, those whom he called the "weaklings" of a village. This judgment must have been inspired by his experience of Nam Tien where the unregistered made up the largest contingent. Schreiner, elsewhere so attentive and sympathetic, did not speculate upon the motivations of these unregistered emigrants. Obviously, though, this category of inhabitants, while not participating in the responsibilities or reaping the benefits of living in a village, shouldered many of its burdens, including taxes and prestations. It is hardly surprising that such people would attempt to escape these obligations in order to live a freer existence—or, more precisely, in order to become the registered inhabitants of a new village.

During the colonial period, similar motives produced the same effect. Following an inspection tour in the region between Bac-lieu and Ca-mau in 1898, an administrative secretary reported that a number of registered people had abandoned their villages because they "ended up paying exorbitant taxes." Elsewhere he observed that

> To require the land tax from these people for the areas they really possess would be to prevent them from working. They would simply move further away and the results would be lost. When the land is in full cultivation, when it is yielding, when risk is no longer dreaded, then they know full well, without anybody forcing them, that they must request registration at the *bo*, for fear that someone passing by might harvest what they have planted.[94]

Avoidance of taxes that were too heavy, or were so judged, was probably the strongest motivation for departures and nomadism. The intolerable character of the taxes resulted in large part from unfavorable climatic factors: what was tolerated in a time of good harvests was not tolerated when floods, drought, or parasites destroyed any hope of a successful crop.

Another source of instability was land-grabbing. The peasant who cleared the soil on his own behalf was seldom the owner of the plot he developed but only its possessor. Far from administrative centers, he could not always have his work validated. Even when he had his parcel registered, he was only considered a provisional concessionaire in a precarious legal situation. If he possessed a receipt, he could lose it or it might be stolen. If he did not have a receipt, the land could be seized by any remote Frenchman whose request was ratified by the Colonial Council and who was powerful enough to displace the pioneer. In this struggle of pygmy against giant there remained little choice for the peasant except to embark again upon the road to adventure (there were some who moved four or five times before settling permanently) or capitulate by signing a rental contract with the legal concessionaire. Sometimes the peasant's lack of resources and especially his precarious position vis-à-vis the authorities forced him to join the "clientèle" of a large landowner even if he did not enter the landowner's labor force. In 1917, landowner Vo Van Thom described a group of wanderers without official papers who hid themselves with him.

> The proof, he adds, is that this fine little canal and these immense rice fields, forest a year ago, are the work of all these people. I made them the necessary advances for the payment of the fine inflicted on them for lack of a "tax" card and for the amount of the latter. They are now supplied with tax cards and they have repaid me in work. They have been very happy and so have I. . . . But there are still many vagabonds in these regions, just so many hands lost to the community.[95]

Of course, there were also positive motivations for migration.

> Life is more vast, and easier. The forest is close by. Gigantic straw huts rise at the edge of the waterways, and the digging of ponds and fish pools is easy. There are numerous and vast glades. The land is easy to work there. And then, if one desires some additional comfort, one may retire into the forest to hunt the honeybees, to gather plants, or, when the season comes, hire out as an oarsman.[96]

Finally, if the settler could hold out long enough to triumph over adversity, if luck supported his obstinacy, he passed into the category of landowner. If he was vanquished, he became a *ta dien* or an agricultural worker.

The *ta dien* was in many cases—and perhaps in the West the majority of cases—a vanquished pioneer. He might also be an immigrant without resources or a small landowner whose plot was not sufficient to feed his family. For all of them, there only remained acceptance of the contract that put them under the thumb of a moneylender. If the rental contract was not exploitive at the outset, it rapidly became so through the *ta dien's* accumulation of debts and interest whenever nature amused itself at the expense of the peasants. The *ta dien* was tempted to flee if he had preserved the taste for wandering or if he felt his back was to the wall. That decision taken, he would carry off both his advances and the harvest. Sometimes he took time to settle other accounts, as did four tenant farmers who assaulted Duong

Hoa Lai, a landowner at Ca-mau, in 1928, taking from him sixty bills of debt worth $20,000 and $2,000 in cash. That evening they also made off with 1,600 *gia* of paddy.[97]

If the *ta dien* chose to stay, he could make the harvest disappear in little packets. In this way, if the *dien chu* or his agent did not notice, the *ta dien* could claim a reduction of the rent on the pretext of a natural calamity. Once he began to practice this strategy, the *ta dien* became an expert. A *dien chu* who suspected a *ta dien*—and he suspected them all on principle—watched him (or had him watched) in order to surprise him in a flagrant offense. To insure himself against all these risks, many *dien chu* increased the interest on advances and used false weights to measure the rice that was used to pay the rent. In 1939, the court of Bac-lieu found a *phu* by the name of Yen guilty of this fraud, and it was established on this occasion that the practice was common among landowners.[98]

This master-farmer dialectic was a far cry from the "old-fashioned relations of confidence between the employer and the workers" that Le Quang Liem recalled.[99] The rental contract, which was little more than a "reciprocal squeeze" according to one administrator, involved a balance of forces that were fragile and often disrupted. It revealed and caused reciprocal distrust. If the landowner did not limit his demands, if he pushed his tenant to extremes, he forced him to pass from docility to resentment, and eventually to revolt.

There was little improvement in the condition of the *ta dien* during the colonial period. His circumstances left him no opportunity to save, even in favorable years, and inevitably he became the victim of bad harvests, indebtedness, sickness, or other calamities.

Labor

A seasonal laborer was a *ta dien* or a settler who supplemented his resources with work undertaken on someone else's land, sometimes outside his home province. Gérard noted this in his description of the pioneers of Ca-mau.

> The life is hard, taxes heavy, the soil barren, and in order to conquer it, in order to feed the household, you must go far away to search for a few piasters that will permit you to increase little by little the plot of land that you have made your own by your labor.[100]

Although seasonal workers were indispensable, they had a reputation for being demanding and quarrelsome. In general, they were feared by the landowners and watched by the authorities.

The middle-sized and large landowners who directly cultivated the whole or part of their lands, also hired permanent workers whose tasks were varied: guarding the water buffaloes, rowing on the sampans, digging canals, maintaining embankments, and fighting predators. Wage laborers also made up the category of *canh dien* (laborers) who prepared the soil and sowed and maintained the seed beds. These domestic jacks-of-all-trades were sometimes recruited from among the nomadic immigrants whose uncertain legal status often led to exploitation by unscrupulous landowners. On the other hand, they might come to be considered part of the family, particularly on the estates of the middle-sized landowners.[101]

Before the Great Depression, both permanent and seasonal agricultural workers in the West received comparatively high wages. Permanent workers received an annual salary of $80 to $100 for men and $40 to $50 for women.[102] Scarcity of labor allowed workers to demand advances in money and such advances in kind as lodging, food, clothing, tobacco, and betel. These salaries were hard hit by the depression, descending to $40 or $50 for men, and many laborers were thrown out of work altogether.[103] By 1938, it was possible to employ a seasonal laborer for 10 centimes and two meals per day. Moreover, the wage earners who were not *ta dien* or small landowners lacked the means to enter the subsistence economy.

Gambling and Other Distractions

The independent settlers, the *ta dien*, and the wage laborers were the agricultural proletarians of the West. They were encumbered by heavy obligations to the internal revenue and the *dien chu*, and these debts were virtually impossible to pay off.[104] They rarely succeeded in improving their standard of living. The pioneer who cleared the forest had to content himself with driving stakes of *tram* into the earth and erecting a light framework on which he arranged tree bark in place of a roof. Later he might build a straw hut of the type that was easy to move: "*la maison à coups de pieds.*" Most of these resembled rude shelters more than dwellings.

The monotony of an existence devoted entirely to pursuing a frugal subsistence was broken only by the theater and gambling, mainly on the occasion of the New Year, the Tet Nguyen Dan. Other opportunities arose during feasts honoring the guardian spirits of the village. These generally occurred during lulls in the agricultural work when the peasants had a little spare time. Villages consulted with one another in order to celebrate the feasts in turn. The villages would host two theater troupes, which performed in turn, day and night. Families might travel ten to twenty kilometers to attend a performance, to eat, to sleep, and to gamble. The theater troupes set up in even the most remote places and gave their performances over several days. The stage was a mound of pilings and sometimes the "orchestra pit" was made up of spectators on their sampans.[105]

Mien Tay is considered to be the birthplace of the *cai luong*, or modern Vietnamese opera, which differs from the classical *hat boi* and the popular northern *hat cheo*. Around 1914–15, in Vinh-long, a man named *thay* Tu Than founded the Academie Sa-dec, an amateur group of comedians and singers that performed in all the provincial towns and many villages in the delta. Given that theater is a cultural expression of a people, some troupes and performances were used by the nationalists and communists to appeal to patriotic feelings or diffuse propaganda.

At the same time, new sports found their way into the delta. Tennis was favored by the upper classes. Commoners took up soccer and bicycle racing. As early as 1918, a soccer team was organized at Cao Lanh, in Sa-dec, and newspaper editor Ziep Van Ky, already active in the Khuyen Hoc Hoi (Association for the Promotion of Education), founded the Hoi The Thao (Physical Training Society). In 1922, Cao Lanh built a soccer field, and groups of players, some without shoes, swarmed throughout the Hau Giang area. In 1930, a soccer "cup" competition was established at Can-tho, the Truong Thanh Quang Cup.

Games of chance also were popular in a society accustomed to risk and with a strong belief in good and bad fortune. The poorest played with the few piasters they possessed, if not with their shirts or their plots of land. There were Chinese merchants who were rumored to be operators of gambling dens. Gambling sometimes accompanied the theatrical performances, and the organizers and *notables* appropriated part of the gains.

Religion

Religion also provided a means of relief for peasants who employed it to ward off evil and gratify desires unfulfilled in their everyday existence. One component of Vietnamese religion was well integrated in village organization and corresponded to the predominant agrarian character of the society. In the West, where the population was dispersed, it was not easy to maintain cohesion between the different hamlets (*ap*) that made up a village (*xa* or *lang*).

This led to decentralization of the village cults, for each *ap* might have its own temple (*dinh*). In 1942, Bui Quang Chieu noticed a decline in village cults, which he interpreted as posing a danger to the established social order.[106]

Many agrarian beliefs and rites remained viable, however. One such was geomancy, the respect for ancient trees, which the settlers protected from the ax.[107] Ceremonies accompanied the farm work, especially at the beginning, the middle, and the end of the harvest. Others were undertaken to attract rain or to expel cholera and epizootics.[108] At the New Year, a rite of exorcism was undertaken to temporarily shield debtors from their creditors.[109] Nor was the forceful use of magic limited to the Cambodians. The Vietnamese took up new magical-religious practices in great numbers, influenced by Khmer folk religion (with its sorcerers, potions, talismans, and recourse to divination) and the secret societies of the Chinese. Nor should one underestimate the influence of the proto-Vietnamese religion, although it usually has been disregarded in light of the impact of Buddhism and Confucianism. It plodded along, borrowing new elements from the Chams, the Khmers, and Taoism. In Mien Tay, and elsewhere, it bore witness to the permanence of an Austro-Asian religious substratum.[110]

In addition, the hills, or *nui*, like the *phnom* of Cambodia, were places of retreat for hermits who were celebrated for their meditations and miraculous healings. The *nui* became the objects of pilgrimage and hotbeds for the spread of new religious movements, some more ephemeral than others.[111] One involved a woman claiming to be a bonzess who was arrested in 1940 after an aborted plot in the region of Ca-mau. Answering to the name of Vo Thi Nam, she had come from a sacred hill on the plain of Chau-doc and Long-xuyen. She had been tattooed for the first time in 1926 by the schoolteacher of a village tainted with "communism and theosophy." In 1933, a Cambodian woman is known to have tattooed her chest with Cambodian characters and cabalistic signs to render herself invulnerable. Also found among her tattoos were Masonic insignia and the motto "Liberté, Egalité, Fraternité."[112]

In another instance, in March 1940, two bloody crimes in the province of Bac-lieu revealed the existence of a religious sect in Song Phu village. A former boxer, Ba Quac, had founded this sect, which was known as Dao Tuong. Ba Quac had a shaven head and dressed like a bonze. He was a vegetarian and led an austere life but he also possessed healing powers. He worshipped the Buddha but also venerated the great Chinese military leader Quan De, and his disciples aspired to invulnerability. Eventually they ritually assassinated an elder on the day of the feast of the Emperor of Jade, a Taoist deity. Another "enlightened one" was Huynh Phu So, who had been born at Hoa Hao in the province of Chau-doc. Besides its political influence, which will be examined below, this sect offers an example of the coexistence of Buddhism and popular Taoism, with the latter furnishing its most spectacular practices.[113] In 1942, in the region of Chau-doc and Long-xuyen, the sect of this "mad bonze" numbered forty thousand members, of whom 90 percent were *ta dien* or agricultural workers. The leaders of the sect, which was known as Hoa Hao, were recruited from among the schoolteachers and the itinerant drivers and conductors of the motor coaches and river launches.[114]

The disappearance of traditional protections and the new social ascendancy of the rich had left the humble defenseless. The success of these kinds of religious sects, though brief, responded to a need to establish new communities of interest.[115]

Links to the Towns

The agricultural labor force was similar in some respects to the proletariat of the towns. The latter was composed primarily of artisans; of workers involved in recently available services such as water and electrical plants and repair shops; and of an unskilled work force of servants and coolies who labored at construction sites, in the mills, and in transport and administration. Their rural ties were still strong, and many of these wage earners also tilled a plot of land or returned to their villages for seasonal work. Although they may have considered themselves to be in a social category different from that of the peasants, their mode of living and behavior presented many similarities.

Although few figures are available concerning the remuneration of workers, some information is available for those employed by the administration and in the electrical plants. The method of payment (by the piece, by the day, or by the month) and the wages vary from one province to another. While the statistics are fragmentary, one can deduce that most wages were paid by the piece or by the day and that employment was unstable.

It was a common practice for employers to reduce wages in retaliation for some venial offense. A decree of 30 December 1937 prohibited the withholding of wages, as well as the imposition of fines, except in cases of lost tools or materials. There were no fixed limits on working hours, the need for weekly rest was ignored, and overtime hours were not recognized as such.[116] There were arbitrary firings, an absence of safety measures, no indemnity in case of personal accident, abusive treatment, and loans (advances on salaries) made at usurious rates of interest.[117] Manual laborers suffered greatly during the early 1930s, and, because high prices were accompanied by currency devaluation, the depression was not followed by a noticeable recovery. In October 1936 alone, prices of consumer goods sold by Cochinchinese retailers rose by 20 percent.[118]

The only comprehensive figures available for this period concern the wages of the quarry workers of Nui Sam. These are reproduced in Table 16. In addition, it is known that in February 1936, on the public works sites at Rach-gia, a coolie earned 30 centimes per day without food or lodging. Tools were supplied at cost. In 1927, coolies had received 80 centimes per day for construction work on the road between Lobe and Ca-mau. A decree of 5 June 1939 set the minimum wage for artisans in central and western Cochinchina at 40 centimes for men and 28 centimes for women.

Protest

For a long while, approximately to the time of the Great Depression, the laborers of the West suffered their condition stoically. Brawls and attacks, though sometimes spectacular, were rare. But they were symptomatic of a restrained violence. Explanations for this state of affairs are not lacking. There was unoccupied land for those who had not settled as tenant farmers. Flight was another safety valve for less patient elements of the proletariat. Even if the prosperity of the West in the 1920s principally benefited the *dien chu* and the moneylenders, some of it diffused to the rest of a population whose behavior sometimes masked their real condition.[119] Confucian teaching advocated obedience and endurance of suffering. This, combined with the malaise of powerlessness, inclined the population toward fatalism and passivity. Bui Quang Chieu addressed this last phenomenon with a frankness that borders on cynicism, stating that the people's "silence, stemming from ignorance or fatalism, is the only guarantee of the social order."[120]

After 1931, the proletariat broke its silence, and workers began to express themselves with more and more conviction. The tenacity with which the pioneers and *ta dien* had overcome natural obstacles was turned upon the men they judged to be their exploiters. Protests and demands continued to intensify until the outbreak of World War II. The *Tribune Indochinoise* was alarmed by a situation it described as follows.

TABLE 16: Wages of Quarry Workers at Nui Sam in the Era of the Great Depression (piasters per cubic meter of rock)

Occupation	Prior to 1931	Early in the Depression	Mid-Depression	1936
Breaker of rock	$.80 to .90	$.50 to .60	$.25	$.30
Miner	.70 to .80	.45 to .50	.30	.35
Carrier	.25 to 45	.18 to .25	.12 to .16	.18 to .22

Source: *Monographie de Chau-doc* (1937), ANVN.

The greater portion of the cultivators, tenant farmers, and sharecroppers no longer want to recognize rental contracts drawn up in the traditional manner, considering them to be just so many scraps of paper. They refuse to take notice of the rents indicated or of the clauses and conditions provided for in the documents. They pay their landlords whatever quantity of paddy they wish, or they pay them nothing at all. Others agree to deliver to the owners only half of the paddy remaining after they deduct what they pretend is essential for their nourishment and for that of their families during the coming year, for seeds for the next agricultural campaign, for the clothing and maintenance of all the members of their families and of people in their charge, and finally for the feeding of their draft animals. Still others usurp the right of ownership to land they have rented for several years under the pretext that they put the land under cultivation, ignoring the fact that they put it under cultivation with the money of their landlords. Others, finally, allow themselves to consider that the draft animals (buffaloes and oxen) rented to them at 50 or 60 *gia* of paddy per year per pair, belong to them on the pretext that they already have paid to their landlords quantities of paddy whose price greatly exceeds the purchase price of these animals.[121]

Nor was the spirit of reform limited to the rural workers. In 1936–37, employees of the Electricity Company of Can-tho, a hundred drivers at Cho-moi, a group of young weavers from the same place, and the tailors of Can-tho and Ca-mau presented lists of demands and went on strike.[122] In particular, they denounced poor working conditions and the abusive behavior of the authorities. In January 1939, eleven peasants of Vong The (in Long-xuyen) went to Saigon to file a complaint with the inspector of political affairs against a rich man who had robbed them. Unable to find the office of the inspector, they wandered around the Inspection du Travail until they were taken off to jail.[123] The boldness of their actions, which were not isolated, was inspired by the naive belief that the administration would intervene on their behalf.

Most of the large landowners attributed all this erratic behavior to the interference of agitators outside the peasantry and even outside the country.[124] Although a few recognized that economic conditions, and even the landowners themselves, must shoulder some responsibility for the general disorder, bolshevik agitation and the machinations of the Front Populaire, with its "hideous retinue of disrupters," were accepted as the principal causes.

The partisans of the menaced social order were not entirely wrong, for one can distinguish two separate aspects in the peasants' and workers' demands. One reflects a response to the immediate situation, but the other, in its call for an eight-hour work day, a forty-hour work week, and paid holidays reflects the influence of the Front Populaire. It was also the existence of the Front that allowed some relative freedom of expression. After 1933, the workers found lawyers willing to defend their cause. They also were given a warm reception by four communist municipal councillors.

The most unusual development, however, was the appearance among the peasants themselves—the small landowners, *ta dien*, and wage laborers— of self-educated spokesmen and organizers. These stepped forward to intercept the ardor that previously had erupted in brief, anarchistic explosions, and guide it into channels of effective organization. The appearance of these grassroots cadres was an indication of a psychological change in certain elements of the proletariat. Suddenly ignorance and fatalism were no longer dominant characteristics of the peasantry, and once this change occurred the established social order was no longer secure. This subject will be taken up in greater detail in the following chapters.

"White-Collar" Workers

There was another category of worker, one that does not find a place in any of the preceding groups. These were the master artisans and the clerical workers, the "white-collar" employees of the administration: secretaries, accountants, cashiers, schoolteachers, security agents, police, and the foremen (*cai*) who acted as the recruiters and overseers of the unskilled labor force. Master artisans aside, these men did not perform manual labor, and their presence illustrates an important division in Vietnamese society between the *thay* (nonmanual, educated workers) and the *tho* (who worked with their hands). Traditionally any Vietnamese who possessed a modicum of education strove to gain the type of employment to which the prestige of *thay* was attached. In 1918, for example, the administrator of Bac-lieu Province observed that agricultural courses had no appeal for young, educated people.

> The sons of the rich covet the *baccalauréat* in order to augment the number of lawyers and doctors. Those from well-off families limit their ambition to becoming minor functionaries, or secretaries of *inspections*, if they are among the most capable. In this situation, appeals and advertisements are useless.[125]

The large landowners were always complaining that the Ben-cat school of agriculture, as well as the Xa-no school on the Gressier estate, failed to furnish them with middle-level employees willing to work on the land. The former students of Ben-cat and Xa-no preferred to work in agriculture departments where they filled bureaucratic, or at least sedentary, positions.

In 1927, a schoolteacher at Bac-lieu complained of the insufficiency of his salary and of the material difficulties encountered in his profession. When an engineer of the public works responded that most other workers received even lower wages, the teacher pointed out that these workers' wives were "for the most part traders, making their own living. Our own, on the other hand, for the sake of our dignity, cannot do the same."[126] Here is a clear illustration of the status bestowed by *thay*.

The wages or salaries of office personnel varied according to certain categories (title holder or assistant, local or regional official) and by province. In 1900, at Long-xuyen, a student secretary of the Revenue Department received around $14 per month. In the corresonding department in Ha-tien in 1905, one secretary received $20 per month and another received $15. But, as a *conseiller d'arrondissement* observed, it was difficult for a civil servant to survive on that salary in Ha-tien because of its remoteness and the high cost of living.[127] Prior to 1908, secretaries at the regional level in Ha-tien did not collect uniform pay and were not categorized. A 1909 reorganization classified secretaries into six categories with movement from one category to another allowed after two years of service (see table 17).

Some information on the salaries and expenditures of a schoolteacher and a family of civil servants at Bac-lieu is available also but the figures are too scattered to allow comparison between categories and periods. The existence of additional income from rice fields, gardens, small plots, and the

TABLE 17: Secretarial Salaries and Classifications in
Ha-tien Province, 1909

Monthly Salary	Title	Classification
$12-$15	student secretary	—
$20	assistant secretary	third class
$25	assistant secretary	second class
$30	assistant secretary	first class
$35	chief secretary	second class
$40	chief secretary	first class

Source: Arrondissement Council of Ha-tien, meeting of 5 September 1909.

economic activities of spouses complicate the picture. It is clear, however, that the white-collar social category, which could be described as "middle," was hardly homogeneous. It settles into several social strata based on material conditions, status, and self-image.

There were similarities between the upper stratum of the white-collar workers and the class of large landowners. In fact, white-collar workers were sometimes landowners themselves. In March 1930, for example, in the magistrate court of Soc-trang, a seizure of property was authorized against the person of Tran Van Luong, a *phu* third class and an accountant residing in the chief town of Can-tho Province. This functionary possessed fourteen plots of land consisting of 125 hectares, 96 ares, and 50 ca of unclassified rice land; 19 hectares of first-class rice land; 5 hectares and 34 ares of first-class garden; and 99 ares and 50 ca of second-class garden.[128]

White-collar workers also shared with the large landowners a taste for borrowing from the western world. To whom, if not to them, were addressed the notices in the Mien Tay press advertising such establishments as the "Restaurant of the West"?[129] In 1926, the restaurant of the Central Hotel at Can-tho City hailed itself as the "meeting place of the Annamite bourgeoisie of Can-tho."[130] Tennis was a popular pastime. In 1923, the occupations of the best players of Can-tho were given as clerk for the administration, first lawyer's clerk, director of the Vo Van Institute, merchant, settler, and technical agent.[131]

Some of these bourgeois possessed French nationality. The visiting card of one, Charles Nguyen Cao Man, proudly bore his titles: French citizen and retired chief telegraphist. However, unlike the large landowners, Vietnamese bureaucratic functionaries were treated differently than their French colleagues. Discrimination was conspicuous both in salaries and in the allocation of offices. With equal qualifications, a Vietnamese possessed far fewer advantages than did a Frenchman. Nonetheless, the offices these bureaucrats filled, particularly in the administration, did confer prestige in the eyes of the humble as well as in their own. Many abused the authority they had been granted and bribery was widespread.

As great importance was attached to titles, it was customary to give such a worker a title superior to the tasks he actually performed. If he functioned as a *thay* (secretary) he was given the title *ong* (monsieur); if he was an *ong,* he was called *quan lon* (Your Excellency). The category to which a functionary belonged also determined his place in a tacit hierarchy. Thus, a secretary of the Cochinchinese government was ranked above his uncommissioned colleague who would have been recruited from the provincial ranks. The farther a bureaucrat resided from the urban centers, particularly from Can-tho, the lower he descended along the white-collar hierarchy and the more mediocre and precarious was his position.

Much of the administrative correspondence contains requests for assistance from faithful employees rendered unfit for work by age or sickness, most commonly due to tuberculosis. Although the administration almost always responded, its contributions were small—around $40 or $50 after ten to fifteen years of service in 1910. This permitted survival, provided that the employee was also aided by his children. The amount could be smaller still. In 1918, for example, a midwife in the *arrondissement* of Ha-tien was discharged after eight years of service because of her advanced age. She received $20 in aid.[132]

Schoolteachers in the cantons and villages made a bare living compared to their colleagues trained in the *écoles normales.* The latter taught in the chief towns, often finding their way into secretaryships. The poor teachers of the countryside often had to borrow money at interest while waiting to be paid, and the most destitute resided in their open schools where they were frequently the victims of robbers. If they wished to travel to the chief town they were required to submit a written request to the chief administrator of their province. In the villages they were held in little regard by the *notables* who coopted them as secretaries during school hours and sometimes even attacked them physically. Lacking the status of a literatus, the rural teacher was considered a failure by *notables* and the pupils' parents alike.[133]

Confucian virtues were preached and practiced with the greatest fidelity among the *thay*. That the importance of the family was paramount is demonstrated by the number of transfer requests submitted by teachers that refer to the need to care for parents or parents-in-law. Solidarity also came into play when the family honor was at stake, as in cases of debt or tax arrears.

The *thay*, however, were also exposed to experiences that did not wholly conform to tradition. Many adopted the Caodaist religion, which was founded in the province of Ha-tien by three *thay* men: the *phu* Ngo Van Chieu; the government secretary turned *conseiller colonial* Le Van Trung; and the former customs secretary Pham Cong Tac. The rise of this religion in Mien Tay was not coincidental, for the essential feature of Caodaism was not syncretism but spiritualism. This spiritualism corresponded to an ancient tradition typified by consultation with mediums (*ba dong* and *ong dong*) and by the evocation of the immortals (*cau tien*), a practice favored among the literati of old Annam. The *cau tien* ceremony featured poetry readings between the living and the spirits. These practices, nearly everywhere abandoned, were preserved in Mien Tay. They were particularly common in Can-tho Province where two *dan* were consecrated to the healing spirits.[134] It is possible that the introduction of European spiritualist books into the bourgeois milieu created a renewed interest in these ancient practices.[135] It is also possible that the refined character of these practices, which were popular among the Vietnamese of the delta, attracted the landowners and *thay* to the sect. Recruitment from different social ranks also may account for the quarrels and schisms that plagued the sect from the beginning.

Conclusion

French domination of Nam Bo helped accelerate and consolidate the Nam Tien of the Vietnamese people. The growth of a colonial economy maintained the society's multiethnic structure, though it strengthened the numbers and the role of the Vietnamese, reducing the Khmers to a minority position. It also helped codify and rigidify the hierarchical class structure.

A new phenomenon was the emergence of a bourgeoisie whose wealth was grounded in land ownership (the Vietnamese) or trade (the Chinese). Laterally, bureaucrats and members of the liberal professions often were linked to (and sometimes were) the offspring of the landlord class. Though something of an exaggeration, in Mien Tay the French may be seen as a kind of epiphenomenon. But they engineered a configuration of social classes that sometimes transcended, overlapped, or blurred ethnic-national loyalties, creating a society that seems relevant to a marxist vision of social relationships and a Leninist strategy of social change. The division of labor and power attribution along ethnic-national lines resulted in an "antagonistic symbiosis." Although the French did not create the ethnic and cultural differences and antagonisms, they used them, as any conqueror would, to divide and rule, claiming at the same time the role of protector of the weak.

In their struggle against the French colonialists, and later against the *My Nguy* (the Americans and their puppets), the Vietnamese communists pointed out the common interests of Khmer and Vietnamese peasants and Vietnamese and Chinese workers. In doing so, they tended to underrate the interethnic conflicts or attribute them to the oppressive "feudal policies" of the Nguyen dynasty or to the divide-and-rule policies of the French, the Americans, and the puppets.[136]

In any case, one cannot reduce the historical relationships between Khmers and Vietnamese, rich and poor, to simple patterns of rivalry and conflict or harmony and cooperation. The history of Vietnamese political movements, which follows, sheds light on the intricacies, ambiguities, and paradoxes of social and political interplay.

CHAPTER 5

Society
and Politics,
1908-1930

THOUGH THE ANNEXATION of Nam Bo by the French provoked fierce resistance, the repeated defeats of the insurgents and the submission of the Court of Hue led their leaders to refrain from additional uprisings. The last serious act of "primary resistance," led by the Muoi Tam Thon Vuon Trau (18 Villages of the Areca Plantations), occurred in 1885 when peasants from various districts around Saigon marched on the city and nearly succeeded in overthrowing the French. In the same year the Phong Trao Can Vuong movement emerged in the center and north and expanded into Nam Bo. Although many French troops were engaged in southern Cambodia at the time, those remaining were barely able to hold Saigon. The vengeful "pacification" campaign that followed in 1886 ensured the end of armed insurgency.

Although the spirit of resistance never disappeared entirely, it changed form. The transformation of Nam Bo's land and commerce during the last quarter of the nineteenth century created a dual character for the region. On one hand, the vastness of Mien Tay provided places and opportunities to escape, roam, and plot, or to settle down, clear land, and (sometimes) to become rich. Sufficient economic options were available to pacify the population for a time, though many opportunities and motivations for resistance also emerged. By 1900, the most serious form of resistance had developed among men who had benefited from the spread of rice cultivation and the rice trade. Even in the midst of dramatic economic improvement, the people of Nam Bo drew inspiration from the period of anti-French resistance, from movements still in existence in the center and north, and from other Asian countries.

The Anticolonialism of the New Class

One of the more significant events for the new class of landlords and government officials in Nam Bo was the Japanese victory over imperial Russia in 1905, which was perceived as a tremendous blow to the white man's prestige. Shock waves spread throughout Asia and the colonial world. The Vietnamese Prince Cuong De, supported by the literatus Phan Boi Chau, chose Japan as a base from which to inspire and direct resistance against the French. Phan Boi Chau, who also had been influenced by Chinese reformist thinkers such as Liang Qi Zhao and revolutionaries such as Sun Yat Sen, recruited young patriots to attend school in Japan. This movement was called Dong Zu, "the trip to the East." By 1906, as many as three hundred young Vietnamese were studying in Japan.[1] The majority came from Nam Bo, often born to well-to-do and even rich families of the provinces of My-tho, Go-cong, Can-tho, and Long-xuyen. After the Japanese government expelled the Vietnamese students in 1908, France (and later the Soviet Union) became the sites of study abroad, and "the western trip" (Tay Zu) replaced the Dong Zu.

Many landlords, *notables*, and colonial bureaucrats retained a nostalgia for the lost unity of their fatherland, even as they were growing rich in the economic boom of the delta. The general cultural and political resurgence led by Phan Boi Chau and Phan Chu Trinh, and organized in the north by the Dong Kinh Nghia Thuc, was known as Zuy Tan ("Modernization") and in Nam Bo as Minh Tan ("New Light").[2] The men who committed themselves to this movement were not of the classes of the tenants, peasants, and laborers. Tran Chanh Chieu (also known as Gilbert Chieu) was representative of the new class of landlords. Chieu owned a thousand hectares in the province of Rach-gia where he employed more than two hundred tenants. He had been awarded French citizenship and the honorific title of *doc phu su* (chief of the province in the south). Typical of the class of Vietnamese landlords who were attempting to expand their activities beyond the agricultural sector, he owned two hotels and a soap factory. He was editor in chief of three vernacular newspapers owned by Frenchmen. Though by all appearances he was a collaborator, he became one of the leaders of the anticolonial movement. With the help of a literatus, Bui Chi Nhuan, an emissary of Phan Boi Chau in Nam Bo, he joined in the anti-French activities and became a prominent figure in what the authorities called "le complot Gilbert Chieu," uncovered in 1908. With the profits from his commercial and manufacturing enterprises he subsidized the studies of many Vietnamese in Japan. In the delta there existed several associations, known as the *khuyen zu hoc hoi*, which encouraged studies abroad. The *hoi* at Cao Lanh (in Sa-dec) was led by Nguyen Quang Zieu, the one at Tan An by Bui Chi Nhuan, the one at Hatien by Nguyen Than Hien, and the one at Rach-gia by Chieu himself. Acording to Nguyen Quang Zieu's biography, Nguyen Than Hien succeeded in collecting more than twenty thousand piasters to subsidize students in Japan.[3] Chieu sent his own son, Jules Triet, to a Catholic school in Hong Kong and eventually during a visit there he contacted Phan Boi Chau.

Chieu's activities embodied a conception of Vietnam inspired in part by the Japanese Meiji and Chinese reformers. His goal was to develop a modern Vietnamese economy that could function without Chinese traders, Indian moneylenders, and French political rule. Chieu and his fellows wished to be treated as equals by the French (they were, it will be remembered, refused equal treatment even when they enjoyed French citizenship) and the inequities of French policy had a powerful impact on their political evolution.[4] They also hoped to become as economically diversified as the French, and to be considered full members of the bourgeoisie, not just landlords and government functionaries. This compelling "syndrome de Gilbert Chieu" endured, and it continued to influence the Vietnamese elite of the twentieth century. Some saw an opportunity for armed rebellion during World War I when France's military forces were primarily engaged in Europe. Probably encouraged by the German embassy in Bangkok, and anticipating German assistance in the form of weapons and troops, the Viet Nam Quang Phuc Hoi emissaries and activists began to organize. Tran Cao Van managed to convince King Zuy Tan to take the lead in an insurrection to be launched in Hue in 1916, though the conspiracy was unmasked before it went far and the king was exiled to the island of La Réunion in the Indian Ocean.[5]

Finally, the great landlords of Nam Bo, having learned the lessons of Chieu's conspiracy of 1908 and the king's of 1916, began to channel their energies into their own businesses. They organized the first Vietnamese bank in 1927, the Société Annamite de Crédit, and made new investments in rice culture and such para-agricultural enterprises as motorized transport and cold storage. Those who remained committed to political change kept their dissent within the bounds of loyalty to the French government. The landlord and agronomist Bui Quang Chieu, along with another landlord and publisher, Nguyen Phan Long, created the Constitutionalist Party in 1917 and operated the *Tribune Indochinoise* and *Duoc Nha Nam*.[6] These newspapers promoted the aspirations of the new class, claiming the legal right to express their views. Children of the elite, returning home as engineers, doctors, and lawyers, considered themselves the modern leaders of Vietnam but chose to cooperate with the French up to a point. They exposed the abuses of French domination (what they called *le colonialisme à la trique*) and protested when the regime raised obstacles to their assumption of public responsibilities. They were not a homogeneous group, divided as they were between conservatives such as Bui Quang Chieu and liberals such as Nguyen Van Thinh and Nguyen Phan Long, but their theory of social relations sprang from family oriented, traditional patterns. Landlords, they believed, must behave like fathers toward their tenants. By and large, like any educated elite, they assumed that they were the "natural" leaders of the lower classes.[7]

Their political activities, though elitist, drew in much of the Vietnamese population. In 1925, the French police captured Phan Boi Chau, and his subsequent trial gave birth to a vast campaign of solidarity. The following year Phan's alter ego, Phan Chu Trinh, a modernist reformer and republican personality, passed away. In honor of these men, people in the delta, especially the young, organized demonstrations at which they expressed their patriotic feelings. Deep in countryside, villages such as Vinh Kim (in My-tho) and My Tra (in Sa-dec) also paid tribute. A future communist, Tran Thi Nhuong, a female teacher in the village school at Hoa An (Sa-dec), recalled that

> My life, my ideas, and my thoughts entered a new stage. It was 1926! The sudden news reached our school: Phan Chu Trinh was dead. In both schools, boys and girls organized a commemoration ceremony in honor of *cu* Phan [*cu* being a term of respect]. . . . I had new thoughts: we must act, and not be satisfied with mere patriotic feelings.[8]

New Religions and Secret Societies

Organization among the lower classes of Nam Bo tended to take the form of secret societies. In the mobile and unstable world created by the expansion of rice cultivation and trade, where debt, poverty, seasonal unemployment, migration, and heavy taxation were widespread, such societies flourished. Two organizations often confused by the French authorities, and even by the Vietnamese, were the Thien Dia Hoi (Heaven and Earth Society)[9] and Buu Son Ky Huong (Strange Fragrance from the Precious Mountain). The former reflects the heavy Chinese influx into Nam Bo. Originally created to oppose the Manchu dynasty, *thien dia hoi* expanded among the Chinese in Vietnam. We can only guess how it was Vietnamized: either the Chinese opened their

Figure 3

Political and Religious Groups in Nam Bo

	Revolutionary Nationalists	Reformists
1925	Revolutionary Party of New Vietnam (Tan Viet cach mang Dang) established	Constitutionalist Party of Indochina founded
	Association of Revolutionary Youth (Thanh Nien cach mang dong chi Hoi) established	
1926		Emergence of the Cao Dai religion
1927	Secret Society of Nguyen An Ninh (Thanh Nien Cao Vong Dang) formed	
1929	May: schism in the Association of Revolutionary Youth; establishment of the First Indochinese Communist Party	
	August: the Revolutionary Party of New Vietnam renamed Communist League of Indochina (Dong Zuong Cong San Lien Doan), but one faction (in Hue) kept the former name	
	October: Communist League renamed Communist Party of Annam (An Nam Cong San Dang)	
1930	February: Nguyen Ai Quoc, a delegate of the Third International, unified the three groups as the Communist Party of Vietnam (Dong Cong San Viet Nam)	
	October: As directed by the Third International, the Communist Party of Vietnam renamed the Communist Party of Indochina	
1939	Rise of the Hoa Hao	Restoration of Vietnam (Viet Nam Phuc Hoi) founded
1946	Formation of the Social Democrat Party (Zan Xa Hoi Dang)	

doors to the Vietnamese and eventually were absorbed by them, or the Vietnamese insurgents chose Thien Dia Hoi as a conduit for their underground struggle. In the province of Rach-gia, for example, where Chinese settlers were fairly numerous, the leader of the resistance against the French, Thu Khoa Huan, had the support of local Thien Dia Hoi chapters. The Buu Son Ky Huong cooperated with the Thien Dia Hoi in 1913, and again in 1916, to stage rebellions in the delta.[10] The Buu Son Ky Huong adepts were particularly active in the village of Hoa Hao in the province of Chau-doc.[11]

Insurgents received support from all sectors of society, a circumstance that encouraged cooperation between classes. The story of Nguyen Quang Zieu (1880–1936) is illustrative in this regard. Born in the district of Cao-lanh (in Sa-dec), and educated as a literatus and writer, he tried to join Phan Boi Chau in China in 1913. Captured by the French, he was imprisoned in the penitentiary of Cayenne in French Guiana. In collusion with a Chinese trader, he managed to escape in 1917, returning home via the United States and Hong Kong. Later he spent ten years (1926–36) in the village of Vinh Hoa (Sa-dec), dividing his time between teaching, healing, and writing poetry. In all that time no one reported him to the police, and he was already dead of typhoid by the time the authorities learned of his return in 1941.[12]

In the 1920s, the Vietnamese elite, searching for a way to assert itself politically outside the Constitutionalist Party, began to graft itself onto this popular world of secret societies and mystical traditions. Neither Governor General A. Sarraut's policy of "Franco-Annamite association" (*Phap Viet de hue*) nor the subsequent appointment of the radical socialist A. Varennes as governor general in 1925 brought notable changes in the colonial regime (although Varennes gave the French in Vietnam a fright). Since neither legal dissent nor armed rebellion appeared to be effective, new forms of organization were attempted. Many among the new class (such as Zuong Van Giao and Nguyen Phan Long) joined or subsidized the new religion Dai Dao Tam Ky Pho Do (the Great Way of the Third Era of Salvation) popularly known as Cao Dai.[13] Its original founders and leaders, as well as its high priesthood, were drawn from the same social milieu as were the constitutionalists—an amalgam of landlords, urban bourgeoisie, and government functionaries. Also known as Caodaism, the new religion appeared in 1925 among a small circle of men that included Ngo Van Chieu, Le Van Trung, Le Ba Trang, and Pham Cong Tac. Most of its founders were born in the delta and owned estates or performed their government functions there.[14]

Cao Dai revitalized Vietnam's three dominant religions (Confucianism, Taoism, and Buddhism), borrowing beliefs, doctrinal ingredients, and ritual practices from each. But the most prominent feature of Cao Dai was the spirit worship and communication with the dead practiced by young mediums. These components, inherited from Taoism, imparted creativity and vitality to the new faith. A belief in prophets and messiahs inspired followers and leaders alike to concern themselves with secular issues and the collective destiny of the country. Ralph Smith has pointed out the connection between Cao Dai and the Buddhist sect Minh Su, which played a role in anti-French resistance in Nam Bo during the first decade of the twentieth century.[15] Amid all the borrowing from other traditions, the only innovation of Cao Dai was the odd presence of foreign personalities in its syncretic pantheon, a roster that included Jesus Christ, Victor Hugo, and Joan of Arc. Smith considers their inclusion to have been a ploy intended to divert French suspicions but it might better be seen as an attempt by the Nam Bo elite to gain the respect of the French.[16] The presence of European spirits was not a tactical cover but a transcultural reference with political content. (Similarly, the prophet of the Tai Ping Rebellion in nineteenth-century China, Hong Xiu Quan, pretended to be Jesus Christ's brother, not due to fancy or mimetism but because he wished to assert parity between yellow and white Christs.)

Though Cao Dai initially appeared in Ha-tien, not far from the mountains of Chau-doc, the cradle of the Buu Son Ky Huong tradition, it was clearly distinct. Adopting a tradition of the Chinese literati, who used to call upon the poet Li T'ai Po's spirit, Ngo Van Chieu made a practice of climbing a *dan* to consult with spirits.[17] But the fortunes of the new religion truly began to rise when Le Van Trung and Pham Cong Tac transferred its center of gravity to the province of Tay-ninh in eastern Nam Bo. Cao Dai temples sprang up in many provinces in the delta as the struggle for power at the top of the ecclesiastic hierarchy generated schisms and at least four sects. The My-tho and Ben-tre sects remained loyal to the Holy See of Tay-ninh, while the sect in Bac-lieu refused to do so.

The true novelty of Cao Dai lay in the way it enabled a mass religion, well organized and highly structured, with a clergy and affiliated agencies for administrative and social purposes, to spread throughout society. In some ways it resembled the Catholic Church and even the colonial administration. As it developed, Cao Dai did not restrict its membership to the class of functionaries, landlords, and traders. Many peasants joined. In fact, in numerous cases the success of Cao Dai in recruiting members might be ascribed to the interpersonal relations prevailing between the elite and its dependents, specifically between landlords and tenants. A significant role also was played by overlapping kinship and patron-client networks.

We even find attempts by some landlords to use the new religion to rejuvenate the traditional social contract. Cao Trieu Phat, who founded the Bac-lieu sect in 1932, was reputed to be a benevolent landlord. Born into the family of a well-to-do Sino-Vietnamese landlord of Bac-lieu who had been awarded the honorific title of *doc phu su*, he was trained as an interpreter at Chasseloup-Laubat College and volunteered to go to France during World War I with a commission as a *sergent-major interprète*. There he apparently familiarized himself with democratic and socialist ideas, for back home in Nam Bo he founded the short-lived Parti Travailliste (Labor Party) and the newspaper *Nhut Tan Bao* (New Daily) in 1926. In another example, Nguyen Van Ca, owner of five hundred hectares in Can-tho and also a *doc phu su*, asked his tenants to call him "brother" rather than "my lord."[18]

The Cao Dai's mass recruitment of members stirred up suspicions among the French authorities, although some of the administrators perceived only certain sects and leaders as posing a threat.[19] When Pham Cong Tac and other high dignitaries were exiled to Madagascar in 1941, some French authorities advocated the total suppression of the Cao Dai. The governor of Cochinchina was opposed to such drastic measures, however, on the grounds that the religion's social networks were so entrenched among the population that its banning would produce a dangerous vacuum.[20] The ambiguous character of the Cao Dai, with its elite leadership and mass base, also posed a difficult problem for the Indochinese Communist Party (ICP). The ICP denounced the "tricks of the landlords and feudalists" but it also called upon Cao Dai peasants to unite with communist peasants in light of their common anticolonial interests.

> Consciousness comes to the Caodaists. . . . Our comrades realize now that benevolent or wicked geniuses don't exist. There are only capitalists, landlords, intellectuals, and functionaries who in creating Cao Dai have but one goal: to lull the credulous masses in order to enslave them.[21]

The Cao Dai leader, Nguyen Phan Long, in effect confirmed the communists' assessment of the religion when he wrote the following to a French deputy who was preparing to lead an investigation committee in Indochina.

> The Caodaists have always respected the authorities. Because of their number, their style of life, and the ethics they practice daily, they neutralize, though involuntarily, the harmful effects of the extremists on the masses.[22]

The Emergence of the Communist Movement

The Cao Dai religion did not pose a danger to the propertied class of Vietnamese since the movement tended to consolidate links between the "haves" and the "have nots." But the religion's democratic and egalitarian doctrines contributed to a general social discourse on political change. The 1920s witnessed a profusion of organizations that took the ideals of democracy and equality much farther than did the Cao Dai. Intellectuals such as Nguyen An Ninh returned from France in 1927 conscious of the failure of the French to transfer the political ideals that governed the mother country to the colonies. Ninh organized a revolutionary nationalist group commonly known as the Hoi Kin N.A.N. (Secret Society Nguyen An Ninh) but formally entitled the Thanh Nien Cao Vong Dang (High Aspirations Youth Party). According to Hue Tam Ho Tai, Ninh recruited many followers from among the Thien Dia Hoi[23] and his cells were based in such suburban villages surrounding Saigon and Cholon as Hoc Mon, Ba Diem, and Go Vap, already famous for resistance. The Vietnamese have since memorialized these places as the Muoi Tam Thon Vuon Trau (18 Villages of the Areca Plantations). From there anti-French sentiments diffused among a host of truck drivers, gardeners, craftsmen, rickshaw operators, and later pedicab drivers, coolies, and even hoodlums (zu con) who formed the ubiquitous and uncontrollable elements of demonstrations and riots. From that half-urban, half-rural, plebeian population, Ninh's movement spread into the delta, mainly in the province of My-tho on the fringe of Dong Thap Muoi. It does not seem, however, that Ninh's influence reached as far as Mien Tay.

Nguyen An Ninh, as well as the Caodaists, illustrate the fertility of the tradition of dissidence and rebellion that originated with the Buu Son Ky Huong, Thien Dia Hoi, and other Buddhist sects. The communists emerged from the same mold. As one communist, Zan Ton Tu, related in his *hoi ky* (memoirs), when he was twenty-one he left his village of Vinh Kim to ramble through Nam Bo in search of the meaning of life. He took refuge in a pagoda in Nui Ket, the birthplace of the Buu Son Ky Huong tradition, and his journey awakened him to social iniquity.[24] The primary appeal of the communist groups over other organizations, however, was that they proposed to accomplish, as Paul Mus put it, "one cosmic reorganization couched in rational terms."[25] Lenin's theories linked analysis of society with a strategy of action and provided a paradigmatic form of revolutionary organization. Finally, the Russian Revolution began to have an impact in Vietnam in the 1920s.

Of the two nationalist revolutionary groups represented in Nam Bo (Tan Viet and Thanh Nien) the latter seems to have been the most active in the delta. When it split in 1929, its offshoot, the ICP 1, expanded under the leadership of an eminent propagandist and organizer, Ngo Gia Tu.[26] The initial cells of the ICP 1 were established in 1929 in three places in Nam Bo that had symbolic and practical value: the arsenal of the French navy at Ba Son in Saigon (a seat of industrial labor), the rubber estate of the Michelin Corporation at Dau Tieng (a seat of agro-industrial labor), and among the rural folk of the village of Vinh Kim (in My-tho) in the heart of the delta.[27] The main focus of the party's efforts to organize the delta's peasantry was the province of My-tho where many rebellions and plots against the French had been launched in the past. During the 1930s and 1940s, My-tho was the stronghold of the ICP. It was also a geographical pivot. Less than 100 kilometers from Saigon-Cholon, My-tho City was linked to the metropolis by rail, road, and canals. From My-tho the party's directives could be diffused throughout the delta. Thus, as early as 1929, the geography of communism was fairly clear. Beginning in My-tho, by the 1930s the provinces of Sa-dec, Ben-tre, Vinh-long, Long-xuyen, Rach-gia, Tra-vinh, and Bac-lieu had districts or villages in which communists were present.

An analysis of the *hoi ky* of five communist militants provides a glimpse of their social background and political experience. While we must be careful not to overgeneralize from this sample, some significant common characteristics emerge in the stories of these four women and one man. Each grew up within family and neighborhood networks like *giap* (often interconnected) whose history was closely intertwined with Vietnam's collective past. In this environment, they were exposed to the memorials of such heroes of the early anti-French resistance as Thu Khoa Huan and Truong Cong Dinh. All were born in provinces in the central or western part of the delta. Theirs were not impoverished families nor did they grow up in districts dominated by rice.[28] Rather, they sprang from a small peasant society of rice cultivators and fruit growers. Yet even in these zones the contrasts between the well-to-do and the poor were sharp and resented. A song popular among rice transplanters expresses this resentment well.

The rich wear sapphire jewels and dress in cashmere shirts.
We, the poor, bear the harnesses of horses and the yokes of buffaloes.

Although they were not rich, none of these five was illiterate, and most had completed their primary education. Unlike the religious faiths that could be diffused by means of esoteric poems and magic formulas, which did not need to be elaborated, or even understood, by their followers, communist propaganda required well-argued discourse and instruction. For this reason, teachers trained in Vietnam and activists trained in Moscow played a major role. The stories of two such persons illustrate well the profile of communist activists compared to that of prophets, healers, and magicians. The first, Chau Van Liem, was born into a well-to-do family of farmers in Can-tho. He graduated from the École Normale d'Instituteurs, a training college for primary teachers in Saigon. After a career as a schoolteacher in Long-xuyen, he resigned his post to commit himself to revolutionary action in Thanh Nien before organizing the ICP 1 in the delta. He was killed by police on 4 June 1930 while leading a peasants' demonstration in Duc Hoa (Cholon).[29] The second man, Nguyen Van Tran, studied in France. After four years there, he spent two years in Moscow, returning home in 1929. He was sent by the Communist Party to the provinces of Sa-dec and Long-xuyen to lecture on communism but was captured by the police after only two months.[30]

Communist propaganda castigated both the French colonial regime and the Vietnamese elite. The French were accused of supporting the rich landowners and evil *notables* and ignoring their exactions. The local establishment was stigmatized for collaborating with the colonial authorities. Both the French and the Vietnamese raised taxes and rents and increased the burden on the lower classes. The communists had some difficulty replacing the commonly understood terms *rich, poor, powerful*, and *weak* with *capitalism, proletariat*, and *class struggle*. They also struggled to analyze the class structure of Nam Bo society and reconcile class conflict and national resistance. After all, many rich peasants and even landlords were anti-French as well. During its early years, 1930–32, the ICP cautioned its militants to take into account the different social classes when organizing peasant associations (*nong hoi*). Party documents complain that poor peasants and laborers shunned the *nong hoi*, which came to be controlled by well-to-do farmers, craftsmen, teachers, and healers. Available documents suggest that the party's *nong cong doan* (laborer trade unions) never existed.[31] The world of Nam Bo was very fluid and the ever-changing fortunes of most inhabitants made it virtually impossible to distinguish between different classes at the village level. While large landlords and rich peasants could be identified, further attempts at class analysis inevitably ended in failure.[32] Thus, the party faced serious problems in its efforts to develop a coherent tactical line and an effective class alliance.

CHAPTER 6

Depression and Recovery, 1931-1940

THE HIGH EXPECTATIONS of the Vietnamese elite for economic development were dashed by the Great Depression. The depression revealed existing colonial structures and dysfunctions the way an earthquake lays bare the inner framework of the earth and forces the eruption of its deepest materials. Before 1930 no trace is found in the annals of the West of a widespread depression. Episodic bad harvests and slumps in rice cultivation had affected one province or another but never the whole region. The fragility of the economy of rice culture was manifested principally in the distributive sector, through the failures (as in 1910–11) of trading firms and mills in Cholon. While these incidents left the rest of the economy intact, they indicated where its Achilles heel was located.

The relative prosperity that preceded the Great Depression must have increased the ease with which the Chinese wholesalers obtained credit from commercial houses and banks. And it must have augmented their propensity to speculate and work on the margin as well. In December 1929, failures among several Chinese rice wholesalers in Cholon led first the exporters and then the banks to cut off their customary cash advances. This tightening of credit did not have an immediate effect on prices and production but it was a disturbing symptom. In the bond that connected the rice grower to the mill, and finally to the market, the weakening of the commercial link could result in a chain reaction. At the time, however, the closure of the Chinese establishments was thought to be unrelated to the beginning of the world depression, and it alarmed neither the public nor the authorities. The governor of Cochinchina declared to the Colonial Council that the "general economic situation is at the present time satisfactory. Some failures have occurred during these last months. But this crisis . . . superficial and passing, does not testify to any weakening of the productive forces of the country."[1]

There is no reason to believe that this was officially constructed optimism, and the governor's conviction that these difficulties would pass was shared by many others. In early 1930, the economy of Mien Tay continued to flourish. It was the inaugural year of the Can-tho branch of the Banque de l'Indochine, of the first mechanized brick works in Can-tho, and of the Rach-gia to Ha-tien canal. Developments during the first half of the year seemed to give cause for optimism, and the price of rice remained firm. Uneasiness only began to appear when prices collapsed in August. But, although stockpiles of 250,000 tons of rice were reported in the following year, they were absorbed when China, devastated by floods, increased its imports.[2] In 1931, both the euphoria and the serenity ended when it became increasingly clear that the depression in Cochinchinese rice culture was going to be neither a local nor a short-lived phenomenon.

The principal manifestation was a dramatic fall in prices. In July 1931, rice sold for $6, then $5, and in 1932 for $4.40 per *gia*. It is true that, according to certain authors, prices on the eve of the depression were not normal, and if one agrees with them that the normal price of rice was roughly $6 or $7, then the figures for 1932 show an average drop of only 35 percent. But prices alone do not convey the situation in the West. There the drop in prices might have been absorbed if the farms had been "without financial burdens" but "it was these three words that all of Cochinchina came up against."[3]

Initially, although the disorganization of the market and the fluctuations in prices spread the perturbation, growers with access to SICAM credit had the means to stockpile rice. But waiting for better conditions proved to be futile, for the collapse of world cereal prices, particularly that of wheat, forced down the price of secondary cereals, including rice. In addition, Indochinese rice was subject to heavier export charges than that of other countries. Finally, the announcement of a projected surtax of 45 percent on rice exports, and of 6 percent on paddy, precipitated the fall in prices and halted the sale of futures.

In 1930, stabilization of the Indochinese piaster further aggravated the depression in Nam Bo. The French government, wishing to guarantee the stability of the Indochinese economy and the security of European capital invested there, had planned since before World War I to abandon the silver standard in favor of gold. The postponed reform was finally implemented in 1930 even though the effects of the depression were beginning to be felt. Currency reform soon resulted in speculation in the silver piaster. It was reported, for example, that the Chinese transferred several millions to foreign

TABLE 18: Depression-Era Paddy Prices on the Cholon Market
(per quintal)

	1929	1930	1931	1932	1933	1934
	$7.15	$5.54	$3.79	$3.32	$2.30	$1.88

Source: Saigon Chamber of Commerce.

currency. The resulting scarcity of money accentuated the prevailing credit restrictions, further paralyzing commerce. Taxes, payments for required service, and debts contracted during the era of the silver piaster did not become any easier to pay.[4]

The principal studies undertaken of the economic depression in Indochina, and particularly of the depression in the rice economy, have emphasized internal causes.[5] They declare that overproduction of rice was the nearly fatal result of the boom years of 1925–29, and claim that the first symptoms were visible as early as 1928 (although they offer no proof for this). They seek to demonstrate that the rice growers, and above all the large landowners, were responsible for their own disasters because they had taken and given credit indiscriminately and had extended the area under cultivation rather than improving the techniques of production. To these reproaches, first made at the time of the depression, the rice growers responded by placing the blame on the credit institutions and their bidding wars, on tariffs, and above all on the monetary policies of the government. The polemic became so bitter that the worldwide depression was nearly forgotten.[6]

There was every indication that the years of prosperity had come to an end in Cochinchina. Considering that the rice economy was burdened with debt and had turned toward exports, a prolonged drop in prices to a level below the cost of production was certain to disrupt it. Perhaps the arrival of the world depression coincided with the beginnings of the ebb in prosperity. Certainly it found in Cochinchinese rice culture a very sensitive organism. In closing off the usual markets and provoking the slide, and then the fall in prices, the world depression revealed these weaknesses but it did not create them. Stabilization of the piaster only worsened the slump.

In Cochinchina, the depression lasted from 1931 to 1934. It was around May or June of 1931 that the rice growers began to feel its effects. Then, as shown in Table 18, prices continued to drop. In the provinces a *gia* of paddy sold for $1.20 to $1.40 from 1927 to 1930. At Ca-mau in 1932, a *gia* changed hands for $.50. In 1933, $.40 represented a purely nominal value, which in fact was reduced to as little as $.25 depending on the distance from markets. In 1934, the BCAC cites a case in which paddy was offered at $.10 per *gia* at the village of Phu Loc in Soc-trang.

The value of land also depreciated quickly. Records of numerous sales at public auction establish that the price of land in Bac-lieu fell from 150 piasters per hectare in 1929 to only 50 three years later. The price in Can-tho dropped from 200 piasters to 150, while in Soc-trang a hectare of land that sold for 350 piasters in 1929 brought only 180 in 1932.[7] After 1930, domanial plots no longer found takers. A plantation at Cay Dua (on the island of Phu Quoc) estimated to be worth 2 million piasters before the depression was acquired in November 1932 for $12,000 by a former overseer. In the course of foreclosure sales in the provinces of Rach-gia and Bac-lieu, rice land previously worth $200 to $250 per hectare sold for $30 or $40.[8] There also was a general decline in the amount of land under cultivation. Cultivated land in 1930 was estimated to have been 2,225,000 hectares; by 1932–33 it was only 1,961,000 hectares. While this decline primarily involved the more recently developed rice land, other areas suffered from poor maintenance as embankments collapsed and canals became choked with silt and debris.

Tax Collectors and Creditors: Attempts at Business as Usual

For its part, the administration was principally occupied with ensuring the payment of taxes. Following the petition of a landowner in Ca-mau whose harvest had been seized because he had not paid the land tax for the years 1929–31, Governor Eutrope expressed his point of view.

> It has never been my intention and I have never written that I will allow installments in the matter of payment of taxes by those who are in arrears with the internal revenue in the matter of their taxes for the 1931 fiscal year. . . . It must be understood that overdue taxes for the 1931 fiscal year must be settled with the least possible delay after the first realizations from the harvest.[9]

This rule was applied by the tax collectors through intimidation of either villagers or their *notables.* At one point the newspaper *Duoc Nha Nam* published an anecdote, which, though censored, was reprinted in the *Tribune*

Indochinoise of 18 June 1934. It described Governor Pagès on an inspection tour in the town of Bac-lieu and a rickshaw operator he met there. The two men engaged in a dialogue.

> Governor: How much do you earn?
> Rickshaw operator: I earn 1.6 piasters per day and I pay 20 centimes in rent.
> Governor: So you make a profit of 1.4 piasters. Have you paid the poll tax?
> Rickshaw operator: Yes, Monsieur.

The governor concluded from this that

> The province of Bac-Lieu is not poor since a rickshaw operator manages to earn 1.6 piasters per day. The thousand rickshaw men who live here therefore earn daily the sum of 1,600 piasters. Thus, there is no depression. There is no reason to decrease the license fees.

The rickshaw operator was ostracized by the population and lost his means of livelihood. Accused of having played the governor's game, he defended his actions, claiming that "I believed this high functionary wanted to negotiate an agreement with me to make a tour of the town. So I raised my price; in bargaining he would have reduced it to a fair level."[10] Regardless of whether this story is true, it illustrates two facts: the conviction of the governor that the depression had not reduced the capacity of the populace to pay its taxes; and, more profoundly, the essential falseness of relations between an official and a citizen under the colonial system even when their meeting was amicable.

The longer the tax crisis lasted the worse it became. Cultivators could not cope with the pressure of both creditors and tax collectors. The demands of the latter in the end took the form of coercion by the gendarmes and the militia who inspected poll-tax cards, jailing those who were not paid up. At Rach-gia and Bac-lieu the unfortunate who could not acquit themselves numbered in the tens of thousands. They became veritable outlaws hunted by the militia.[11] In 1934, in Bac-lieu, a French gendarme disguised himself as a Chinese peddler in order to surprise the peasants in their fields.[12] In one instance, M. Idylle, a landowner at Can-tho, protested against the incursions of a group of militia that had invaded his estate and threatened his laborers with imprisonment.[13] Illegal searches were common. In 1934, for example, numerous landowners of Long-xuyen complained of nocturnal visits during which doors, wardrobes, and chests were smashed and people beaten. In Rach-gia Province, three hundred persons were imprisoned for two days. At Soc-trang, those found to be without their poll-tax cards were detained at the police station until they could appear before the chief of the province or his deputy. If they could pay 2 piasters they were released with a permit valid for 30 days, at the end of which time they had to pay the balance. Those unable to pay stayed in prison for two to five days.[14] There were so many arrests that a well-known member of the Chamber of Agriculture, Truong Van Ben, suggested that prisoners employed in the maintenance of the gardens of the administration had performed required service that should have released them from prison or relieved them of a part of their poll tax.[15] As a result, the governor of Cochinchina requested that

> Messrs. the administrators, chiefs of provinces, will make all necessary arrangements so that, within the limit of budgetary feasibility, the taxpayers in question may be used as coolies on the works now in progress, in order to permit them to recover all or part of the amount of their tax.[16]

M. Chêne, the president of the Chamber of Agriculture, thanked Governor Eutrope "for the benevolent spirit with which he has received the suggestions of the Assembly."[17] But he also expressed indignation at the methods employed, deploring "the degrading role that the gendarmes of Lower Cochinchina are made to play," recalling that "the *gendarmerie* was once one of our most beautiful institutions."[18]

Creditors, principally the *chettys*, put heavy pressure on debtors in the provinces of Bac-lieu, Rach-gia, and Can-tho. At times they allied themselves with Chinese wholesalers in order to force landowners to sell their harvests, even at a low price. In other instances they used the courts to force the sales. They pursued their debtors with a ferocity that impressed their contemporaries, as in the story of a debtor who, having obtained a restraining order in the province of Can-tho, found himself proceeded against in a Saigon court. One *chetty* at Can-tho was known to have had several debtors executed; he became a very large landowner.[19] The expulsion of several *chettys* in March 1933 did not resolve the problem. They were soon permitted to return to Cochinchina, though they began to suffer setbacks in their turn. Some went bankrupt and found themselves proceeded against at the request of their backers in India. Others were arrested by the internal revenue. At

Soc-trang in 1934, the offices of Meyappachetty and Soccalingamechetty were searched and sacked by the gendarmes. These incidents scandalized the Vietnamese in spite of their generally low opinion of the Indians.[20]

Not only the *ta dien* and the small landowners but also the middle-sized and large landowners were exposed to the predations of the internal revenue and creditors. The same methods were applied to them without concern for their social status. Seizures of crops were carried out at the request of the SICAMs, private creditors, or tax collectors. Harvests were seized with no distinction made between the landowner's portion and that of the *ta dien*, endangering the latter still further. The seizures disrupted production, with the result that many landowners refused to furnish advances to the *ta dien* who then abandoned the land or refused to repay existing loans (see appendix 5). Finally, with public opinion running high against the crop seizures, on 13 January 1934, the internal revenue began to require the conclusion of written contracts between landowners and *ta dien*. In addition, the *trat* of a *doc phu* to the canton chiefs of Soc-trang Province prescribed the direct appropriation of the taxes from the harvest but also required the delivery of a withholding certificate to the *ta dien* for the amount of the rent.[21]

Landowners, particularly the large ones, who had borrowed to invest in nonagricultural enterprises were hit hard. Many had to reduce their expenses and abandon the exterior signs of wealth. Women pawned their jewelry, automobiles no longer left the garages, and children were withdrawn from school. The days passed in apprehension of a visit from the bailiffs. The newspapers cited the social decline or the downfall of large landowners, some of whom had occupied or were occupying the office of *doc phu*.

The most callous or hard pressed of the landowners turned to their tenant farmers, pressuring them to the extreme. Conflicts at harvest time multiplied. In rarer cases landowners renounced their rents, even going so far as forgiving arrears. They had no choice; their tenants were destitute. And if the landowners could not meet their contractual obligations how could they require the *ta dien* to meet theirs?[22] The rupture in the economic and so-called moral solidarity of the landowner-tenant relationship inevitably had wide-ranging consequences in the social and political spheres.

It was after 1932 that the deadlines for repayment of debts were the hardest to meet. The rice growers had to pay the poll tax, the land tax, and numerous others, and they also had to repay short-term loans and finance the next season's agricultural campaign (see appendix 5). Offers of new credit were scarce. On 15 May 1933, a group of rice growers of the Cau Ke *circonscription* (in Can-tho) submitted a petition to their administrator. Addressed to the governor of Cochinchina, it solicited a reprieve in the payment of taxes, arguing that the landowners, if caught in a bind, would be obliged to abandon their *ta dien* at the risk of provoking social turmoil.[23]

A portion of the population returned to the subsistence economy. *Ta dien* and small landowners contented themselves with planting an area just large enough to feed themselves. Peasants sold their water buffaloes and placed themselves at the head of the plough. In Rach-gia, cultivation itself was abandoned when the ferocity of the creditors, the demands of the landowners, and the relentlessness of the internal revenue forced many peasants to flee. Thus, the depression aggravated the existing instability of the most disadvantaged sectors of the population. Rather than sow and reap, it was lift the net and set the snares. The yield from fishing and hunting or paddy was bartered for cloth and kerosene for the lamps. In many cases the latter was replaced by rat grease or the oil of the castor-oil plant.

Permanent agricultural workers who had received salaries of $120 per year before the depression, received no more than $60 to $80 in 1932. Seasonal workers were subject to the same drop in wages. A typical harvester was paid one *gia* per *cong* in 1929. Although he received the same amount in 1932, the *gia* of paddy was worth only 20 or 30 centimes instead of $1.20. The suspension of much off-season work removed this source of income altogether, with the result that day laborers began to accept work for miniscule wages.[24]

The agricultural depression had repercussions throughout the economic spectrum, especially among small merchants and artisans. The decline of purchasing power in both the urban and rural populations, as well as the recourse to hunting and fishing, explains why fish and chickens offered at ridiculous prices still found no buyers. The "Malays" or Chams of Chau-doc ceased importing cattle and pirogues from Cambodia.

The retreat of the cultivators, particularly the poorest, into a familial economy of subsistence and barter was a peaceful process. But another alternative was banditry, the growth of which frightened both landowners and the authorities. Nonetheless, the rupture in the normal course of existence did not necessarily carry with it rebellion and the brutal seizure of property. In 1933, and again in 1935, bands of roving Cambodians and Vietnamese begged grain from landowners who gave it to them more out of fear than charity. They also applied to the administration of the chief towns, which resulted in a few grain distributions. Though a few other groups assaulted granaries and convoys of junks, seizing sacks of paddy or rice, they did so without bloodshed, and many of these "requisitions" were limited to just the quantity of grain judged necessary for subsistence.[25]

The Limits of Administrative Reform

Throughout the course of the depression the Chamber of Agriculture voiced with vigor, and sometimes with violence, the complaints and demands of the cultivators. Its opinions are contained principally in two documents dated June 1931 and April 1932. The chamber demanded that the authorities adopt certain measures, which it grouped under three rubrics: urgent measures, those to be realized as soon as possible, and questions to be put under study. Urgent measures included the demand that seasonal loans be extended, that prosecutions of debtors and those who owed taxes be suspended, that the export of rice and paddy be facilitated by abolishing the 45 percent surtax, and that taxes on rice and paddy be reduced. The second series concerned the extension of government land credit, the granting of sufficient funds to facilitate mutual agricultural credit, and technical aid to cultivators. Lastly, the rice growers called for the establishment of a compensation fund and a study of the monetary question.[26]

The colonial administration could not accede to the demands of the Chamber of Agriculture on all points, for in doing so it would have encouraged general fiscal flight and injured the creditors. But neither could it allow the latter to proceed with unrestricted seizures, for such license would favor the speculators and bring about a massive transfer of property, and it was feared that this would lead to dangerous social disequilibrium.

On 22 July 1932, Governor General Pasquier renewed the policy of Governor Eutrope: "No general moratorium on debts." This being accomplished, the authorities attempted to establish equilibrium between debtors and creditors. In response to a petition signed by 611 Vietnamese landowners to the governor general,[27] Attorney General Bourayne had a memorandum transmitted to the justices of the peace of Cochinchina recommending that they proceed with attempts to mediate between debtors and creditors and grant delays to debtors if they appeared to be acting in good faith. This latter condition was difficult to determine. How was one to distinguish between good and bad faith? The directive was vague enough to leave a great deal of latitude to those who executed it, and rice growers complained of its frequent nonapplication.

Beginning in 1931, the government made attempts to ease the credit situation. Having suspended ordinary lending practices as early as March,

Governor of Cochinchina Krautheimer authorized the granting of emergency advances to the SICAMs, which were required to redistribute them in the form of loans for the 1931–32 season. The loans were to be granted in the amount of $6 per hectare and required security of 15 *gia* of paddy per hectare. These provisions excluded a considerable number of cultivators.

> Other possessors of rice land with any title-deed whatever, simple occupants, tenants, and *ta dien* whose landowners have not received advances can only obtain direct loans. . . . No one will be able to obtain a direct loan or a loan on discount if the request is not accompanied by a certificate issued by the *notables* of the village and countersigned by the chief of the canton attesting that he does not have in his possession from the latest harvests a quantity of more than twelve measures of paddy per hectare.[28]

If they were requesting a loan of more than a thousand piasters, they had to be members of a SICAM or an agricultural union. It seems certain that this 1931 program permitted the cultivation of most of the existing rice land. But the poverty of the borrowers prohibited repayment, and by 31 August 1932 less than 30 percent of the cash loans and 22 percent of the crop loans had been repaid. In many cases the security had disappeared as well. For the 1933–34 season, only the Chau-doc Fund was authorized to grant new loans, and these could be dispensed only to cultivators who had met their previous obligations.[29] In 1934, among all the SICAMs of Mien Tay, only the one at Soc-trang granted new loans, and then only two, for a total of $450. In 1935, out of a total of $4,447,880 in outstanding loans, those considered uncollectable or completely lost amounted to $2,333,000. Rach-gia led with losses of $700,000. The SICAM of Ha-tien had suspended its loans.[30]

To revive the SICAMS the government reduced the interest rate charged to their borrowers in 1934. The SICAMs had recorded a shortage of 4 million piasters resulting from unpaid interest, and on 22 June 1934 Governor Pagès asked the administrators to lighten the burden on the SICAMs by lowering interest rates from 10 to 7.5 percent.[31] This reduction was to be compensated for by a general reduction in the expenses of the SICAMs (Pagès went so far as to specify that the pay of an orderly ought not exceed $10) and the relinquishment of half the rebate paid by the Banque de l'Indochine to the government. Unpaid interest for the years 1929 and 1930 was to be written off as a loss and the interest due for the years 1931 and 1932 was figured at the rate of 6 percent.

Another important measure concerned mortgages on land. The land debt being estimated at 70 million piasters, a decree of 29 April 1932 instituted a long-term loan program and allocated 10 million piasters to it. The government of Indochina concluded an agreement with the Crédit Foncier Agricole and the Compagnie Foncière d'Indochine with the aim of granting mortgages to owners of rice land and eventually returning the management of the long-term loans to members of the SICAMs. This program was formally launched in 1933, with the establishments making land loans receiving a premium of 1.5 percent per year in exchange for their participation.[32] The program excluded a large proportion of the rice growers, however, since it prohibited the granting of loans for less than 5,000 piasters. In the end, the number of recipients was low. De Feyssal writes that only 2,400 landowners applied, while Melin gives a figure of 4,000 to which he adds the debtors of the SICAMs, or at most 20,000 people, 8 percent of the owners of rice land in Cochinchina. Of the allocation of 10 million piasters, 9,930,000 were utilized by only 335 landowners between 1932 and 1937.[33]

The government also tried to rein in the *chettys*. After a September 1932 decree of the governor of Cochinchina, which declared his intention to deport the *chettys*, they accepted the conditions laid down by the Service des Prêts Fonciers. The government further neutralized the *chettys* by expelling six of the most active among them.[34] The others agreed to abatements of 22 percent on debts of first priority and of 35 percent on those of lesser priority. By the end of August 1933, a total of 3 million piasters had been distributed through these loans.[35]

The lot of the majority of the population was not ameliorated, however, and the situation worsened to such a degree during 1932–33 that Governor Pagès was moved to greater efforts. Noting that "The administration ran after the shadow of the taxpayers. . . . [and] the taxpayers in real difficulty faded into the brush," he provided figures that showed a serious decline in the number of taxpayers. Between 1929 and 1934, the number of Annamite taxpayers was reduced from 1,200,000 to 850,000, while the number of Chinese taxpayers dropped even more drastically—from 80,000 to 38,000.[36] The government attempted to halt this decline by working out an arrangement that would adjust the fiscal system to the reduced income of the populace. In August 1934, the governor decreed that any taxpayer in the western provinces who acquitted himself of his entire tax assessment for the current year would be freed of his obligation to the internal revenue for past years.

Finally, in 1935, the poll tax was reduced to $5.50 in all provinces, new tax rates on rice land were adopted in the provinces of Rach-gia, Bac-lieu, Soc-trang, and Can-tho, and the tax on licenses was reduced by 10 percent.[37] Budgetary cutbacks accompanied these tax reductions. The administration reduced the pay of medical assistants, of the Garde Civile, and of teachers in certain provinces, and it abolished bounties for destruction of harmful animals. Governor Pagès was able to declare, "I have diminished the public or quasi-public tax arrears by $1,425,000, or 34.5 percent, reducing them from $4 million to $2,575,000."[38]

The government even began to consider some type of land reform during the crisis. Though the initiative ultimately came to naught, the Office of Colonization was created by decree on 22 April 1932. The administration assigned it a dual role: to stabilize property ownership and avoid monopolization and depreciation by intervening in sales under writs of execution; and to buy back and redistribute land by dividing the large estates into lots (thereby enlarging the class of small landowners) and establishing new settlement villages. It can be said that the Office of Colonization wished to avoid upheaval in the land and social systems by correcting the inequities of the agrarian regime. This is certainly how the large landowners interpreted it, and they denounced it as more administrative interference at the expense of the landed bourgeoisie, the "social bulwark against communism." They further predicted "the destruction of export commerce by the creation of small ownership."[39] These fears were groundless, a high civil servant wrote in a self-congratulatory manner, and the initiatives of the office were "prudent."[40] In 1934, in any case, the landowners and everyone else had determined that in reality the office was of more nominal than practical significance.

The Character of the Recovery

Over the course of the years 1930–34, less than 13 percent of Cochinchina's rice land, or 132,494 hectares, passed into new hands (see Table 19). The transfers involved about a thousand landowners, most of them the insecure or the less fortunate. Under the prevailing conditions of agrarian indebtedness in the West, many considered the change of ownership to be natural and the result of a "cleansing" of the system. In fact, there was a marked trend toward concentration of ownership, a phenomenon over which Governor Pagès confessed some uneasiness. The situation was aggravating the instability of an already floating population, and the increase in absentee landlordism further distended the relationship between the owners and the *ta dien*. In

TABLE 19: Changes in Ownership of Rice Land in Mien Tay,
1930–34 (in hectares)

Province	Amount of Cultivated Rice Land	Amount that Changed Hands				
	1930	1930	1931	1932	1933	1934*
Bac-lieu	330,000	9,836	9,700	5,355	7,762	11,273
Can-tho	174,271	7,249	3,523	5,443	2,416	438
Rach-gia	337,500	23,292	10,870	6,338	3,761	1,526
Soc-trang	194,300	5,219	4,053	5,053	6,281	3,116
Total	1,036,071	45,596	28,146	22,189	20,220	16,353

*January to September only.

Source: Speech by Governor of Cochinchina Pagès to the Colonial Council (1st session, 9 October 1934).

consequence, the squatter movement revived. The already slow and difficult regularization of ownership and concessions was not going to be hurried. Moreover, even though some Vietnamese had rid themselves of Chinese merchants and provincial mill owners, the bonds of dependency had not been greatly eased.[41] And, through its participation in the recovery of the landowners and the rice culture, the Banque de l'Indochine and its affiliates were becoming in effect the beneficiaries of the depression.

All social classes were affected by the stagnation. Imprudent large landowners and middle-sized and small cultivators alike were ruined. Many resorted to suicide. Agricultural laborers were forced to accept work with only their nourishment as remuneration. Civil servants became the victims of budgetary cutbacks, and elders, normally provided for by the collection of taxes and debts to the SICAMs, followed close behind. And behind the financial worries, the bankruptcies, and the loss of property and employment lay a psychological shock that profoundly traumatized the West: the belief in uninterrupted prosperity had vanished.

The depth of the depression was reached in 1932, and by 1934 it was believed that Indochina had emerged from the crisis. Life began to return to normal and exports of paddy and rice resumed their ascending curve (see Table 20). An even better indicator of the course of the recovery is the price of rice. The price of a quintal of paddy hit bottom in June 1934 ($1.88). Later that year, however, the Dutch East Indies reopened its ports to

TABLE 20: Indochinese Rice Exports, 1928–38

Year	Quintals of Rice
1928	1,792,682
1929	1,471,642
1930	1,121,593
1931	959,504
1932	1,222,233
1933	1,288,816
1934	1,528,154
1935	1,765,585
1936	1,575,000
1937	1,548,000
1938	1,064,000

Source: Melin, L'endettement agraire en Indochine.

Indochinese rice and demand in the Chinese market increased as well. By 1935, the price of a quintal of paddy began to climb, from $1.98 in January to $2.66 in May (it averaged $2.48 for the year).[42] In 1937, it rose to $4.71 and in 1938 to $5.40 (with the piaster devalued by 51 percent). Nonetheless, the net revenues of the landowners did not return to predepression levels. Melin drew up a revenue table (reproduced here as table 21), which recorded the disparities between the regions of ancient cultivation, those of recent settlement, and the zone of floating rice.

The devaluation of the franc in 1936, and the detachment of the piaster from the gold standard in order to link it to the franc, also had an important impact on the Indochinese economy. Depreciation of the local currency, which occurred in conjunction with the depreciation of the franc, benefited the rice growers and rubber-tree planters. The Colonial Council judged, in 1937, that in terms of "the present value of the piaster, agricultural workers, cultivators, and landowners are in a favorable situation."[43] In 1937, the large landowners, previously so bent on combating stabilization, voted against cutting the piaster loose from the franc.

Attachment to the franc permitted the return of profitable predepression prices. It was a fortunate event, a true rejuvenation brought to the Indochinese Union by the Popular Front Government. So we beseech

TABLE 21: Net Revenue per Hectare of Rice Land in the Three
Regions of Mien Tay, 1925–36

Year	Can-tho and Soc-trang	The Far West	Zone of Floating Rice
1925	$30.76	$25.87	$14.88
1926	33.32	28.19	17.16
1927	32.36	27.32	16.68
1928	35.56	30.22	18.28
1929	39.40	33.70	20.20
1930	37.48	31.99	19.24
1931	17.64	13.98	9.32
1932	13.99	10.67	7.49
1933	7.94	5.19	4.47
1934	4.20	1.80	2.60
1935	12.48	9.21	6.74
1936	13.92	10.61	7.46

Source: Melin, L'endettement agraire en Indochine.

the metropolitan government not to remove the link between the
piaster and the franc, in order to avoid a new fall in prices for paddy.[44]

The rice growers finally saw their dream of paddy "at $1 per *gia*" become a
reality, and from June to July of 1937 the price of paddy rose from $3.93 to
$5.00 per picul.[45] It can be said that in the course of 1937 the rice-culture
depression was surmounted. Soon the prospect of a world war appeared as a
reassuring factor, in so far as such a conflict would seem to guarantee a continuous market for rice. At the Third Agricultural Congress, convened at
Saigon on 4 April 1940, the president of the Chamber of Agriculture, M.
Mariani, declared that "Overproduction today, far from being an element of
disequilibrium, is, to the contrary, a considerable force in the service of the
country."

The Effect of the Depression on Land Ownership

The large estates did not collapse as a result of the depression, and the renting out of land remained the rule. Figures published in 1937 by the BCAC and those included in the *monographies* illustrate the continuing importance of the large French estates. In the province of Chau-doc, for example, thirteen settlers or companies held thirteen thousand hectares. The summary report of the fiscal year ending in August 1940 provides an account of the Domaine Agricole de l'Ouest, a large estate in the province of Long-xuyen. Profits had risen from 3,696,095 francs in 1938–39 to 6,156,544. The tone of the report is optimistic and the company seems to have been prosperous. Among the resolutions of the General Assembly there also appears a record of the payment by this estate of a gross dividend of 30 francs per share, or 23.62 francs after taxes. But, although the large estates were rescued and consolidated by means of the long-term land loans, which had been instituted principally for this purpose, their growth had been arrested. For the most part, the fevered years of acquisition and speculation were over. There were a few exceptions, however, as in Long-xuyen, where Le Quang Liem, a landowner with a well-established reputation for voracity, obtained a lease for two plots of 3,100 hectares in April 1936.[46]

Because it was believed that the small owners were "the natural basis of the economic future and the social tranquility of the country,"[47] the colonial administration had long been concerned with encouraging indigenous settlement. The Commission Locale de la Colonisation en Cochinchine, convened on 13 May 1930, had provided for the closing of certain zones to settlement and had reserved certain other areas for small indigenous settlement. The administration was particularly eager to resettle people from the Tonkin Delta in Cochinchina.[48] This was difficult, however, due to regulation and the inflated price of land.

The preference of the administration was for the establishment of "settlement villages." The first initiative of this kind dates from 1907 when 238 Tonkinese (84 families) were resettled at Thoi Binh (in Can-tho), although the program's lack of success led to the repatriation of some of them. During the depression the administration again turned to resettlement projects. When 2,900 Tonkinese were dismissed without wages at a rubber plantation at Phu Quoc they were settled near Ha-tien where they received 5,000 hectares of land. Of this they cleared 1,500 hectares and cultivated 200. Their villages included a Catholic settlement, which disintegrated, after which 600 of these Tonkinese returned to the north. Many others fled on foot to Saigon.[49]

The authorities also were concerned over the condition of the landless Cochinchinese. In the province of Rach-gia, the administration, playing the role of landowner vis-à-vis the *ta dien*, divided 8,000 hectares into 750 lots of 10 hectares each and 750 dwelling areas. It received 700 requests for the land, and the composition of these petitions sheds light on the agrarian situation in Mien Tay. The authors of the requests included 200 people deprived of domanial lands, 100 registered at villages in areas without unoccupied land, 400 unemployed former soldiers, and a few poor families. The settler-candidates signed individual contracts. At the end of six years, if the conditions of the contract were fulfilled, the land was acquired permanently by the settler and remained inalienable for some years.[50] In the neighboring province of Ha-tien, two settlement villages were established in 1933. The first, An Hoa, was populated mainly by Cochinchinese who had been established on 4,428 hectares after the departure of the Tonkinese Catholics. The second village, at An Binh, possessed 1,420 hectares, divided into 10-hectare lots. In 1934, the Tonkinese Colonization Commission promulgated a new settlement program for 5,000 families in the "*casiers tonkinois*" of Chau-doc and Rach-gia.[51]

These projects gave rise to reservations, and even some hostile criticism, on the part of the French. Influential colonists such as Labasthé and Chêne denounced the concession of good land to uncertain elements.[52] They pointed out that the villages were costly to construct and that the taxpayers bore the expense. Most damningly, it was their opinion that small settlements did not favor economic progress. All in all the project was seen as an intolerable manifestation of a controlled economy. The chiefs of the provinces, too, were sometimes reticent, at least vis-à-vis the Tonkinese. The chief of Chau-doc pointed out the absence of hydraulic works (with the concomitant risk of alum soil) and the difficulty of watching over a population far removed from administrative centers.[53] Under the pretext of helping the Tonkinese to become better acclimated, some colonists also advocated placing them as agricultural workers with local landowners prior to their permanent settlement.

Those responsible for the settlement program were aware of all these obstacles but apparently necessity ruled the day. By a decree of 18 August 1938, the governor of Cochinchina reserved seventy thousand hectares of land for the Tonkinese in the provinces of Rach-gia and Ha-tien. In 1942, 750 families (3,800 people) from Nam Dinh and Thai Binh settled on five thousand hectares along the banks of the Tri Ton canal in Rach-gia. Each family received five hectares plus livestock, seeds, and farm implements.

When the experiment turned out to be costly, the government decided not to create additional settlement villages. The existing villages were given the "role of attracting free emigration"and thus a middle course was finally adopted.[54]

The administration was also concerned with communal property. The practice of renting the lands of the West by means of public auction had effectively excluded the small landowners and the landless, for land disposed of at auction could not be divided into smaller plots. When the chief of the province of Go-cong (outside Mien Tay) on his own initiative rented communal land by private agreement to poor cultivators, the governor envisioned the extension of this measure to all of Cochinchina. In Rach-gia Province, in 1937, an administrator by the name of Dufour prohibited the renting of large lots. Communal lands were divided into parcels of five hectares and rented for a piaster per hectare with a renewable lease. This did not neccessarily make these lands secure from the rich landowners, however, and Dufour's example does not appear to have been followed in neighboring provinces.

The regularization of land titles and registration had not been completed when the depression began, and afterward it still was not finished in certain provinces. On the contrary, due to the slowdown in survey work, the resignation of landowners, and the increase in nomadism, stagnation contributed to the confusion of an already unclear situation. Land that had been acquired with great effort was sometimes called into question once more. In Bac-lieu Province, in 1944, 150,000 hectares were still being occupied without title or deed.[55] The administor for Chau-doc pointed out, in fact, that a portion of the land considered open to settlement by Tonkinese immigrants was already ceded or occupied.

Except in Ha-tien, the cadastral survey was considered complete by 1938. But this did not solve the problem of occupancy without title. Sometimes the occupancy was very old and had been accompanied by development of the land. The cadastral survey was hampered and sometimes blocked by the collective efforts of occupants without titles, or with provisional titles, for the appearance of a boundary commission usually heralded an order to quit the land. Such occurrences frequently led to bloodshed—for example, at Rach-gia in April 1939, and at Ca-mau in August 1939.[56]

General Effects of the Depression

The other sectors of the economy remained subordinate to that of rice culture, and did not undergo significant changes after the depression. The ethnic division of labor and Chinese control over the distribution sector continued as before. The most notable incidents concerned attempted monopolies. The administration continued to license a salt monopoly, which it had substituted for direct control. In December 1936, the population of Ha-tien (*notables*, councillors, and fishermen) asked that salt be put within reach of the consumer at a tolerably low price. They complained that the administration resold salt at ten times its original price, and that they had been forced to throw quantities of fish back into the sea for lack of the salt with which to treat them. In 1937, new grievances were voiced against the contractors who ran the markets.[57] In 1936, several motor coach owners tried to establish monopolies over transportation in Rach-gia and Long-xuyen, a practice that involved the use of hired thugs who regularly engaged in knife fights.[58]

In 1934, maize production outstripped that of rice but by 1936 rice had regained the lead, surpassing all previous figures: 110,000 tons as opposed to 75,000 in 1928–29. Even though maize won a significant place in the economy, it is the only example of progress outside of rice culture that one can cite. The 1937 *monographie* of Bac-lieu records the disappearance of secondary crops in favor of rice. Mulberry-tree cultivation, which was found principally in Chau-doc in the framework of the local economy, was reduced from 450 to 250 hectares in 1935. This was the result of the depression and the abolition of ten years of tax exemption.[59] The price of pepper also fell in 1937, certainly not a stimulant to production.

Despite the efforts of the Indochinese Rice Office, methods of rice growing changed little. This office was created by decree in April 1930 and became operational on 1 January 1931 under the direction of a committee presided over by Y. Henry (then inspector general of agriculture, animal breeding, and forests). It brought together large landowners such as Gressier, Bec, Bui Quang Chieu, Truong Van Ben, and Lambert (the latter the president of the Conseil d'Administration de la Société Rizicole de Battambang). Representatives of financial institutions and industrial and commercial firms included Bazil, the director of the Crédit Foncier Agricole de l'Indochine; Thomas, director of the Distilleries de l'Indochine; and Lepervanche, director of the Société Anonyme Rizicole d'Indochine.

The first task of the office was to conduct a scientific investigation to determine which ecological zones were suitable for rice culture, to search for appropriate fertilizers, and to select the best varieties of rice. The work was to be undertaken by a professional association of rice producers, which would exploit the results. The budget of the office was progressively raised from $130,000 in 1931 to $660,000 in 1942.[60] At the time it was the object of virulent criticism on the part of certain sectors of the Cochinchinese population. The principal reproaches concerned a lack of consideration for the realities of life in Mien Tay, a bureaucratic attitude, and some "hermetic and confidential articles" published in the office's *Bulletin.*

Because of the setbacks caused by the depression and maintenance of the quasi-monopoly of agriculture, rice growers were reluctant to increase their yields, and this attitude rendered much of the office's work ineffective. In assessing its progress, its director could claim only that it had reduced the number of varieties of rice in use (400 in the 1940s compared to 1,200 previously, covering 70 percent of the rice land in Cochinchina), and had made some tentative moves toward standardization.[61] The office also suffered from a lack of intermediaries between its staff and the rice producers. The village *notables* who were the office's recognized correspondents were not particularly competent, and we know that many landowners were not interested in modernization. In 1939, the office was forced to cancel the rice-culture courses it had been offering at the College of Can-tho. Another obstacle, one that had impeded agricultural improvement even before the depression, was of a commercial nature. When Devismes complained of the absence of genetic improvements in rice in 1942, he gave as the cause the "defects of domestic commerce."[62] Some remarks set forth two years later sum up the situation well.

> The small peasant looks after his varieties even though the large
> Annamite landowner, who often does not live on his land, takes no
> interest in the quality of rice his tenants cultivate. For this reason, it was
> proposed to group these peasants in a corporate form and to increase
> the number of small cooperatives storing grain. There is no order in col-
> lection and transport. The rice growers and exporters work in the man-
> ner of brokers and quality is secondary to them.[63]

Two other conditions for agricultural progress were not met. First, hydraulic preparation of the soil for agriculture remained primitive. Although in 1935 M. Maux, chief of the Agricultural Hydraulics Service, had grasped the importance of effective irrigation systems and had developed several models, by 1936 only one project had been begun. The floods of September 1937 furnished the Chamber of Agriculture with a pretext for criticizing the meager funding of the administration and the allocation of what funds did exist mostly to Tonkin and Annam. When the floods destroyed the paddy on 240,000 hectares, 400,000 tons were lost, half due to the inundation and half due to damage inflicted by the insect and plant parasites called *tiem* (*tiem sau nach* and *tiem lun*). Control of the water would also have provided protection against the *tiem lun*, for it would have permitted the paddy fields to remain in a muddy state throughout the season, without a layer of water over the soil.[64]

The second condition hampering agricultural modernization was the credit situation. Following the depression, the administration was able to partially restore the health of the SICAMs and place them under stricter controls. On 11 August 1934, Governor Pagès had an account for the Treasury opened at the Caisse Centrale and ordered the transfer of all the SICAMs' liquid funds, and all their collections, into it. This move had two benefits: first, the deposits, which up till then had been unproductive, would bear interest; second, the funds would augment the treasury. The SICAMs were no longer required to register receipts and expenditures from day to day and could devote themselves to the collection of loans. Another step was taken with the decree of 26 February 1934. Henceforth, the elected members of the Administrative Council of a SICAM took office only with the approval of the governor of Cochinchina. During their term of office they could be replaced (following new elections or through the appointment of a new member by an administrative commission presided over by the chief of the province). With the permission of the governor, the *directeur du cabinet du gouverneur* could dismiss technical personnel and he was given the power to set their pay and conditions of work.

Simultaneously, the discounting practice of the Banque de l'Indochine was replaced by lump-sum advances on current accounts. On 31 August 1936, an agreement was signed with the bank: the Caisse Centrale (acting as agent for the SICAMs) and the Caisse Française took charge of the whole of the debt that the Banque de l'Indochine had discounted in order to deposit promissory notes in a special account in the name of the Caisse Centrale. This liability was to be paid off by annual installments of $500,000, which would be deducted from the principal. Interest of 5 percent per year was added. The payments would be due as long as the balance of the special account was greater than 5 million piasters.[65] Six years later, agricultural credit was administered by the Office Indochinois de Crédit Agricole et Artisanal Mutuel (OICAAM), which had its headquarters in Hanoi. At the local level, the control exercised by the chief administrator of the province was strengthened.[66] OICAAM was conceived not only as a credit agency but as an organization charged with promoting small settlement schemes and developing projects for agricultural improvement. A decree of 14 January 1943 replaced OICAAM with the Office du Crédit Populaire.

The progress of mutual agricultural credit toward centralization in its administration, as well as toward more severe and direct administrative control, may be explained by the concern of the colonial administration to shield agricultural credit from two perceived threats. The first was the Banque de l'Indochine, which during the depression, according to one observer, had "supported agriculture like the rope supports the hanged man."[67] The other hazard was felt to be the rural Cochinchinese bourgeoisie who kept the government "completely defenseless vis-à-vis some elected leaders whose goodwill or disinterestedness left much to be desired."[68] For these reasons it was believed that agricultural credit must become an institution of the state. However, although the agreement of 1936 substituted the Caisse Centrale for the Banque de l'Indochine in dealings with the SICAMs, it also consolidated the credit of the bank. One may even speculate that the transfer of operations to the Caisse Centrale was engineered by the bank itself, which not only lost very little in the process but was relieved of a function in which it had never had much interest.

The procedures of the new organization were more complicated than those of the SICAMs, which resulted principally in a tightening of credit. Nor did the new arrangements satisfy the landed bourgeoisie. In addition, of the ten seats on the Administrative Council, only five were reserved for representatives of the Crédit Agricole Mutuel and of the Associations de Coopératives d'Artisans—one for Tonkin, one for Annam, one for Cambodia, and two for Cochinchina.

In 1942, Governor of Cochinchina Rivoal reported to the governor general that the Caisse Centrale had absorbed the debt of the SICAMs and that the functioning of the SICAMs had improved. But he noted that the "elite country gentlemen" were displeased by the linking of the communities to OICAAM. He informed the governor that SICAMs in the provinces of Chau-doc, Long-xuyen, and Soc-trang still existed, although they had ceased all loan operations after 1932. It had been decided that the administration would found branches of OICAAM at Can-tho and Bac-lieu but the transitional difficulties had not yet been overcome. He also reported that in Rachgia the SICAM had been liquidated and replaced by a branch of OICAAM. Finally, Rivoal concluded his report with the revealing phrase: "Cochinchina has been deprived of agricultural credit since 1932."[69]

CHAPTER 7

Movements and Insurrections, 1930-1941

DURING THE DESPERATE YEARS of the depression, small and large landowners, Vietnamese as well as French, found a scapegoat for their troubles in the Banque de l'Indochine. To them it seemed as if the entire financial system of the colony had been designed to benefit the bank. In addition, that institution appeared to be more preoccupied with making commercial loans and indulging in foreign investments (especially in China) than in supporting the agriculturalists of Cochinchina.[1] While this critique was hardly new, the economic crisis gave it added strength. The "stabilization" of the Indochinese piaster crystallized the landowners' opposition. Linking the value of the piaster to the gold standard was designed, they said, to favor only the bank and the urban financial groups that had invested in mines and plantations. Stabilization was denounced as the primary cause of the depression in the rice industry, making rice expensive to export and cutting Indochina off from its principal markets in the Far East.[2]

The Landowners Respond

In response to these real and imagined grievances, the landowners launched a campaign to return the piaster to the silver standard. An early example of their demands may be found in a leaflet that circulated in the western delta in early 1932 urging rice growers to protest against stabilization. At the Chamber of Deputies in Paris, at the time of the debate on the general budget for the colonies, the deputy for Cochinchina, E. Outrey, condemned the stabilization. In Saigon, two demonstrations were organized in 1934. The first took place upon the return of a delegation from a Monetary Commission meeting held in Paris on 2 April. Fifteen hundred French and Vietnamese landlords and their supporters marched in a procession with banners reading

Cochinchina wants to live!
Long live the silver piaster!
Save our rice!
Down with the gold standard—destabilize!

Two weeks later a second rally was held in front of the Saigon Town Hall (see appendix 6).[3] According to the *Tribune Indochinoise,* there were five thousand demonstrators in spite of police obstructions designed to limit rural participation.[4] Banners raised at the Town Hall rally carried the inscriptions

Down with the swindlers!
Down with the gold standard!
Revoke the privileges of the bank!
Cochinchina wants to live!

The mayor of Saigon, Dr. Biaille de Langibaudière, convened and presided over the rally. His speech indicted the financial oligarchy. The *doc phu* Le Quang Liem then denounced the Banque de l'Indochine, and the pharmacist Sarreau presented the following demands.

1. Implement the monetary reforms adopted by the representatives of 20 million Indochinese at the Grand Conseil Indochinois.

2. Arrange for debt relief and suspend court-ordered sales of property.

3. Lower interest and discount rates.

4. Review Indochinese tariffs, particularly those affecting trade with China.

This list reflected the principal concerns of the members of the Chamber of Agriculture of Cochinchina. After the speeches, the demonstrators made their way down Catinat Street to the Quai de Belgique where the bank's imposing edifice stood. There the procession halted, shouting "Down with Gannay! Stavisky! Stavisky!" A third demonstration was planned to coincide with the arrival of newly appointed Governor General Robin but it was postponed. The landlords explained that they were "not revolting against the established order" but placing their trust in "the honesty and determination of the new leaders of Indochina to rescue the country."[5]

It was not accidental that these demonstrations took place in Saigon rather than in the delta, for the largest landowners, merchants, and bureaucrats often congregated there. In the front ranks of the march of 2 April, the *Tribune Indochinoise* reported the presence of Khuong Binh Tinh, a pharmacist from Can-tho City; Dr. Nguyen Van Thinh; Le Van Dang, a forestry inspector; Nguyen Hien Nang, *doc phu* at Rach-gia; and Nguyen Hien Than, provincial councilor of Rach-gia. The newspaper went on to describe the scene.

> The considerable procession walks down rue Catinat without a shout or a gesture. It is not made up of hoodlums recruited for the occasion. The principal French and Annamite personalities are in fact followed by many people whose behavior and clothing indicate a certain social class. It is indeed the honest laboring population of Cochinchina which follows its leaders. . . . Peasants and landowners have the same interests. This is neither a class nor a racial struggle.[6]

Not only did the *Tribune* recognize "its own" but it depicted them as the spokemen for the whole Cochinchinese population. The last sentence expresses both the upper class's ideology and recognition of the potential for class and racial struggles.

The echo of events then occurring in France is discernible in the rhetoric aimed at the financial establishment and accusations that the Indochinese administration was a captive of it.[7] The most prominent Vietnamese landowners shared the opinions of the French concessionaires and colonists who were familiar with the political discourse in France. At the time the French extreme right was denouncing finance capital, in hyperbolic style, as the source of all evil. There even emerged, from the pen of a Vietnamese man, an anti-Semitic diatribe against a colonial bureaucrat, Mr. Diethelm.[8]

Some protesters went so far as to envision independence for Cochinchina, including secession from the other Indochinese territories, which, they complained, paid less than their fair share of taxes. J. Boy, secretary of the Syndicat des Riziculteurs of Cochinchina, upbraided "the small shopkeepers of Hanoi, the fat prebendaries, the government of Indochina and the French metropolitan government, the Banque de l'Indochine, the sharks of Lyon, Bordeaux and elsewhere," declaring that

> You must know that we, Cochinchinese citizens of Annamite as well as French origin, are fed up! Remember that in 1776, England lost America because she wanted to subject her young colony to the financial and economic tyranny of the merchants of the City of London. . . . We will not hesitate if the French government continues to exploit our new land of Cochinchina for the profit of a gang of hooligans and swindlers. We will not hesitate to declare economic war on France with the watchword: "Don't buy French!"[9]

Boy's declaration of economic warfare was taken up in the *Tribune Indochinoise,* though nothing came of it.[10] The demand for the independence of Cochinchina was quickly dropped. As the economy revived, slowly but surely, the growth of a more radical anticolonial movement forced the elite back into the protective arms of the government.

Emergence of the Indochinese Communist Party

While the causal relationship between the Great Depression and the landowners movement is obvious, the great wave of peasant unrest that erupted in 1930 does not appear to have been related to that economic crisis. Some believe that it began much earlier and cite the fall of rubber prices in 1928 and the bankruptcies of the Chinese rice traders in 1928–29 as the first indications of its onset. One can then suppose that the economy had an impact on political behavior at least through a diffused discontent. As we shall see, the movement that spread in the countryside from northern to southern Vietnam obeyed a logic of its own.

Dramatic uprisings that broke out in 1930–31 were preceded by four years of unrest following Phan Chu Trinh's death in 1926. The year 1929 was marked by labor strikes organized by the Tan Viet and Thanh Nien (then the ICP 1). The latter organization had instructed its members, most of them intellectuals, to proletarianize themselves in 1928 in order to infiltrate and organize mines, plantations, harbors, industrial plants, and work sites in general. One cannot understand the 1930s explosion without keeping in mind the methodical, if not always successful, preparation of the communists during the preceding years.[11]

The three communist groups of Vietnam's north, center, and south were merged in February 1930 by the Third International's delegate Nguyen Ai Quoc (Ho Chi Minh). Although these groups had been competing with one another, their geographical and social bases were sufficiently disparate that they were able to settle most of their differences. Unification gave them renewed impetus, a wider scope, and a new strength of action, despite the fact that there were no more than a handful of active communists involved. In the town of Saigon, each cell consisted of three or four members; in Cholon, there were five cells with three or four militants each. In the provinces of Sa-dec, Can-tho, and Vinh-long, fifteen people were affiliated with five cells; and there were only known to be five "comrades" in all of My-tho City.[12] Thus, the ICP stepped into a vacuum in the radical movement. The nationalist revolutionary party Viet Nam Quoc Zan Dang (VNQZD) had collapsed. It had organized the mutiny of Vietnamese soldiers in Yen Bay and a terrorist campaign in the north but the failures of these actions and subsequent repression by the French led to its virtual disappearance. Many of its militants subsequently joined the ICP.

The uprising of 1930 in central and southern Vietnam began on 1 May, International Labor Day, which was commemorated by communist parties throughout the world. Paradoxically, however, it was not the working class that was involved in the large Vietnamese demonstrations, meetings, and riots. In fact, one source states that there were 2,791 peasants, 374 industrial workers, 28 primary school teachers, 18 bureaucrats, and 341 unemployed. The administrator of the province of Rach-gia summed up the feelings of the French authorities when he lamented that "Formerly so docile, the Annamite of the countryside has become harder to handle during the last few months."[13] The entire districts of Nghe-an, Ha-tinh, Quang-ngai, and Quang-nam in Trung Bo flared up.[14] However, in Nam Bo, no soviets were organized in the villages as they were in Nghe Tinh in central Vietnam. In Nam Bo, all around the Saigon-Cholon area and in Mien Trung in the delta, synchronized groups of demonstrating peasants (numbering in the hundreds, even thousands) marched on the communal houses and administrative bureaus. Acts of violence were limited to material installations, however, and aggression against individuals was rare. One administrator even wrote that the leaders of the groups of demonstrators he encountered were "polite."[15]

The central target of the demonstrators was the hated poll tax. But the burden of the poll tax was aggravated by market taxes and ferry charges. In an economy in which petty trade was an indispensable complement to the peasants' low and episodic incomes, such taxes were particularly burdensome. As the administrator of the province of Sa-dec pointed out,

> Except for the liberation of those who have been jailed, the demands of the demonstrators are not excessive. Extraordinary levies to build roads

are a burden on a population impoverished by two years of bad harvests and they are unpopular. Dissatisfaction generates a favorable ground for the ringleaders.[16]

The French response was harsh. Though officially very few people were killed, many were arrested and jailed or sent to the penitentiary of Poulo Condor. Once more, the marshes of Dong Thap Muoi and the forest of U Minh provided refuge for those who were able to evade the police.[17]

The revolt created a chasm between the peasants and the large landlords. And, although propertied Vietnamese were often critical of the French administration, they were frightened enough by this uprising among the masses that they began to voice more support for the regime. The governor general, for example, reported that *conseiller colonial* Nguyen Tan Zuoc, a landlord in the province of Sa-dec, had experienced a change of heart.

> One of the constitutionalist leaders well known for his strong opposition to our administration . . . is ready to cooperate. He did not conceal that the demonstrations aimed to threaten the local social class of which he is a spokesman.[18]

The *Tribune Indochinoise* criticized the communists for dividing the Vietnamese, declaring that "Rather than fight imperialism according to their fundamental principles, [the communists] attack the rich Vietnamese landowners who are just as dominated."[19]

The communists were not the only ones involved in the revolt. In the vicinity of Saigon-Cholon, for example, affiliates of Nguyen An Ninh's "secret society" organized processions and riots. In the delta, the center of gravity was located in the districts of Cao-lanh (in Sa-dec) and Cho-moi (Long-xuyen) where the Cao Dai had numerous adherents. Caodaist peasants demonstrated alongside everyone else. At times there were ties of kinship between communists and Cao Dai members. When Nguyen Van Thanh, alias Axinovitch, arrived from France, for example, he found shelter in a Cao Dai temple in Cholon whose warden was his aunt.[20] There were also cases of the tactical use of Caodaist or Buddhist institutions by the communists as fronts. Finally, we must recall that French authorities were prone to lump all the opponents together, as did a lieutenant of the *gendarmerie* in a report on the events at Cao-lanh.

There the constitutionalists were very strong and the Caodaists controlled the place. One group of people is connected with Prince Cuong De. Soon the communists infiltrated the nationalist organizations.[21]

The crucial years 1926–31 exposed the Mekong Delta and Vietnam as a whole to global crises and movements: the economic crisis of the capitalist world market, on one hand, and the international communist mobilization on the other. Both would become even more important during the next forty years.

The Popular Front and Popular Struggles

By 1936, the depression was over. The ICP had tended the wounds of its 1930 defeat, rallied its scattered or hidden militants, and reconstructed its cells. The genius behind its resurgence was Tran Van Giau, alias Ho Nam, a young returnee from Moscow where he had sojourned after pursuing studies in France. One party committee representing Nam Bo was created, along with three "special committees" representing the region's three sections. The Transbassac Special Committee (Xu Uy Dac Biet Hau Giang) was initially based in Chau-doc and later in Long-xuyen. It published a newspaper, *Cung Kho* (Commiseration).[22] During this orthodox phase in ICP politics, more attention was paid to the working class than to the peasantry.[23] Its strategy was grounded in anti-imperialism and agrarian revolution (the Asian version of "class versus class"). As soon as this line was endorsed by the second congress of the ICP (held in Macao in March 1935), however, it was contradicted by the seventh congress of the Third International convened in Moscow in September. Confronted with the victory of fascism in Europe and the militarist expansion of Japan in the Far East, the Comintern had developed a new political line. Henceforth, all communist parties would strive to create a united front in opposition to fascism. The class struggle was to be downplayed in favor of broadly based alliances. When a coalition of French left-wing parties triumphed in the elections of July 1936 and the new government (known as the French Popular Front) began planning colonial reforms, the ICP altered its policy in favor of legal, united action aimed at the fulfillment of democratic goals and opposed to potential Japanese aggression.[24] In the countryside the ICP adopted a moderate stance in line with the new directives of the party.

It is not yet the time to prepare the anti-imperialist and agrarian revolution. But we must build the united people's front to obtain urgent reforms for all. So, we must prevent daily laborers from fighting the well-to-do and poor peasants and we must convince them to be tolerant of rich farmers. To avoid a collapse of the people's front, it will sometimes be necessary to adopt watchful behavior toward the landlords.[25]

In October 1937, a directive of the Central Committee further encouraged the militants to attract "landlords and rich farmers" into a "united anti-imperialist front if there is common ground such as the antitax demand."[26] The new strategy of the ICP was sharply criticized by those on the far left, primarily the Trotskyites with whom the Stalinists had united in a front organization called La Lutte.[27] Rooted in the intelligentsia and in the urban Saigon-Cholon area, the Trotskyites paid little attention to the peasantry. Their leaders, Ta Thu Thau and Pham Van Hum, made trips through the delta but these were for the purpose of investigating the situation rather than mobilizing the masses.

The communist militants moved to exploit the new tolerance of the colonial authorities under the policies of the French Popular Front. Although the police continued to watch the anticolonialists and harass them with fines, arrests, and detentions, the communists and nationalists no longer hesitated to propagandize, hold meetings, and contest the authorities on the local level.

The years 1936–37 were rife with popular unrest in Indochina, as strikes and demonstrations followed one after another.[28] Amid the huge swell of people's movements, the militancy of the villagers of Nam Bo did not lag behind that of the city dwellers. In the countryside, the social and political movements were two-pronged, one aimed at opposing the colonial regime and the other meant to foster agrarian reform. The poll tax was the main target. In 1937, there also was a campaign against the tax on tobacco plantations. Supposedly corrupt and harsh *notables* were exposed. Some were beaten; one was murdered. Demands for democratic reforms were found along with the antitax slogans.

The confrontations shifted to Mien Tay—something that had not occurred in 1930—mainly to the provinces of Rach-gia and Bac-lieu where large tracts of land were held by absentee speculators. Small-scale settlers lacking formal title to their own land occupied fallow fields and claimed ownership. Where the settlers had cleared and cultivated land, they now refused to pay rent to the legal owners. They fished in "private" ponds, and opposed the survey and demarcation of plots taken from them. In 1937, following floods and lost harvests, tenants in Chau-doc, Long-xuyen, and Rach-gia refused to pay rent even to the small landlords.[29] In the period following the depression, unemployment had increased and salaries had been lowered in the towns as well as the countryside. Meanwhile, the devaluation of the piaster in 1937 led to a rise in prices. This situation provoked strikes by rice transplanters and harvesters demanding higher wages.[30] Long-repressed frustrations surfaced. The French administration and its local officials clearly recognized what was happening and it is worth quoting the observations of one official who conducted an investigation in the province of Rach-gia.

> When I explained to the ringleaders Nguyen Tan Buu and Luong Van My that they could not obtain legal ownership of plots already granted to others but that they may be granted plots elsewhere, the latter replied: "Then I shall tell the newspapers in Saigon, we know that the administration favors the rich and not the poor." I read the same thoughts in the eyes of the hundred Annamites who surrounded me. . . . Accustomed to the deference that Cochinchinese peasants usually exhibit toward the administrators and representatives of the governor . . . I realized then how deep this change was in some minds.[31]

The colonial administration was aware that the agrarian inequities, tensions, and antagonisms constituted a crucial issue for the continuation of French domination,[32] as well as for the success or failure of the Vietnamese communists. Active opponents of the French might not be in the majority in the countryside but the contentious spirit was everywhere. People were in a state of moral outrage over both the French and the Vietnamese establishments. The French were caught in the midst of inescapable contradictions. As Governor General Brévié observed, "When we protect the rights of some, we go against justice and the sense of fairness toward others. When we neglect them, we transgress the law and condemn our own methods."[33]

Insurrection in Nam Bo

When World War II broke out in Europe, the period of liberality in the French administration ended. But the agrarian problem, "a capital one" as Vo Nguyen Giap and Truong Chinh had written, was still unsolved; this was "the Dragon in the bathtub."[34] Even before the war, the climate of relative freedom had eroded badly. In France, a split in the Popular Front coalition between the French Communist Party and the far left had been exacerbated by the Nazi-Soviet Pact of August 1939. In Indochina, 1938 had been a year of tightening repression. In 1939, laws enacted against the French Communist Party were applied in the colonies, targeting such "seditious" elements as the left-wing and nationalist parties.

In June 1940, when the French army capitulated, the Wehrmacht occupied France. In September, Japanese troops from Guangdong in China attacked French garrisons on the Sino-Vietnamese border. The French government of Vichy, unable to reinforce its military position in Indochina, signed agreements with Tokyo to put Indochinese territory and resources at the discretion of Japan. Phibul Songkram's government in Thailand soon reconquered the Cambodian and Lao territories that Siam had been obliged to surrender to France at the turn of the twentieth century.

The reactions of the Indochinese appear to have been mixed. Nationalists felt that the opportunity to oust the French was at hand but they were puzzled by the official Japanese line, which recognized the Vichy French as partners (though minor ones). The communists and others who had been alarmed by Japanese aggression in Asia since 1937 denounced the Japanese fascists and the French colonialists alike. The bulk of the population waited and watched. However, a widely shared feeling was that a French collapse was inevitable.

On 8 November 1939, the Central Committee of the ICP met in the Saigon suburb of Hoc Mon. In line with the Third International's recommendations, the committee decided to create an anti-imperialist united front on the grounds that the war was interimperialist and offered an opportunity for colonized peoples to free themselves. Consequently, communists must be ready to undertake the immediate task of national liberation (*Nhiem vu truoc mat la giai phong zan toc*). Agrarian revolution (*cach mang ruong dat*) would be replaced by confiscation (*tich ky ruong dat*) of the property of the French and their lackeys. The strategic goal was no longer to create a government composed of workers' and peasants' soviets but to forge a government to be known as the Federation of Democratic Republics of Indochina.

In 1941, faced with the Japanese occupation of Indochina, the communists abandoned their planned anti-imperialist front to forge a formal coalition, the Viet Nam Doc Lap Dong Minh Hoi, commonly known as the Viet Minh.[35] The new organization would fight both the Japanese and the French. With this new strategy in hand, and with the French defeated in Europe, the ICP plotted a national uprising for the nights of 21–22 November 1940.[36]

Unfortunately, some of the best cadres of the party and most of the Central Committee leadership had been jailed by the French in 1939 and early 1940. In 1941, the party was being led by a faraway, reconstituted committee operating in northern Vietnam. According to the figures of the Sûreté Indochinoise (the police),[37] eight hundred experienced cadres were in the Central Prison of Saigon and the penitentiary of Poulo Condor while two thousand had been interned in two "workers' camps" in Nui Ba Ra and Ta Lai in northern Nam Bo.[38] Despite the lack of leadership in the party in the south, the Xu Uy Nam Ky issued a "Program of Preparation for Insurrection" on 3 March 1940. The Xu Uy took another step in July 1940, gathering representatives of the provinces in the village of Tan Thuan (in My-tho) to coordinate preparations for the uprising.

Having learned the lesson of "revolutionary defeatism" taught by Lenin and the bolsheviks, the Vietnamese communists were eager to take advantage of the opportunity offered by France's war with Thailand to continue spreading propaganda among Vietnamese soldiers in the colonial army so as to incite upheaval in the rear guard. It radicalized the propaganda launched by the Central Committee on 30 December 1939, which may be summed up by the slogans "Down with the imperialists' war!" and "Don't send soldiers to France and abroad!"

But there was not yet a call to mutiny.[39] While preparations were being actively pursued, a Central Committee conference convened at Dinh Bang (in the north) calculated that the insurrection would be premature. The committee decided to postpone it. Nevertheless, a revolt was launched. The official explanation of the ICP as to why the revolt was attempted is ambivalent, hovering between two causes: either the leaders of Nam Bo disobeyed the Central Committee's directive to postpone the revolt or they never received it. Either it was a putsch attributable to the "adventurism" of second-rank leaders in Nam Bo or to the late arrival of the committee's messenger, Phan Dang Luu, whose train from Hanoi was delayed.[40]

French authorities had been alerted to the insurrection on 26 September 1940 during a search conducted in the province of Vinh-long. The Sûreté discovered two documents, one detailing "local uprisings and street fighting" and the second giving the Xu Uy's "directive for insurrection."[41] Thus, the police knew that the revolt was to begin with a soldiers' mutiny in Saigon-Cholon from whence it would spread throughout the delta. The police ensured that the soldiers' mutiny was thwarted and that the couriers of the revolution were captured. As Nguyen Thi Thap remembers it, the realization of defeat came at My-tho City where the insurgents waited for the morning train that was to be brimming with mutinied riflemen: "On the twenty-second, at 9 o'clock, we realized that the uprising had already collapsed when, observing the arrival of the Saigon train, we saw only the usual passengers."[42]

Figure 4

Structure of the Indochinese Communist Party, 1940

(as determined by French police following the arrest of communist militants
in Nam Bo in April 1940)

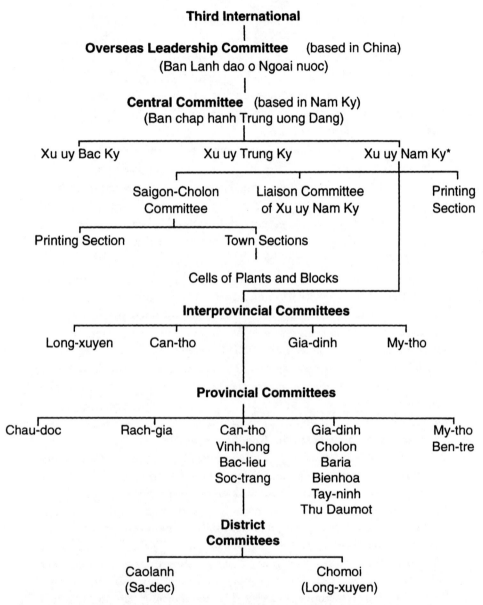

Third International

Overseas Leadership Committee   (based in China)
(Ban Lanh dao o Ngoai nuoc)

Central Committee   (based in Nam Ky)
(Ban chap hanh Trung uong Dang)

Xu uy Bac Ky   Xu uy Trung Ky   Xu uy Nam Ky*

Saigon-Cholon   Liaison Committee   Printing
Committee   of Xu uy Nam Ky   Section

Printing Section   Town Sections

Cells of Plants and Blocks

Interprovincial Committees

Long-xuyen   Can-tho   Gia-dinh   My-tho

Provincial Committees

Chau-doc   Rach-gia   Can-tho   Gia-dinh   My-tho
                         Vinh-long   Cholon   Ben-tre
                         Bac-lieu   Baria
                         Soc-trang   Bienhoa
                                        Tay-ninh
                                        Thu Daumot

**District
Committees**

Caolanh   Chomoi
(Sa-dec)   (Long-xuyen)

* *Xu uy* is a committee for the country. There was one *xu uy* for each *Ky* or *Bo*.

Note: After the 1939 crackdown and the repression of mid-1940, some of these
committees and cells were only embryonic or had been decimated.

The places where the insurrection did occur coincided closely with those of the unrest of 1930–31 and 1936–37. Vinh Kim and Cay Lay (in My-tho), Cho Moi (Long-xuyen), Cao-Lanh (Sa-dec), Phuo Clong (Rach-gia), Cau Khe (Can-tho), and Can Long (Tra-vinh) experienced ruthless suppression by the French who sent European soldiers of the Colonial Infantry and the Foreign Legion and three companies of Cambodian riflemen into the region. As in the days of conquest in the 1860s, French riverboats were employed. Airplanes bombed villages.[43] Dozens of prisoners were publicly executed in the marketplaces. Newpapers reported that Ngo Huu Hanh and Ly Hong Thang, who led the insurrection in Can-tho, were executed on 5 June 1941 before a crowd of 2,000 onlookers. Ha Chanh Ngo and Doan Van Vang were shot down in Soc-trang in the presence of 400 people, and at Ca-mau 10 murderers of the lighthouse warden of Poulo Obi were executed before 3,000 on 8 July 1941. Hundreds were sent to the penal island of Poulo Condor, so that from May 1940 to August 1941 the number of prisoners held there leapt from 2,119 to 4,203. Small groups of insurgents who managed to escape the net took refuge in Dong Thap from whence, the French complained, "they cannot be ousted."[44] From there they fled to Cambodia or to the U Minh forest where they joined others who had taken refuge there in 1930–31. According to the French authorities, more than 30 militiamen and village elders were killed, and 20 wounded. Three Europeans were killed and 3 wounded. A hundred insurgents were killed and 5,848 arrested.[45] The Vietnamese historians Tran Huy Lieu and Van Tao calculate that 5,248 were killed and 8,000 were imprisoned.[46]

Thus, in 1940 the events of the 1930s repeated themselves. *Notables* and district functionaries were attacked by the insurgents but the landlords and rich peasants were largely spared. Momentarily defeated, the ICP abandoned the struggle to organized forces better able to channel peasant resentment and expectations. One Vietnamese, a stalwart partisan of Viet-French collaboration, sadly commented that

At Cai Lay, where the Foreign Legion plundered and raped, the repression was too ruthless. . . . Surely it was difficult to separate the wheat from the chaff but the hatred that has been sown will be reaped in the future. Between government and the people an abyss has opened again . . . [and] it suits the troublemakers. The task of the collaborators will now be much more difficult.[47]

....

CHAPTER 8

War in the Delta, 1941-1960

IN THE WAKE OF THE Great Depression, economic ties between France and its colonial empire, particularly those with Indochina, were strengthened so as to preserve outlets for Indochinese commodities in France and its other colonies. Soon after, under the growing threat of world war, the French felt compelled to strengthen imperial ties (*la solidarité impériale*) as well. In the process, the "natural" relationship between Indochina and the Asia-Pacific customers for its rice, coal, and rubber was disrupted. World War II suddenly reversed that situation. Maritime communication with France was severed by the end of 1940 and economic exchanges in the Far East and the Pacific region increased. By the end of 1941, after the bombing of Pearl Harbor, French Indochina had become one of the major suppliers of rice, rubber, and coal to Japan. According to formal agreements concluded between Vichy and Tokyo, Japan was to deliver in return the manufactured commodities, such as engines and chemicals, that formerly had come from France. Indochina was going to be an important participant in what the Japanese called the Greater East Asian Co-Prosperity Sphere.

Though from the beginning Japan failed to meet its commitments, to meet their own the French authorities progressively introduced strict economic controls. A French-Japanese agreement on rice concluded on 20 January 1941 obliged the French to meet a quota each year, supplying rice at a fixed price. When the French began to limit price controls to the volume of rice destined for Japan, the dual pricing (one for the Japanese quota and the other for domestic trade and consumption) induced hoarding and speculation. This compelled the French to gradually extend the price controls to both domestic and export rice. For this purpose, they created an official agency known as the Comptoir du Riz et du Maïs.[1] As the documentation covering this period is scarce and piecemeal, I rely only on J. Decaudin's report, "Essais de contrôle du marché du riz en Cochinchine, 1941–1944," which, though it is not dated, quotes statistical figures up to 1945. According to Decaudin, from 1941 to 1944, state control was strengthened until it finally became comprehensive. Early on, the rice market of the delta remained free, with only Cholon subject to controls on processing and trade. But hoarding and a black market soon provoked a rise in the price not only of rice but of all commodities: prices in Saigon from 1941 to 1945, for example, increased by 60 percent. In 1943, in spite of the rice producers' protests, and in order to secure food for the urban population, the French authorities decided that the Comité des Céréales d'Indochine would become the sole buyer of paddy from the producers and the sole rice broker in Cholon.[2]

Nevertheless, the French administration was driven to raise prices. By the end of 1943, they had reached 4.5 piasters for a *ta*, or picul, of paddy. In April 1944, bridging the gap between two harvests, paddy was selling for 5 piasters a picul in Mien Tay.[3] Indeed, things did not go as forecast: from 1943 onward no rice was delivered anywhere overseas, not even to northern Vietnam, which always had a shortage. In addition to these internal problems, Allied submarines and planes were sweeping the Pacific of steamers and seagoing junks, as well as destroying sections of the railway from Saigon to Hanoi. In 1945, "the year of all menaces" for Indochina, Mien Tay and the delta at large were still the colony's "rice basket" but the figures reveal a marked decrease in cultivation. Between 1943 and 1945, 197,800 hectares were abandoned.[4] The situation deteriorated further during the war of resistance against the French. One 1951 report estimated that the amount of rice land lying fallow was 600,000 to 700,000 hectares.[5]

The Japanese and the Vietnamese Nationalists

The Japanese presence in Indochina gave full scope to the noncommunist nationalists in Nam Bo, especially the Caodaists and the Hoa Hao religious movements that involved themselves in politics and tried to seize power. The Tay-ninh sect of the Caodaists chose to cooperate with the Japanese military, while the Hoa Hao group, a relative newcomer, was ambiguous in its dealings with the Japanese. The Hoa Hao religion was popular in the delta, especially in the provinces bordering the Mekong. The formal name of the sect was Dao Xen. Hoa Hao was its popular appellation, commemorating the birthplace of the charismatic prophet Huynh Phu So, the "Buddha Master of the Western Peace," who headed the Buu Son Ky Hong movement. During the war, So became involved with the Hoa Hao sect,[6] which was molded by the combined influences of messianism, the millenarianism of the Maitreyan Buddhists, the secular preoccupations resulting from French domination, and the doctrines of marxism.[7]

Although the political vacuum resulting from the weakness of France, the decline of the ICP, and the exile of Cao Dai leaders might logically have vaulted the new sect into the forefront of Nam Bo society, its influence was limited mainly to the provinces of Chau-doc, Can-tho, Long-xuyen, and Bac-lieu. In 1943, a French administrator wrote the following concerning the diffusion of the Hoa Hao faith.

> Communism was wiped out of the province of Long-xuyen in 1940–41. . . . Communism no longer plays any role, and the Caodaists have no weight, but the Dao Xen [Hoa Hao] have chosen Long-xuyen as a base from which they can confront the authorities. . . . The Dao Xen are numerous; in the district of Cho-moi they comprise at least 20 percent of the population. If we include sympathizers, they may be seen as a homogeneous group settled in a limited number of villages. . . . The majority of Dao Xen are honest and sincere people but the clique of agitators existing among them is dangerous.[8]

Similar observations were made in the province of Chau-doc in 1944.[9]

Although most Hoa Hao adepts were recruited from among the poor peasantry, the leaders and financial donors were bureaucrats such as Nguyen Giac Ngo or landlords such as Lam Tho Cu and Huynh Phu So's uncle Le Cong Bo. The future general Tran Van Soai, then a steam-launch operator, played an important role in the expansion of the sect.

One wonders why the Hoa Hao sect never spread beyond the area of Mien Tay and central Nam Bo. My hypothesis is that the new faith was closely associated with the geographic and sociocultural complex that Hue Tam Ho Tai calls *subculture*, the pivot of which is the "mountains" near the Cambodian border. In addition, as a latecomer, the political activities of the sect had no foreign support—neither from the Third International nor from the Japanese military.

To the French, the prophet Huynh Phu So had been a troublemaker. To the Japanese, though they considered him unreliable, he was a political factor they could not afford to overlook. Jailed by the French in November 1942, he was freed by the Japanese. Though protected by them, he was also their hostage. Nonetheless, his new situation increased his aura and strengthened the self-confidence of his followers in confronting the French authorities. This sparked a remarkable change in the orientation and fortunes of the Hoa Hao sect. As So became more and more interested in secular and political goals, his desire to play a national role grew.[10]

In all his actions Huynh Phu So seemed to rely essentially on his charisma. In 1945, Nguyen Hien Le, a writer skeptical of Hoa Hao effectiveness ("they are a great force but they lack organization and a blueprint for action"), was introduced to the Master by a nephew who was on So's staff. So was then residing in Saigon in a cottage in the rue Miche. Le described him as looking "like a young student . . . with a pretty white complexion, a frail, weak and pale man. . . . His physiognomy was harmonious, his manners and language were courteous." But he confided to his nephew that "Mature, polite, and quiet as he is, I cannot understand how the Master can attract and fascinate the masses as you and other people say. His cottage looks like a solitary scholar's retreat not like the premises of a revolutionary party."[11] Nonetheless, in public meetings So seems to have exerted a real magnetic attraction.

Although the Japanese supported such nationalist parties as the Dai Viet and the Phuc Quoc Hoi, and recruited their labor gangs through the Caodaists and paramilitary units, they left the French to manage the Indochinese rear guard while they occupied themselves with the war in Asia and the Pacific. What the population in the provinces thought of all this is not well documented. On one hand, the communists' *hoi ky* describe a unanimity of resentment directed against both the French and the Japanese. On the other hand, the reports of French political inspectors shed light on the attitudes of the upper classes. The worried French authorities sent inspectors to the delta periodically (maybe every year). Though fragmentary, their reports allow glimpses of the situation. Inspector Renou, for example, reported from Long-xuyen in April 1943 that "the condition of the tenants, owing to the lowering of rents, has not worsened, but it is at a very low level." In the same month he noted that in Rach-gia the French were very concerned about Franco-Annamite intercourse because "they fear the impact of Japanese propaganda on the Annamite elite." In June 1943, back in Long-xuyen, Renou heard the landlords' complaints about the requisitioning of paddy by the Comité des Céréales. A Vietnamese lawyer regretted that there was still de facto segregation between Frenchmen and Vietnamese even in the Cercle Franco-Annamite, although some individuals maintained good relations. And Dr. Zuong Van An observed that the Vietnamese elite resented the racial arrogance of the French. The province's most powerful landlord and former colonial councilor Dang Van Zan (who owned eight thousand hectares of rice land) complained of the condescension of the lower-ranking French functionaries. But, Renou added, "Dang is a demagogue; he protects the Dao Xen sect whose many adepts are his tenants." Finally, it was noted that, although in Long-xuyen the landlords were more flexible and had agreed (in December 1943) to lower rents, this was not the case in Tra-vinh Province where "the landlords are harsher."[12]

The year 1943 also brought Japanese military defeats that heralded a reversal of the situation in Burma and the Pacific. Anticipating that the French would soon switch their allegiance to the Allies, the Japanese overthrew French rule.[13] After they took control, the situation grew increasingly anarchic. In Nam Bo, only the Caodaists, the Hoa Hao, and the communists maintained a modicum of law and order. After determining their respective spheres of influence, these forces sometimes united in one front and sometimes fought the others in their attempts to seize overall power.

Each faction had its own trump cards. Perhaps the Caodaists were strongest in the beginning. Wholeheartedly supported by the Japanese, they had recovered their temple, only eighty kilometers from Saigon. They claimed more than 600,000 adepts, 3,000 of whom were militarized. But their collaboration with the Japanese was a serious handicap in Allied eyes.

After 1943, the Hoa Hao had grown stronger, and its leaders, too, were eager to play a political role.[14] They had organized "protection groups" (bao an doan) under Tran Van Soai and Le Quang Vinh (alias Ba Cut). Many outsiders served Huynh Phu So as political ideologues and advisers, among them the Trotskyite Pham Van Hum, the Stalinist Bui Van Zu, and the nationalist Tran Van An.[15] Since they played in the same yard, relations between the Hoa Hao and the communists were strained but that did not prevent them from cooperating when the need arose. A delegation sent to the national conference convened by the Viet Minh in Tan Trao in August 1945, for example, included at least one Hoa Hao representative according to Nguyen Thi Thap's *hoi ky*. Thap notes that "In early July 1945, comrade Bui Lam, a special envoy of the central committee of the party, along with comrade Cao Hong Lanh, arrived to choose delegates to the conference of Tan Trao." Ly Phu Xuan, a representative of the Hoa Hao of Can-tho was chosen because

> Comrades of the group Giai Phong, or the so-called old Viet Minh, had already convinced Huynh Phu So that his adepts and organizations must join the Viet Minh front if they are to save the Fatherland. During

Hoa Hao militia women at prayer; note the unadorned
altar and simple characteristics of the Hoa Hao
(Credit: ECP-Armées France).

his trip, the Hoa Hao delegate will discover the strength of the Viet
Minh throughout the three *ky,* and come to respect the united and reliable leadership of the Central Committee.

It was crucial, therefore, in light of an impending national uprising, "to rally
the precious personality of Huynh Phu So and his respectable mass organization."[16]

Thap's statement acknowledges the immense popular strength of the
Hoa Hao sect as well as the charisma of its leader. It also confirms French
police reports concerning talks undertaken in the fall of 1944 between a
communist emissary, the Hoa Hao sect, and the nationalists in Tra-vinh and
Vinh-long,[17] in which local communists had emphasized both the strong
position and role played by the Hoa Hao in Mien Tay. The topsy-turvy
political situation also gave rise to outpourings of patriotic enthusiasm, the
paying off of old scores, and an increased incidence of arson, racketeering,
and murder. Amid the chaos of the summer of 1945, Baron Minoda, the
Japanese governor of Cochinchina, cautioned the Vietnamese chief of the

*The "First Regiment" of Hoa Hao militia women,
led by the wife of General Tran Van Soai alias Nam Lua
(Credit: ECP-Armées France).*

province of Chau-doc that "The Hoa Hao sect is not to be formally acknowledged, only tolerated. Its provincial committees have no legal standing and they are authorized neither to organize village chapters nor to exert pressure on the authorities."[18] Though its claim of a million followers was certainly an exaggeration, the Hoa Hao was very strong within its sphere of influence. Its weakness lay in the fact that its power base was remote from the populated and developed areas of Nam Bo and from the Saigon-Cholon area.

The ICP militants, having rebuilt their cells, concentrated their efforts on the regions of Mien Trung and Mien Dong that included the Saigon-Cholon metropolitan area. Monthly reports of the police, the heads of the provinces, and the governor of Cochinchina for the years 1943–44 offer glimpses of the party's reconstruction.[19] The rebuilding was slow, often interrupted, and twice it regressed. By mid-1943, however, the communist resurgence was a matter of fact. The French police vigilantly followed its progress in Nam Bo, and the police archives document vigorous hunts for guerrillas, the arrests of militants such as Vo Van Kiet, and the seizure of documents and weapons. Meanwhile, the leaders of the 1940 uprising were executed: six in October 1943, two in June 1943, four in February 1944, and two in July 1944.

Drawing upon this chronicle of repression, we may sketch some features of the ICP's revival. First, the connection of the ICP with the communist Central Committee (in Bac Bo) was confirmed when the police captured the Viet Minh Manifesto, as early as December 1942, in Mien Tay. The police also discovered that a new interprovincial committee of the Hau Giang had distributed the fourth issue of *Cuu Quoc* (printed in Bac Bo and dated 23 August 1942) in March 1943. Second, the ICP was publishing the newspaper *Giai Phong* (Liberation) the sixth issue of which (January 1944) exhorted the people to unite under the Viet Minh banner. Dozens of these papers were distributed in Mien Tay. Third, provincial committees and local cells are described in captured documents. In addition to those of Saigon-Cholon, Gia Dinh, and Thu Dau Mot, organizations blossomed in Mien Tay. In July 1943, the party claimed 104 militants and 5 cells (with 43 members) in Rach-gia, 3 cells (16 members) in Can-tho, 3 cells (13 members) in Vinh-long, 2 cells (6 members) in Long-xuyen, 2 cells (14 members) in Chau-doc,1 cell (6 members) in Tra-vinh, and 1 cell (6 members) in Sa-dec. Every province had 2 to 4 Peasant Associations for National Salvation (Nong Hoi Cuu Quoc), each with 20 to 100 members. There also were associations of sympathizers. Finally, in August 1944, the police claimed to have proof that the connection between the communists of Nam Bo and the Central Committee of the party had revived. In September of the same year we find the term Viet Minh used in police reports, maybe for the first time.

The second set of available documents is Nguyen Thi Thap's *hoi ky* and Giau's version of the story.[20] According to these, there was much mutual distrust among the communists. In Nam Bo, the defeat of 1940 made them more defiant and their remoteness from the top leadership raised many obstacles to reunification. In 1942, for instance, when Nguyen Huu Xuyen, an envoy of the Central Committee to the south, was arrested, the link was severed until 1943. In that year two groups emerged, one gathered around Tran Van Giau, who built the party in Nam Bo in the early 1930s, and the other under the influence of a new envoy from the Central Committee, Nguyen Huu Ngoan. Among the latter were Tran Van Zi, Bui Van Zu, and Tran Van Tra (the future general of the People's Army of Viet Nam). They publicized the policy of the United National Front (the Viet Minh) by distributing copies of their newspaper *Giai Phong* and they tried to rebuild the *xu uy* of Nam Ky. When the police arrested them and killed Ngoan in October 1943, Giau escaped from the camp of Ta Lai, hidden in My-tho. Later he organized a new *xu uy* but some communists (such as Thap) refused to join because, she said, a *xu uy* already existed under the leadership of the delegate of the Central Committee. Hence, in April 1945, there were two communist *xu uy* in Nam Bo, which corresponded to two parties known as the Dang Cong San Dong Zuong (Thap's party) and the Dong Zuong Cong San Dang (Giau's party). These were commonly called the Viet Minh Cu (Old Viet Minh) and the Viet Minh Moi (New Viet Minh). In June 1945, the two groups began to cooperate on the provincial level, merging in a single *tinh uy* (provincial committee) in My-tho.

Nevertheless, when Thap returned from the Tan Trao conference on 22 September 1945, the division was still acute. She angrily observed that two flags were to be seen everywhere: the yellow and red star of the Thanh Nien Tien Phong (Vanguard Youth), led by Dr. Pham Ngoc Thach, a member of Giau's *xu uy*, and the red flag with the gold star of the Viet Minh, controlled by the Central Committee's partisans. Thap also regretted the sight of the Cao Dai and the Hoa Hao with their own standards.[21]

In the end, it was September 1945 before the two factions healed their rift. In the meantime, there were disagreements over tactics and strategy. Should the communists, for instance, fight both the French and the Japanese fascists or only the Japanese? This controversial issue was hotly debated in print. On one side was the *Tien Phong* (Vanguard), the journal of Hau Giang and the voice of Giau's group. On the other was *Giai Phong*, the Viet Minh and Tien Giang's paper. The former advocated fighting the Japanese, the latter fighting both the Japanese and the French. Truong Chinh, the general secretary of the ICP, straddled the fence by declaring that the decision would depend upon the unfolding of events. After 9 March 1945, of course, when the Japanese usurped what was left of French power, the question became moot.[22] There was also much discussion over which flag to adopt, the Viet Minh's or the Vanguard Youth's. Giau argued that the red would be most shocking to the Allies when they came, the yellow looking more nationalist than communist.

These controversies seem too trivial to explain the rift. There were also sharp cultural differences between the urban, educated leaders who had studied abroad, men like Tran Van Giau and Pham Ngoc Thach, and rural peasants such as Nguyen Thi Thap and Nguyen Van Zi who were not formally educated and had closer ties to the masses. Neither Thap nor Giau are explicit about causes, though Giau's recent account of the events of 1943–45 may provide a clue. The *xu uy* founded in October 1943 on Giau's initiative in My-tho (without links to the Central Committee) declared that the national insurrection must begin in Saigon, the bulwark of the enemy. It must not appear to be the revolt of a minority (as occurred in 1940) nor an encirclement of the town by rural guerrillas (a reference to Mao in China but also to the planning then underway in Bac Bo).[23]

Whatever their disputes, in the end the communists of Nam Bo did not fight each other because they reached a consensus within the wider reality of the Vietnamese nation of that time. In 1945, the Vanguard Youth joined the Viet Minh. Another link was forged when the ICP took power in Tan An, half-way between Saigon-Cholon and My-tho, in order to test the reaction of the Japanese. Thereafter it seized power under the banner of the Viet Minh in Saigon on 2 September. On 8 September, thousands of Hoa Hao supporters attempted to capture Can-tho City, the capital of the delta, but they failed.[24]

Summing up what he believed to be the reasons for the communist paramountcy, Giau listed the victories of the Soviet Red Army, which enhanced the prestige of the ICP, and the collaboration of other nationalist forces with the Japanese. He adds that when hundreds of communists were freed after March 1945 they reinforced the party and its satellite organizations. Last, but not least, he notes that in the end the former colonial constabulary (Garde Civile de Cochinchine, or *miliciens*, similar to Garde Indigène of the north and center), with its weapons, switched to the Viet Minh's side. With the exception of those areas controlled by the Hoa Hao and Caodaists, the communists easily took power in Mien Tay. On 27 August 1945, a schoolteacher named Tran Thi Nhuong and Dr. Ke, who led the Vanguard Youth in Sa-dec, called at the provincial chief's office and proposed that the bureaucracy join the new people's movement. Street demonstrations soon convinced the chief and his deputy and they joined the Uy Ban Nhan Zan (People's Committee) of Sa-dec. Of all the officials, only the police intendant refused to comply.[25]

Anarchy or Union?

The communists quickly achieved hegemony over competing political forces. They overcame their adversaries without suppressing all of them. In spite of bloody mutual fighting in the fall of 1945, they even convinced Huynh Phu So to join their united front against the French in 1946—before assassinating him the following year. The reconquest of the delta by French troops following the Japanese defeat obliged the Vietnamese to unite, or at least to refrain from fighting each other. A second factor was the signing on 6 March 1946 of agreements between the French government and Ho Chi Minh, which gave Ho and his party de facto if not formal recognition.

It was a short-lived truce, however, and the war never really ceased in Nam Bo. The French played upon internecine divisions and strife. The united front against them was not a coalition of political parties but a loose confederation of political and politico-religious groups defended by their own military forces. As early as 1946, the Caodaists opened negotiations with the French military command and soon after signed an agreement of cooperation.[26] In 1947, when the prophet was murdered, the Hoa Hao commander Tran Van Soai also began treating with the French.

The *hoi ky* of the writer Nguyen Hien Le affords us a glimpse of the situation in Mien Tay. When the French, with the aid of British troops, recovered Saigon, Le managed to escape to the chief town of Long-xuyen, his family home. In a rented boat he passed through the canals, crossing Dong Thap. At one checkpoint a Vanguard Youth girl asked him: "What's that book you keep with you? A French book? You still have a French book? Follow me to the People's Committee." Le was fortunate enough to meet a revolutionary committee member who had once been a colleague in the Agricultural Hydraulics Department. Although he was freed, his colleague warned him not to "keep anything colored blue, white, and red, or you will be accused of being a French spy or a sympathizer."[27]

After a six-day journey, Le reached the road to Long-xuyen where he saw dozens of youngsters, barefoot and dressed in black, enthusiastically undergoing martial training. Upon his arrival in Long-xuyen, he found the town nearly destroyed because the People's Committee had implemented a "scorched-earth" policy.[28] By the spring of 1946, French soldiers and their *partisans* (local supplementary troops), reinforced with a number of bandits, looted several homes. Interethnic feuds also arose between the Vietnamese and the Khmers. Wherever the Khmers outnumbered the Vietnamese, as in certain districts of Chau-doc and Tra-vinh, they attacked. According to Le,

> The Khmers rose up, got drunk, and went on a looting spree, and when they encountered a Vietnamese they cut his throat. In times of peace, the Khmers are quiet and mild but when troubles occur they become pirates.[29]

The French soon found volunteers among the Khmers to organize units of *partisans* who helped French troops reconquer parts of the delta. Looting, murders, and rapes sparked a lethal round of reprisals and counterreprisals. M. Solier, a French civil administrator recently arrived in Soc-trang, left a vivid description of these interethnic clashes.

> We arrived in the province on 4 January 1946, and by May or June it was nearly pacified. That process went quickly because there were eighty thousand Cambodians there. The Vietnamese joined us, seeking protection from the Cambodians. The Viet Minh having fled, the Vietnamese were uneasy, for they had oppressed the Cambodian minority while we were absent. . . . In 1946, our task was to limit civil strife. In this we had to curb our allies who were too enthusiastic. Often we were compelled to use force against the Cambodians. There were also unfrocked monks who acted as prophets and who drove us into actions we regretted afterward; it was later proved that we were lured by the Cambodians' vengefulness.[30]

When that orgy of blood had spent itself, it left behind a festering hatred that drove many subsequent events.

From One War to Others: Mien Tay and the Anti-French Resistance, 1945–1954

With the exception of Allied bombings of selected targets, Indochina was not a battlefield in World War II. Rather, Indochina (and particularly Vietnam) were devastated by military operations after the war. In its attempt to reconquer Vietnam, the French armored division of General Leclerc launched an offensive through the delta in Nam Bo. It did not go well, as H. J. Loustau, a French noncommissioned officer, remembered: "The top brass believed that the offensive in Cochinchina would be a devastating and glorious route. Now our losses have led us to see that the war has just begun and it promises to be destructive."[31]

Franco-Vietnamese agreements concluded on 6 March 1946 were not followed by a general cease-fire in the south (Nam Bo and Nam Trung Bo), for the combatants' aims were diametrically opposed and the situation in the field was out of control. The French were obsessed with erasing the humiliation of their earlier defeats and restoring their imperial identity, even under a new guise, for without it France would never recover its status as a world power. For the Vietnamese, independence and reunification of the country were nonnegotiable objectives. One of the first stumbling blocks in the attempt to implement the agreements of March 1946 was Nam Bo itself. The French army was attacking there even while its diplomats were negotiating with Ho Chi Minh at Fontainebleau. High Commissioner Thierry d'Argenlieu engineered a phony Autonomous Republic of Cochinchina but it immediately collapsed. On the other side, we can suppose that the southern Vietnamese exerted sufficient pressure on Ho Chi Minh's government that it could not bargain away Nam Bo.

The signing of the agreements had little effect on the combatants, who fought on. Loustau recalls that in October 1946 he received the order to cease fire. "For the first time in my soldier's life," he writes, "I decided to disobey."[32]

The Strategic Role of Mien Tay: A Stronghold of the Resistance

The French never wholly reconquered Nam Bo. Control of the south was either steadily or temporarily shared between the French and their allies (the Caodaists, the Hoa Hao, the Catholics, and the Binh Xuyen mafia) on the one hand, and the Uy Ban Khang Chien Hanh Chanh Nam Bo, or UBK (Committee of Resistance and Administration of Nam Bo), on the other. The UBK was dependent upon Ho Chi Minh's central government. In 1947, General Valluy, chief commander of the French troops in Indochina, summed up the situation as follows.

> If all the Vietnamese are not members of the Viet Minh, nor communists, they are all, broadly speaking, resistants. All ask us to pay the same bill, and their requests are identical to those Ho Chi Minh presented at the Fontainebleau conference. . . . The brutal and acknowledged fact is that the whole populace, even if passively, are accomplices of the Committee of Nam Bo [the UBK]. . . . Except for the Caodaists and our widening yet still limited occupation and influence, the true authority in Nam Bo is the committee, an emanation of the former government of Hanoi. It has a genuine administrative machinery that, publicly or underground, asserts itself through its armed forces, and it does not hesitate in the choice of means.[33]

The factors and constraints of the geography of Nam Bo have never been so obvious as during that period. To take control of the delta was a matter of paramount importance to the belligerents. The "rice basket" could provide food not just for the south but for the entire country. Exported rice could provide hard currency with which the resistants could buy weapons, drugs, fuel, and clothing. The Resistance was determined to control such strongholds as the Mien Dong forests, the Dong Thap swamps, and the U Minh forest. There they built *lang rung* (forest villages) in which they hid from the French army. To maintain their communications and transport links with central and northern Vietnam, by land and sea, they had to exploit the advantages of topography and hydrography, and keep the border with Cambodia open.[34] On the border they also trained the future Khmer cadres of communist-led guerrillas. Finally, through Mien Tay, they kept open the sea lanes of the Gulf of Thailand, connecting Vietnam with Bangkok and Singapore, using the islands of the gulf as relay points and shelters.

Another War Economy

"One *gia* of paddy for the Fatherland is one gunshot against the Enemy" ran the motto of the UBK. By 1949, the Resistance had control of the "rice basket" of Nam Bo. From there they harassed and intercepted the convoys of boats and trucks that supplied Saigon-Cholon and the smaller urban centers occupied by French troops. But at the same time the French-allied Caodaists (with their military posts established along the Hau Giang); the Hoa Hao of Sa-dec, Long-xuyen, Can-tho, and Chau-doc; and the Catholic self-defense militia of Ben-tre seized the sources of production and built a buffer zone between the western delta and the rest of Nam Bo. There the anti–Viet Minh forces controlled a portion of the paddy harvests from 1949 to 1953 and maintained the French "blockade of the Transbassac." By then the Transbassac, or Mien Tay, was the last stronghold of the UBK.[35]

Because of the blockade, the Resistance could no longer freely sell paddy, wood, and charcoal, nor even the pepper of Ha-tien and Kampot. The French navy continued to strengthen its hold over the coastline and the rivers. On 28 August 1949, troops from a French gunboat boarded a ship purchased by the Vietnamese in Thailand and captured a key resistant, Benoit Trong. The proceedings against Trong, who was head of the Committee of Logistics of Nam Bo (which maintained communications with Thailand by sea), sheds light on the importance of Vietnamese activities in Bangkok and reveals the workings of maritime transport. It was found that

Thai crews had been bringing small boats to the edge of territorial waters, at a place called Mai Ruot, where Vietnamese crews would replace them.[36]

Though the UBK launched its own economic "blockade of the enemy's zone" (*Bao vay kinh te dich*), the French blockade was damaging. The Resistance headquarters and its best fighting units were forced to abandon Dong Thap and flee to Mien Dong and Mien Tay, paradoxically at the same time that French troops were suffering their first serious defeats in the north.[37]

The new situation forced the UBK to adopt an authoritarian policy under which it attempted to produce enough rice to satisfy the needs of the liberated areas, imported only the bare minimum of commodities, and banned all luxury goods. This economic reply to the French blockade was consistent with the political discourse of popular mobilization, and with the promotion of the virtues of equality, frugality, and self-reliance. But, if this policy had a sincere ideological face, it also had a tactical aim: to weaken the hard currency of the opposition. The *piastre indochinoise* issued by the Banque de l'Indochine was outlawed in the liberated zone and replaced with "Ho Chi Minh piasters." Cadres and soldiers also were called upon to commit themselves to self-sufficiency, manual labor, mutual aid, and frugality.

Cadres were exhorted to increase production in the fields of agriculture, animal husbandry, and textiles. A program of land redistribution was launched in the areas firmly controlled by the resistants, particularly in Mien Tay. The UBK announced the confiscation of all land owned by the "French and traitors" and encouraged "patriotic landlords" to give up their land as well. Those who did were highly celebrated. Dr. Pham Ngoc Thach, to give one example, donated 420 hectares in the province of Sa-dec to the Fatherland.[38] Some Viet Minh documents hint, however, that these donations were not always free of self-interest, as many plots were situated in places where it was impossible to collect rents even though the owners were still responsible for the taxes.[39]

In July 1949, a decree of Ho Chi Minh's central government declared its intention "to temporarily distribute the rice fields of the French colonialists and traitors to the poor peasants" (see table 22). In 1950, it "temporarily redistributed the land of landlords who had taken refuge in areas occupied by the enemy." In 1950, the government also requisitioned fallow lands. These were allocated to poor peasants who were allowed to keep the harvest for themselves and were exempted from the payment of tax. In March 1952, it was decreed that all communal lands and rice fields would henceforth be shared by poor peasants and women.[40]

TABLE 22: Anticipated and Actual Land-Tax Revenues
of the Resistance, 1951–52 (in gia)

Province	Anticipated Revenue	Actual Levies
Bac-lieu	700,000	250,047
Vinh-tra	500,000	350,000
Long-chau-ha	12,593	5,559
Can-tho	250,000	200,000
Soc-trang	198,435	145,000

Note: Some provincial boundaries were redrawn by the UBK and the resulting jurisdictions were given new names.

Source: Pham Van Bach, "Cong Tac Thue."

Desperate for funds, the UBK attempted to collect levies from the population of the liberated areas and even from those in the occupied zones. Since the Revolution for many people had seemed to promise freedom from taxation, the UBK was hard pressed to convince its followers that the exacted funds should be thought of as contributions (*dong gop*) rather than levies (*thue*).[41] As taxes were assessed on the basis of the size of plots and their productivity, investigations and local censuses were conducted. Under the conditions of war, such operations were left in the hands of the local authorities, where a great deal of bias came into play.[42] Captured documents reveal that the local cadres often exempted their relatives and friends. Buddhist monasteries and Catholic convents were exempted and the Khmers were granted a privileged tax status.[43] Though fragmentary, land-tax figures provided by Pham Van Bach for 1951–52 illustrate the gap between expectation and reality (table 22). In total, the government collected 1 million of 5 million anticipated *gia*, "just enough to meet minimum needs, including the budget of Mien Tay."[44]

In 1953, when land reform was undertaken in northern Vietnam, the "central government" ordered the UBK to eliminate all exemptions and differential tax rates, including the one that favored the Khmers.[45] Tenants were ordered to again pay rent to their landlords, although the rate was limited to 25 percent of the harvest. As the French administration had done previously, the Resistance government also encouraged peasants and landlords to make

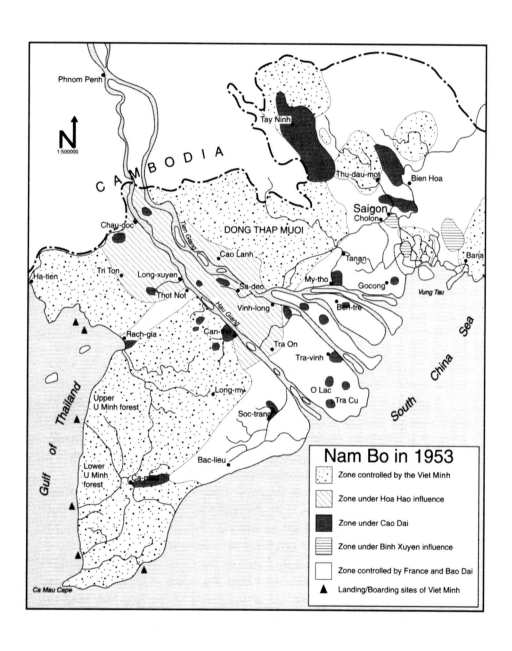

Phnom Penh

N
1:500000

C A M B O D I A

DONG THAP MUOI

Chau-doc

Tay Ninh

Thu-dau-mot

Bien Hoa

Saigon
Cholon

Tanan

Baria

Ha-tien

Tri Ton

Long-xuyen

Cao Lanh

My-tho

Gocong

Vung Tau

Thot Not

Sa-dec

Vinh-long

Ben-tre

Rach-gia

Can-tho

Tra On

Tra-vinh

Upper
U Minh
forest

Long-my

O Lac

Tra Cu

South China Sea

Gulf of Thailand

Lower
U Minh
forest

Ca-mau

Soc-trang

Bac-lieu

Ca Mau Cape

Nam Bo in 1953

Zone controlled by the Viet Minh

Zone under Hoa Hao influence

Zone under Cao Dai

Zone under Binh Xuyen influence

Zone controlled by France and Bao Dai

▲ Landing/Boarding sites of Viet Minh

use of written contracts and it urged tenants to pay their rent regularly so as to help the owners remit the land tax promptly. The fact that such exhortations were repeated over and over suggests that in this matter the Resistance officials were as unsuccessful as the French.[46]

Despite such difficulties, the UBK and the Viet Minh succeeded in implementing some social and political reforms. The grants of land to landless and poor peasants alone created a new "social landscape" that had inevitable political consequences. The scale of this land redistribution in Nam Bo is indicated by Lam Quang Huyen who wrote that "Prior to 1954, the French colonialists' land, traitors' land, and ownerless land that had been provisionally distributed amounted to 564,547 hectares divided among 527,163 beneficiaries."[47]

Mien Tay Prior to the Founding of the National Liberation Front

When the First Indochina War ended with a negotiated settlement in 1954, Vietnam was partitioned into two states divided at the 17th Parallel. Elections were to be held in two years to decide whether the country should be reunified. So many communist troops and supporters left for the north, that of 65,000 Communist Party members residing in the south in 1954 only 15,000 remained in 1955.[48]

Peasants in the areas formerly controlled by the Resistance now had to cope with the southern regime of Ngo Dinh Ziem. Ziem launched a campaign to eradicate the communists, now known as the Viet Cong. Although he also attempted to continue some type of land reform, his main priority was to build a national authoritarian state.[49]

The government in Saigon began its sweep of the delta by suppressing the Hoa Hao. Once that had been accomplished, it faced the invisible but ever-present communists of Rach-gia and Ha-tien provinces (now combined to form the province of Kien Giang) and in Long-xuyen and Chau-doc (now known as An Giang).[50] Previously, however, there had been one last conflict between the communists and the Hoa Hao. According to the official history of the province of Kien Giang, the armed forces of the Hoa Hao tried to seize the U Minh zone late in the war.

> In many places they continued to aggravate the "debt of blood" [*no mau*]. Therefore the party committee and members infiltrated cadres in Hoa Hao units such as the Trung Doan Nguyen Hue and Le Quang,

each gathering nearly a thousand guerrillas. When the Hoa Hao chief Ba Cut surrendered to the government, one Hoa Hao company commanded by communist cadres stayed in the bush.[51]

The official communist line depicts Ngo Dinh Ziem as a champion of the landlords, mandarins, and comprador capitalists. Indeed, if one adheres to the Leninist view of the class state, it is difficult to interpret Ziem's role otherwise. But was Ziem's policy so narrow? When his government forces invaded Mien Tay, one goal certainly was the opening of large tracts of empty or sparsely populated land to the thousands of refugees pouring in from northern Vietnam. In the delta the largest *khu dinh dien* (planned agricultural settlement) was supposed to be in Cai San (in Rach-gia). There 77,000 hectares of rice land were cleared for up to 100,000 refugees, though only 43,000 settled there. It was hoped that these new settlements would contribute to the pacification of the countryside,[52] and in fact the arrival of the outsiders, mostly Catholics, did introduce the culture and values of the *kinh* (lowland Vietnamese) into the fabric of life in Mien Tay.

In the areas still under its control, the Viet Minh's agrarian policy was moderate. It was determined by the Politburo in Hanoi, which forwarded its orders to the Central Directorate of South Vietnam. The directive entitled "The Tasks of 1954" (*Nhiem vu nam 1954*) clearly stressed that "To implement the Land Reform, you must wait for orders from the Central Committee. Do not make any decisions on your own."[53] The directive went on to caution that if a united national front was to be built, religious freedom must be guaranteed, the support of the poor peasants must be won, and an alliance with the middle-level peasants forged. Finally, "you must treat the landlords with discrimination, carefully distinguishing the reactionaries from the resistants."[54]

Nonetheless, in the process of attempting to redistribute land to Catholics and Khmers, many landlords were dispossessed. The documents reveal that many were branded as traitors (*viet gian*) and fled to the towns. When these people returned to the delta, most after an extended absence, they often found their estates confiscated, occupied by tillers who refused to recognize the validity of their legal titles. The return of the landlords also reactivated resistance among the peasants against those they viewed as their exploiters.

By 1956, it was clear that the promised general elections would not take place. With partition now thought to be more or less permanent, the struggle between south and north gradually shifted from the political to the military sphere. The communists by now had lost whatever faith they once had in peaceful political evolution.

Did the Ziem government's campaign of *to cong, ziet cong* (Denounce and Eliminate the Communists) force the north's hand, or was there a long-standing plot to invade the south? Recent Vietnamese publications shed some light on that period. We are told that in Ben-tre, for example, "only a fortnight after the cease-fire," two thousand cadres and soldiers were sent north. But

> already two thousand other cadres, party members, had been selected to
> stay and lead the struggle of the people. The provincial committee
> decided to retain some military cadres along with weapons and weapon-
> making machinery.[55]

By 1955, the party committee of Rach-gia and Ha-tien had organized several armed units of thirty men each. By 1958, there were three *trung doan* (regiments). Le Zuan, who had led the Resistance in Nam Bo since 1951, had stayed on for some time at Minh Hai (in Ca-mau Province) before returning to the north, issuing "directives to the provincial committee to reorganize the armed forces to fight the American imperialists." Consequently, in July 1957, when the South Vietnamese army, aided by American advisers, launched a campaign in Minh Hai to destroy the communists, "The party was ready to fight back."[56]

In the meantime, the Ziem government was attempting to implement its agrarian scheme. This program required the peasants to sign contracts with landlords, called for the distribution or sale of land to the landless, and established *khu tru mat* (centers of prosperity). The purpose of the latter was to keep watch over the population while promoting rural modernization.[57] Ziem also attempted to force the integration of the ethnic minorities into the new national state. He "nationalized" the businesses of the Chinese and tried to Vietnamize the central highlanders (in the process giving birth to the BEJARAKA). For the Khmers of the delta, the study of Pali was forbidden and the practice of Buddhism was discouraged.[58]

According to both Ladejinsky's reports and the socialist Vietnamese version, *Buoc mo dau,* 1958–59 marked the turning point for the Ziem regime. After a drastic campaign of arrests and executions launched to "denounce and destroy" the communists, the government seemed finally to have succeeded in asserting its power in the countryside.[59] The communists never gave up the fight, however. Their armed insurrection against the Republic of

Vietnam, formalized under the title Mat Tran Zan Toc Giai Phong Mien Nam Viet Nam (National Liberation Front of South Vietnam) carried on the opposition despite brutal government suppression.[60] Although its persistence cannot be explained strictly on economic and social grounds, economic factors played a key role. As Robert Sansom tells us, "economic grievances, particularly those arising from land, played a major role in the growth of the V.C. [Viet Cong] support in the Delta."[61] The land that had been provisionally distributed to peasants in 1948 had been permanently granted in 1953–54. In return the peasants gave their unqualified support to the communists when they came under attack by Ziem's troops and the police. Eventually the communist authors would refer to that land policy as their *la bua ho menh* (talisman).[62] After Ziem consolidated his power and the *dien chu* began reclaiming their properties and attempting to collect overdue rents, peasants (including the Khmers and the Hoa Hao) reacted in self-defense. The communists did not arouse these feelings of revolt but they became adept at channeling them. As the peasants made up the bulk of the guerrilla fighters and provided the movement's backbone of logistical and moral support, once more the countryside of Nam Bo became a sanctuary as well as the scene of armed opposition to the state.

CHAPTER 9

Conclusion

DOES THE HISTORY of the Mekong Delta, and particularly that of Mien Tay, shed light upon the long process that has revolutionized—broadly speaking—Vietnamese society in the twentieth century? The "southern drive" of the Vietnamese resulted in a society markedly different from that of the country's settled north and center. The Mekong was to the Vietnamese what the American West was to the United States. The village in Nam Bo was not like those of the north, entrenched behind their bamboo hedges, and its peasants were far less prone to bow to feudal authority or be bound by Confucian ethics.[1] In the twentieth century, attempts at organization among the *don dien,* and even the civilian communes, fell by the wayside as soon as pacification was assured, and the remaining large tracts of fallow land allowed settler families to try their luck and gain some measure of autonomy.

Although village cohesion and solidarity could be observed, it tended to focus upon opposition to the state and to foreigners such as the Khmers and the French. Increased autonomy and individualism brought with them a deterioration in communal values. Communal lands themselves became commodities to be rented or sold, and what traditionally had served as a device for the maintenance of balance and safety inside the community almost disappeared as early as the turn of the nineteenth century. What solidarity remained became focused upon the enduring structure of the extended family. In Nam Bo, family has been at the core of networks of mutual aid and cultural activity. Always present in traditional patron-client relations, today it is employed by the Communist Party. During the French colonial period, the family rather than the village was the underpinning of the ideological discourse of the landlord class.

This rather loose societal fabric helps explain the difficulties encountered by the conquerors of Nam Bo, from the failure of the emperor Minh Mang's efforts to restore a Confucianist state to the attempt of the "Last Confucian" to build a southern state 120 years later.[2] Even the Communist

Party apparently has given up trying to enforce its grip. Buddhism has been a much stronger influence, both the orthodox Cambodian sort and the more unorthodox Vietnamese version, which incorporates Taoism and local creeds. At the same time, Mien Tay exhibits some melding of the Asian and European traditions that met at this crossroads. French capitalism integrated Nam Bo into the world economy, further distancing it from northern and central Vietnam where a more traditional economy prevailed. But the French did no more than build upon trends that had begun earlier.

Although the French administered Nam Bo as a colony directly subject to their laws, they assimilated neither the country nor its people. In 1930, Governor General A. Varenne admitted that Vietnamese culture possessed an irreducible originality and recommended that the French abandon their efforts to impose their ideals on the colony, acknowledging, in effect, that assimilationist policy was a dead issue.[3] The paradox of Nam Bo lies in its blend of individualistic, unorthodox tendencies and the ties that bind it to the "land of the ancestors" (To Quoc). The latter notion, the sense of belonging to a larger community forged over time, has functioned to keep the inhabitants of Nam Bo part of the nation of Vietnam. But the motivation has been less nationalism than patriotism, less rational conceptualization than emotion.

While for the most part the French abandoned their attempts to monopolize (or even control) the economy of the Mekong Delta, they created a plantation economy (based on rubber, coffee, and tea) on the central highlands of northern Nam Bo. Although the financing and markets for these enterprises were essentially European, the cultivation of export rice remained deeply entrenched in Asian networks. The major source of funding for these activities came from the Chinese, Indians, and Vietnamese. European-born French were not major rice producers or transporters, contenting themselves with involvement in its export. Rice milling and trade were left to the Chinese, and this enduring local and regional commerce provided the economic basis for the anti-French resistance of 1945–54. But it is not accurate to label this a dual economy, as conceptualized by Boeke.[4] The Asian- and European-dominated economies of Nam Bo were in reality but two segments of the capitalist world economy.

The growth of export-rice monoculture during the French colonial period bred the *"question sociale"* in the Mekong Delta, just as the rubber estates and mining concerns did in the rest of Vietnam. The great landholdings and large (though fragile) fortunes profoundly affected the inner relations of village communities. Though a "moral economy" certainly existed, peasant solidarity was all but obliterated by acquisitiveness, if not greed, and the drive to maximize income.[5] Throughout Mien Tay, of course, landlords and tenants were the crucial components of social relations. Linked by necessity, their interdependence could take the form of familial, benevolent relations or oppression of *ta dien* by *dien chu*. The quality of their relationship depended upon either the acceptance or rejection of common ideological values.[6]

It took two wars to solve the agrarian quandary of Vietnam. During the First Indochina War the Committee of Resistance and Adminstration in Nam Bo (Uy Ban Khang Chien Hanh Chanh Nam Bo) managed to redistribute about 1 million hectares of land, so much that middle-sized farmers came to outnumber landless peasants.[7] After that war the republican government of Nguyen Van Thieu went further with its Land to the Tiller program (1971), so that, in a way, radical (communist) and moderate (Taiwanese-style) agrarian reformers joined to accomplish the true Revolution in the countryside of Nam Bo by suppressing the absentee and rentier landholders and promoting technological change—the so-called Green Revolution—in the delta. Today, realizing that the collectivization introduced after reunification in 1975 has failed, reformist communists and others are emphasizing the crucial role of the middle-sized farmers of Nam Bo who still retain some knowledge and experience of export-oriented agriculture.

The Vietnamese communist movement was a fabric woven of town and countryside, class and nation. This complex web sometimes worked in harmony, sometimes in contradiction. Conflicts arose from the communists' need to unite as many sectors of the Vietnamese population as possible while satisfying the aspirations of the most wretched. The latter mandate impinged not only upon the interests but upon the feelings and ideas of the other sectors of society. Moreover, was it possible to unite Vietnamese and non-Vietnamese on the grounds that all were victims of the same oppressors: feudals, colonialists, capitalists, and so forth? Tensions mounted as questions were raised. Who would gain hegemony in the resistance movement? Who would rule the embryonic state in the bush, and later the victorious "State of Workers and Peasants"?

The communists succeeded in harnessing the "Green Power" of the peasants as long as both groups faced the common enemy of French rule. In those days it was possible to play upon the fundamentals of historical memory and myth, economic frustration, and racial sensitivity. Later they were again able to mobilize the peasantry in opposition to the domestic masters whose early actions seemed to continue the policies of their old rulers, benefitting the landlord class.

All this changed after the Communist Party reunited the country and cast it in the mold of a planned economy with collectivist structures. Could the tradition of Asian communitarianism ease the transition to such a new order? In 1921, Ho Chi Minh contended that it could. But many changes occurred in the decades following the 1920s, particularly in Nam Bo. The early communist practice of distributing land among the peasants was very popular in the Mekong Delta where the pioneer mentality, so much more individualistic than that held by most Vietnamese, had long prevailed. W. Ladejinsky captured this quite effectively when he recalled a conversation with a peasant in the region of Bac-lieu and Ca-mau. "Would you like to see the landlord back?" he asked. "No," the peasant replied, "Let the government [in Saigon] give me three hectares and a pair of buffalo and I will pay for them in installments." Ladejinsky noted that "clearly he did not want the landlord back, his ideal was a version of the American 'forty acres and a mule.'"[8]

The resistance of the Vietnamese peasants was finally overcome by the authoritarian state. But today the socialist regime is being forced to make new concessions to the "Green Power." It would appear that the peasants who once wholeheartedly accepted the sacrifice of their plots of land will now refuse to submit to the dogmatic and inflexible constructions of urban intellectuals.

APPENDIX 1

Weights and Measures

Although the French authorities introduced the metric system to Nam Bo, Vietnamese weights and measures were retained for the transactions of daily life. During the colonial period, the local (Vietnamese), regional (Chinese), and metric (French) systems were used simultaneously or alternatively. For more on this complex system, see Nguyen Dinh Dau, "Gop phan nghien cuu van de do, dong, can, dem cua Viet Nam xua" in *Nghien cuu kinh te*, no. 5 (1978).

Vietnamese	French	English
Linear measure:		
tam	2.25 meters	
thuoc tay	1 meter	
tac	6 centimeters	
thuoc	6 decimeters	
Square measure:		
mau tay	1 hectare	2.5 acres
mau	50 ares	
cong	10 ares	
sao (1/10 of a mau)	5 ares	
cong (of harvesters)	13 ares (in Mien Tay)	
Fluid and grain measure:		
gia of rice or paddy	40 liters	8.8 gallons
touque	18 liters	3.9 gallons
Weights:		
ta (picul) of paddy	60 kilograms	132.24 pounds
ta of pepper	68 kilograms	

APPENDIX 2

The Ziep Van Cuong Case

On 6 May 1909, a Frenchman by the name of Dr. Flandrin applied for a concession of three thousand hectares in Ca-mau. Although the land was occupied by squatters, the concession was granted to him. Flandrin enlisted the aid of Ziep Van Cuong, an official interpreter and naturalized French citizen, and a French surveyor named Gregoire. It was later alleged that Cuong and Gregoire violently dispossessed legal title holders, stole water palms under cultivation, and confiscated fish from the ponds of Vietnamese and Khmer farmers under the pretext that they came under the jurisdiction of Flandrin's concession. Suit was filed against the conspirators in 1911. On 23 January 1912, the justice of the peace of Bac-lieu pronounced the following sentences.

> Ziep Van Cuong: two months in jail and a fine of 500 francs
> Gregoire: a fine of 300 francs
> Luong Hue Mang: ten days in jail and a fine of 100 francs
> Le Van The: ten days in jail (deferred) and a fine of 200 francs
> Luong Dit Nga: fifteen days in jail and a fine of 100 francs

On 12 December 1912, the Court of Appeals in Saigon, considering only proven allegations, mainly those concerning violence by hired thugs, amended the sentences as follows.

> Ziep Van Cuong: fine of 200 francs
> Gregoire: fine of 100 francs
> Le Van The: fine of 50 francs

In a letter addressed to the Ministry of the Colonies, Governor of Cochinchina Gourbeil commented that

> The administration cannot but accept the sentences of the court. But, as head of the administration, responsible for public order and security, I regret the mildness of the sentences in the face of the proven facts, which deeply moved the local population and which the judicial investigation demonstrated were serious and frequent.

(Governor of Cochinchina Gourbeil to the Ministry of the Colonies, 27 February 1913, CAOM, Indochine, NF 728).

Summary of Trade at the Harbor of Ca-Mau in 1880-81

The register of M. Savignoni, harbormaster at Ca-mau, indicates that in 1880 the port was visited by forty-five seagoing junks, most of eight hundred tons. Imports and exports for the year 1881 are summarized below.

Imported	Commodity	Value
From Kampot (in Cambodia)	tobacco lime for betel wood oil wooden boards watermelon sweet potatoes sugar nuoc mam areca nuts	$4,500
From China	peanut oil water jars ceramics furniture sugar hogs (for fattening and re-export)	$1,400
From Singapore	cotton fabric opium iron silk petrol dates	$1,700

Exported	Commodity	Value
To Kampot	mats wax (in blocks) dried fish	
To China	paddy	$2,800
To Singapore	fattened hogs rice* shrimp	$2,200
To Saigon	215 tank boats loaded with 2,000 piculs of fresh-water fish	

*Rice was by far the dominant commodity in the Singapore trade.
Source: "Rapport sur les cours d'eau de la presqu'île de Ca-mau" of Lieutenant M. Moreau, ER (1881).

Although hard data for subsequent years have not been found, a similar trade was maintained throughout the colonial period. The Mien Tay harbors, including that of Ca-mau, were an integral part of an ancient trading network involving China, Indochina, and the Malay archipelago. Despite the political upheavals of the twentieth century, some semblance of this trade endures even today.

APPENDIX 4

The Fiscal Standing of a Chinese Congregation in 1923

Bac-lieu, 4 November 1923
To M. the Governor of French Indochina at Saigon
Dear M. the Governor,

We, the undersigned, heads of the *congrégations* of Teochiu, Canton, Hainan, and Ca-mau, have the honor to submit respectfully to your distinguished attention the following collective petition asking the State not to increase the amount of tax levied upon the subjects of our *congrégations*.

The reasons for this request are as follows.

Prior to 1921, an increase in the poll tax had already been applied to Asian foreigners, in other words, our subjects and compatriots. It is difficult for them to pay all of the various [monetary] contributions required by the administration, which has always meant that we must cover certain deficits. This is particularly so for the *congrégations* of Teochiew [Teochiu]. They have the highest level of debt, for which they must expend several thousands of piasters in order to pay the taxes for the three to four hundred persons who disappear annually [from the *congrégation*]. As for the other *congrégations*, the amount comes to about a thousand piasters each year. The number of disappearances will not decrease if the authorities resort to increasing the amount of the tax again.

The reasons for many of the disappearances are as follows.

The majority of Chinese who come to Cochinchina do not work in the rice-processing industry. They are simple coolies, earning meager salaries that hardly sustain them. The others, unable to find work, are reduced to becoming small-time, itinerant merchants, which does not advance them far either. In order to meet the demands of the State, they are forced to take advances on their salaries. Finally, realizing that they cannot save enough money, despite their efforts and goodwill, the majority become desperate and save themselves by moving to another place, that is, to China.

We bring this matter to your distinguished attention, M. the Governor, in order to ask you to take our grievances into consideration.

Aware that it is in the interest of all that the administration possess sufficient funds, we would be the first to urge our compatriots to accept [their duty].

Moreover, with an increase in taxes, we could no longer hazard to guarantee, vis-à-vis the administration, the total sum of the contributions payable by our subjects, as we have previously. [In this case,] we would ask to serve the administration but without responsibility for meeting the taxes, which undoubtedly would be very high, representing a sum that we could not cover without putting ourselves in debt.

In the hope that you will respond to our respectful petition, please be so kind as to accept, M. the Governor, the expression of our dedication and appreciation.

[Signed] Leaders of four *congrégations*

Note: In a letter enclosed with this one, the provincial administrator noted to the governor of Cochinchina that the increase proposed for 1924 would do no more than put the amount of Bac-lieu's tax on a par with those of the other provinces, responding to economic necessity and not exceeding "the ability of the foreign Asians to pay."

Source: Bac-lieu, E.7923, Correspondence 1922, 1923, ANVN.

Appendix 5

....

Complaint of a Seizure of Harvest for Arrears on Debt, Ca-mau, 1933

23 February 1932
Ca-mau
To: Chairman, Chambre d'Agriculture de Cochinchine, Saigon
M. President,

Better than anyone, you are aware of the hard conditions under which we farm in Ca-mau, a backward place that suffered the depredations of two typhoons in 1929–30, each resulting in the loss of the harvest.

Consequent to these disasters, I was unable to pay my land taxes for 1929, 1930, and 1931. This year the administration seized the paddy not yet stored in my granaries.

Agents of the Garde Civile invaded my estate of Tan Loi (in Ca-mau) and requisitioned the heaps of sheaves. My neighbor's buffaloes, which had been lent to help with the harvest, have also been seized on the supposition that they are mine.

The harvest was disrupted because my tenants were frightened and ceased to work. . . .

I am known as an honorable man in Bac-lieu and Ca-mau where I have lived for twenty years. I am a French citizen and have made many sacrifices to raise my ten children, six of whom are very young. . . .

Given the present price of paddy, .5 piasters per *gia* at Ca-mau, I am not able to immediately pay four years of arrears in taxes.

It would have been possible, without disrupting the work on my land, to estimate the value of the crop [after the harvest was completed] and then sequester it.

Source: BCAC (February–March 1932): 110–11.

Abbreviations for Sources

AF	Asie Française
AG	Annales de Géographie
ANVN	Archives Nationales de la République du Vietnam
BAEI	Bulletin de l'Agence Economique de l'Indochine (in Saigon, now Ho Chi Minh City)
BAISS	Bulletin Agricole de l'Institut Scientifique de Saigon
BAVH	Bulletin des Amis du Vieux Huê
BCAC	Bulletin de la Chambre d'Agriculture de la Cochinchine
BCAF	Bulletin Commercial de l'Asie Française
BCAIC	Bulletin de Comité Agricole et Industriel de la Cochinchine
BEFEO	Bulletin de l'Ecole Française d'Extrême Orient
BEI	Bulletin Economique de l'Indochine
BIIEH	Bulletin de l'Institut Indochinois pour l'Etude de l'Homme
BSAF	Bulletin du Syndicat Agricole Français
BSEI	Bulletin de la Société des Etudes Indochinoises
BSG	Bulletin de la Société de Géographie
CAOM	Centre des Archives d'Outre-mer (Aix en Provence)
CEFEO	Cahiers de l'Ecole Française d'Extrême Orient
CHEAAM	Centre des Hautes Etudes sur l'Afrique et l'Asie Moderne (in Paris)
DC	La Dépêche Coloniale
EA	Extrême-Asie
EFEO	Ecole Française d'Extrême Orient
ER	Excursions et Reconnaissances
GCEIFI	Grand Conseil des Intérêts Economiques et Financiers de l'Indochine
JMBRAS	Journal of the Malayan Branch of the Royal Asiatic Society
MCI	Monde Colonial Illustré
RDM	Revue des Deux Mondes

RI	Revue Indochinoise
RIJE	Revue Indochinoise Juridique et Economique
RMC	Revue du Monde Colonial
RMEC	Revue Maritime et Coloniale
RP	Revue du Pacifique
SHAT	Service Historique de l'Armée de Terre (in Paris)
SLOTFOM	Service de Liaison avec les Originaires des Territoires Français d'Outre-mer
TDBCPNV	Toa Dai Bieu Chinh Phu Nam Viet

ENDNOTES

Preface

[1]Nam Bo means "the southern part of Vietnam." Here semantics have great political significance, for when the French conquered Luc Tinh (the Six Provinces) in the 1870s, they separated them from the kingdom of Vietnam and called them Cochinchina. In Vietnamese, the French renamed the region Nam Ky, which means "the southern country." The French thus set the linguistic basis for political severance by changing the name from *part* to *country*. When they later created the Autonomous Republic of Cochinchina, in 1946, its Vietnamese name became Nam Ky Cong Hoa, which can be translated as "the Republic of Nam Ky." The nationalists restored the idea of the region as a part of Vietnam by renaming it Nam Phan, meaning "the southern part," during Tran Trong Kim's regime, and Nam Bo under the Democratic Republic of Vietnam (Hoang Xuan Han, interview with the author, November 1992, Paris).

[2]K. Taylor, *The Birth of Vietnam* (Berkeley, 1983), 297–99.

[3]A notable exception is Carlyle Thayer, *War by Other Means: National Liberation and Revolution in Vietnam, 1954–1960* (London, 1989).

[4]Bui Huu Nghia, *Thoi cuoc* [*Events*], in *Tho Van Yeu nuoc* (Ho Chi Minh City, 1977), 193. Bui Huu Nghia (1807–72) was a nonconformist mandarin and poet of the delta who fought the French invasion. He is often evoked along with the blind poet Nguyen Dinh Chieu, the literatus Huynh Man Dat, and Phan Van Tri, all of whom refused to cooperate with the French authorities.

[5]Quoted by Dinh Van Lien, in *Tim hieu von van hoa zan toc Khmer Nam Bo* [To understand the essentials of the Khmer culture of Nam Bo] (Ho Chi Minh City, 1988), 66.

[6]See W. Ladejinsky, *Agrarian Reform as Unfinished Business* (Oxford, 1977), 309.

[7]See, for example, Son Nam, *Ca tinh cua Mien Nam* [The personality of South Vietnam] (Saigon, 1974); and, Son Nam, *Lich su khan hoang Mien Nam* [History of settlement in South Vietnam] (Saigon, 1973).

[8]Y. Henry, *L'économie agricole de l'Indochine* (Hanoi, 1932); P. Gourou, *L'utilisation des sols en Indochine* (Paris, 1940).

Chapter 1

[1]Thus, the lower basin is Cuu Long, Mekong, or Bassac. The central region is Mien Trung, Cisbassac, Tien Giang, or central Nam Bo. The western region is Mien Tay, Transbassac, Hau Giang, or western Nam Bo. The major tributaries of

the Mekong River, both of which flow through Nam Bo, are the Tien Giang, or Fleuve Antérieur; and the Hau Giang, or Fleuve Postérieur. Today the Vietnamese names of the tributaries are also the names of two provinces. Not long before the arrival of the French, Mien Tay had been divided into three provinces: Vinh-long, An-giang, and Ha-tien. The French altered this division in 1875 by creating five districts subdivided into *inspections*. The names and extent of the districts were modified several times thereafter. By a decree of 1912 the region was divided into six provinces: Chau-doc and Long-xuyen (which protrude into the central delta), Can-tho, Bac-lieu, Rach-gia, and Ha-tien. Later the district of Ca-mau was detached from Bac-lieu and three others were created: Soc-trang, Tra-vinh, and Sa-dec. Ultimately the surface area of Mien Tay officially came to encompass 26,300 of the 56,400 square kilometers in all of Cochinchina.

[2]This is according to the *monographies* (monographs) of Long-xuyen, Can-tho, and Chau-doc provinces, published by the Société des Etudes Indochinoises (Saigon, 1901–8); and by *La Revue Indochinoise* (Saigon, 1907). Copies are housed in the ANVN.

[3]*Monographie de Bac-lieu* (1937), ANVN.

[4]In one example, litigation arose in 1920 between an individual, Nguyen Van Lang, and the French administration. In 1907, Lang had acquired a parcel of forty hectares located by a stream in the province of Chau-doc but as a result of alluvial desposits his land had increased considerably. This occurred with such rapidity that by 1914 the accumulation represented an expansion of six hectares. The dispute arose because the administration denied Lang ownership of the additional area (Minutes of the Colonial Council, 2d session, 28 March 1920, BCAC, 1920). See also A. Bonnaud, "Etude sur les voies navigables de la Cochinchine," ER (1881); and M. Moreau, "Les cours d'eau de la presqu'île de Ca-mau," ER (1881).

[5]L. Malleret, *L'Archéologie du delta du Mékong* (Paris, 1959–63).

[6]E. Bruzon and P. Carton, *Le Climat de l'Indochine et les typhons de la mer de Chine* (Hanoi, 1930); Y. Henry and M. Devismes, *Documents de démographie et de riziculture en Indochine* (Hanoi, 1928).

[7]During a crisis in May 1926, for example, in the province of Bac-lieu, water sold for twelve centimes per *touque* (eighteen liters). At Ca-mau it sold for fifteen centimes, the sellers having to draw it at Poulo Obi (twenty miles from the coast) or from the headwaters of the rivers. Boatmen brought it in the same boats that served to transport charcoal (BCAC, January 1932). At Soc-trang, each day at 5 o'clock in the afternoon, the subdivisional agent of the Public Works locked the public wells. The same year a man named Mechin, an engineer, described a visit to a village: "At the village of Tan Hung, on the Song Bay Hap, we visited a few straw huts: most of the men had left in sampans to look for water at a village 30 kilometers away, where it had rained the day before. In the jars there remained only a few liters of water containing 234, 1,735, and even 3,500 milligrams of chlorine per liter" (A. Mechin, "Le problème de l'alimentation en eau en Cochinchine," BEI, no. 184 (1927).

[8]M. Le Louet, "Note sur le barbone en Cochinchine," BAISS, no. 8 (August 1921).

[9]According to E. Lefeuvre, "Etude des terres de la Cochinchine," BSEI (1903); R. Auriol and Lam Van Lang, "Etude sur les eaux et terres alunées," BCAC

(no. 278, 1934); P. Bussy, "Etude agricole des terres de la Cochinchine," BAISS (1920); and Henry and Devismes, *Documents de démographie.*

[10]A. Henry, *Etude sur les forêts de la Cochinchine* (Saigon, 1891).

[11]M. Dugros, "La mangrove et l'arrière-mangrove," *Asie Nouvelle* (February/April/June 1936); M. Dugros, "Le domaine forestier inondé de la Cochinchine," BEI (1937); *Monographie de Bac-lieu* (1937), ANVN.

[12]A. Brière, "Rapport sur la circonscription de Ca-mau," *Excursions et Reconnaissances* 1 (1879):17.

[13]Thoai Ngoc Hau, cited in the *Monographie de Long-xuyen,* BSEI (1928). One *tam* is 8 feet or 2.25 meters.

[14]*Monographie de Bac-lieu* (1937), ANVN; *Monographie de Chau-doc* (1937), ANVN.

[15]Ibid.

[16]Minutes of the Provincial Council, sessions of 1907 and 1910, ANVN.

[17]"I have been speaking of the fevers; they begin to rage when the rain has sufficiently moistened the soil to release the miasma and not moistened it enough to drown them. They are paludal in character and are mortal for an anemic constitution" (extract from a report to the administrator of Bac-lieu (21 January 1898, Bac-lieu, E.12, dossier 51, ANVN).

[18]Brière, "Rapport sur la circonscription."

[19]Ibid.

[20]Thoai Ngoc Hau, quoted in the *Monographie de Long-xuyen,* BSEI (1928).

[21]Quoted from D. Chandler, *A History of Cambodia* (Boulder, 1983), 14–15.

[22]For more on the ancient history of the area, see L. Malleret, *L'Archéologie du delta du Mékong,* 4 vols. (Paris, 1959–63); and R. Smith and W. Watson, eds., *Early South East Asia* (Oxford, 1979).

[23]For a history of the Chinese immigrants, see *Gia dinh Thanh Thong Chi;* P. Boudet, "La conquêt de la Cochinchine et le rôle des émigrés chinois," BEFEO 42 (1943); and E. Gaspardonne, "Un Chinois des Mers du sud: le fondateur de Hatien," *Journal Asiatique* (1952): 2. See also *Monographie de Ha-tien* (1937), ANVN.

[24]E. Deschaseaux, "Note sur les anciens don dien annamites de la Basse Cochinchine," ER (1889); Son Nam, *Lich su khan,* 98–104.

[25]Nguyen Tri Phuong was a great mandarin of the Court of Hue who distinguished himself in the war against the Siamese and the French. He was one of the conquerors of Mien Tay where he founded many settlements.

[26]Son Nam, *Lich su khan,* 64–65.

[27]A. Woodside, *Vietnam and the Chinese Model: A Comparative Study of Vietnamese and Chinese Government in the First Half of the Nineteenth Century* (Cambridge, Mass., 1971).

[28]Chandler, *History of Cambodia,* 123–31.

[29]Son Nam, *Lich su khan,* 104.

[30]Ibid., 108.

[31]Quoted in Nguyen Dinh Dau, "Thu tim hieu dat nuoc va zan toc qua 10,044 tap dia bo" [To understand our country and nation through 10,044 land registers], *Tap Chi Khoa Hoc* (Hanoi) 4 (1988).

[32]French soldiers were rarely sent into the fighting because of the hardships of

the climate. Most of the repression was accomplished by *ma ta* (policemen). In 1880, to fight the insurgency led by Mai Xuan Thuong, Tran Ba Loc mobilized 1,050 *ma ta* (Son Nam, *Lich su khan*, 143).

[33]Hue Tam Ho Tai, *Millenarianism and Peasant Politics in Vietnam* (Cambridge, Mass., 1983), 20, 43.

[34]Son Nam, *Ca tinh cua;* Son Nam, *Lich su khan*, 1; Hue Tam Ho Tai, *Millenarianism*, chap. 3.

[35]Son Nam, *Lich su khan*, 141.

[36]Quoted, respectively, from Governor to Ministry of Colonies, 15 May 1878, CAOM, Indochine, A 30 (21); and Son Nam, *Lich su khan*, 141–42. See also M. Osborne, *The French Presence in Cochinchina and Cambodia: Rule and Response, 1859–1905* (Ithaca, 1969).

[37]Ibid., 68–69; Son Nam, *Lich su khan*, 144. Son Nam reports that Loc owned the island of Nam Thon. Like most of his countrymen, Son Nam believes that collaboration with the French was a stepping stone to the acquisition of land for some Vietnamese. But one must also consider Osborne's thesis that the principal collaborators were already important landowners who cooperated in order to safeguard their wealth (Osborne, *French Presence*, chap. 6).

Chapter 2

[1]Quoted, respectively, from H. Bineteau, "Divisions territoriales et agricoles par provinces," BSG (1864):69; and L. de Grammont, "Notice sur la Basse Cochinchine," BSG (1864):9.

[2]Lt. de Bonneaud, *Etude sur les voies navigables de Cochinchine* (CAOM, Indochine, V100–5, C.306, 1879).

[3]A. Pouyanne, "Les dragages de Cochinchine et l'inauguration du Canal Rachgia-Hatien," EA (1930); A. Pouyanne, *Les voies d'eau de la Cochinchine*, 2 vols. (Saigon, 1911).

[4]Arrondissement Council of Ha-tien, 3d session, 4 March 1905, ANVN.

[5]*Monographie de Long-xuyen* (1907).

[6]According to Pouyanne, "Voies d'eau."

[7]Colonial Council, 6th session, 30 September 1929.

[8]Rear Admiral Lagrandière to the Minister of the Colonies, 30 April 1863 (CAOM, Indochine, M.00 I, carton 233).

[9]"Statistiques de la population de Cochinchine, 1906–1908" (CAOM, Indochine, G01–06, carton 3).

[10]H. Brenier, in "Essai d'atlas statistique de l'Indochine française" (Hanoi, 1914), has enumerated the principal difficulties encountered by the French in establishing a registry office and conducting a census: fiscal aversion, which was the main obstacle; feelings of intrusion; complicated degrees of relationship; and, in many cases, the existence of several names for one individual.

[11]Economic depressions could play a part in such migrations. For example, according to the "Rapport sur la situation économique en 1919" (CAOM, Indochine, NF 1516), poverty and high prices affecting agricultural workers resulted in emigration from the provinces of Ben-tre, Go-cong, Tan-an, and My-tho to the provinces of Bac-lieu, Rach-gia, and Soc-trang.

[12]These figures are taken from *Annuaire de Cochinchine* and *Annuaire général de l'Indochine* for the years cited.

[13]"Dossiers des engagés de Rach-gia, 1915" (ANVN); "Dossiers des engagés de Bac-lieu, 1920" (ANVN).

[14]*Annuaire de Cochinchine* (1886); *Annuaire général de l'Indochine* (1901).

[15]H. Jammes, *Au pays d'Annam* (Paris, 1900), 64.

[16]Extract of a memorandum from M. Boudineau to all colonists, dated 25 September 1918 (Dossiers divers, ANVN).

[17]M. Guery to the Chamber of Agriculture of Cochinchina, 18 May 1900, reproduced in BCAC (1900):521.

[18]Speech of the Governor of Cochinchina to the Colonial Council, 5 December 1918, in *Procès-verbaux du Conseil Colonial de la Cochinchine*.

[19]*Report to the Conseil Colonial* (Saigon, 1881), 10 (pamphlet).

[20]*Courrier Saigonnais*, 18 March 1904. A. Schreiner, a publicist and writer of Alsatian origin, spent twenty-six years in Indochina (1885–1911). He was a surveyor for the cadastral survey, founded the newspaper *Nam Ky* (in a bilingual edition), and collaborated on the *Courrier Saigonnais*. In 1903, he was named director of the Land Registry for Cochinchina, and later served as a professor of land surveying at Chasseloup-Laubat College.

[21]V. Purcell, *The Chinese in South East Asia* (Oxford, 1951), 192.

[22]*Tribune Indochinoise*, 11 April 1927.

[23]Memorandum from the Governor of Cochinchina to the chief administrators of the provinces, no. 255, reproduced in BCAC (1922):206–7.

[24]Administrator of Bac-lieu to Joseph Phuoc (ANVN). Phuoc was a colonist at Dai Ngai.

[25]G. Aubaret, *Histoire et description de la Basse Cochinchine* (Paris, 1883), 18 (translation of Trinh Hoai Duc, *Gia Dinh Thanh Thong Chi*). See also Son Nam, *Lich su khan.*

[26]For the domanial legislation, see A. Schreiner, *Les institutions annamite en Basse Cochinchine avant la conquête française*, 3 vols. (Saigon, 1900–1902); and A. Boudillon, *Le régime de la propriété foncière en Indochine* (Paris, 1915).

[27]Syndicat Agricole, meeting of 30 August 1917, described in the *Courrier de l'Ouest*, 20 September 1917.

[28]After retiring from the administration, Le Bret became a colonist of the West. He was quoted in ibid., 17 January 1918.

[29]He set forth a grandiose plan for this in a pamphlet, *Appel à la colonisation* (Paris, 1895), 68.

[30]Speech by P. Paris, 21 November 1897, Chamber of Agriculture, 1st session, reproduced in BCAC (1897):14. These opinions are actually isolated and quite unusual. Since the beginning of the conquest, the French had judged the climate of Cochinchina to be murderous to Europeans.

[31]A. Schreiner, in *Courrier Saigonnais*, 18 March 1904.

[32]Minutes of the 65th meeting of the Chamber of Agriculture, session of 20 March 1903, reproduced in ibid. (1903).

[33]P. Paris, *Le colon et l'administration en Cochinchine* (Saigon, 1896). The situation of a European colonist in Cochinchina was similar to that of concessionaires in Tonkin. J. Morel, in *Les concessions de terre au Tonkin* (Paris, 1912), stresses the

abusive inequality that marred relations between colonists and tenants (pp. 227–28).

34 *Tribune Indochinoise*, 8 September 1926.

35 BCAC, issues of 1901 and 1913.

36 Colonial Council, session of 22 December 1894.

37 Lieutenant Governor Rodier to the Minister of the Colonies, 1 May 1895 (CAOM, Indochine, F 21[3], carton 108).

38 Records of the Assembly of the Comité du Syndicat, 30 April 1900 (CAOM, Indochine, M 10[2], carton 233).

39 See, for example, a memorandum of the governor general, dated 10 June 1904, which appeared in the *Bulletin Officiel de la Cochinchine* (1904), 462.

40 See Ph. Grandjean, *Le statut légal des missions catholiques et protestantes en Indochine française* (Paris, 1939); and J. Caratini, *Le statut des missions en Indochine* (Hanoi and Paris, 1941).

41 See "Report on the Economic Situation of Indochina for the Year 1918" (CAOM, Indochine, NF 1516, carton 206).

42 *Courrier Saigonnais*, 27 April 1907.

43 For 1926, see the *Tribune Indochinoise*, 25 February 1927; for 1931, see Robequain, *L'évolution économique de l'Indochine française* (Paris, 1939).

44 For Bac-lieu, see various statistics for 1918 housed in the ANVN. For Long-xuyen, see Economic Report (CAOM, Indochine, NF 1516).

45 Later, in the province of Bac-lieu in 1937, rice was cultivated by Europeans on 61,116 hectares, of which 38,961 were under cultivation. Of these, 37,409 hectares belonged to estates larger than 100 hectares and 16,828 belonged to estates larger than 500 hectares. Three estates were larger than 1,000 hectares, and one of these was 5,200 hectares according to Robequain, *L'évolution économique*, 214.

46 According to the inquiry of Boudillon.

47 A. Boudillon, speech of September 1927, Colonial Council.

48 Intervention of Le Quang Liem at the 4th session of the Colonial Council, 31 August 1927.

49 Operations of the boundary commissions were described by Ngo Van Huan, an administrative deputy in 1918 for Gia Rai, in the *Tribune Indochinoise*, 14 September 1928.

50 L. Malleret recounts a misfortune of this kind that struck some Cambodians of Rach-gia Province (see BSEI, vol. 21 [1946]).

51 Le Quang Liem, in the Colonial Council, 6th session, 3 November 1937. See also appendix 2, this volume.

52 *Courrier de l'Ouest*, 30 August 1917.

53 A. Schreiner, *Le livre foncier* (Saigon 1904), 9–10.

54 Ibid., 22–23.

55 In 1934, R. Dumont compared these procedures with those adopted in the delta of the north. See R. Dumont, *La culture du riz dans le delta du Tonkin* (Paris, 1934), 49.

56 *La Voix Annamite,* 15 November 1924.

57 *Tribune Indochinoise*, issues of June and October 1927.

58 *L'Appel*, 10 December 1927.

59 *Tribune Indochinoise*, 25 November 1927.

[60]Ibid.

[61]Inquiry of Le Trung Nghia, in *Tribune Indochinoise*, 30 April 1928.

[62]Extract from the court reporter's shorthand transcript of the trial, published in the *Courrier Saigonnais*, 24 August 1928.

[63]Gourou, *L'utilisation des sols*, 272.

[64]Y. Henry, *L'économie agricole en Indochine* (Hanoi, 1932).

[65]Cited in ibid., 158–59.

[66]*Monographie de Ha-tien* (1937), 129 (ANVN).

[67]In the nineteenth century the emperor Minh Mang, perhaps renewing an ancient practice, had dictated the allotment of communal village lands to the indigent or the weak (such as widows and orphans) and to other deserving subjects. Thus, the *cong dien* served as the instrument of social security for the villagers. Minh Mang went even further in the south where there was much unoccupied land. There, in 1840, asserting an edict of 1804, he required the richest landowners to cede part of their holdings to the villages in order to form *cong dien* (the ordinance of the third month of the twenty-first year of the reign "confiscated" 3/10 of the private property of the province of Gia-dinh). This measure was taken not as a response to demographic pressure but as an application of the fundamental principles of government inspired by Confucianism, in which economic disparities are seen as the source of disorder. Breaking with tradition, Minh Mang abolished the practice of distributing *cong dien* according to social status. Nonetheless, the emperor's legal provisions and Confucian principles were subject to encroachments by landowners (see Vu Van Hien, *Communal Property in Tonkin: A Contribution to the Historical, Judicial, and Economic Study of Cong Dien and Cong Tho in Annam* (New Haven, 1955).

[68]A. Landes, "La commune annamite," ER, no. 3 (1880):105.

[69]Henry, *L'économie agricole*; Gourou, *L'utilisation des sols*. However, when the French arrived, the concept of collective property was still entrenched in the West. In fact, the assembly of the villages of the *arrondissement* of Can-tho, summoned for consultation by Admiral Ohier, expressed itself very clearly on this point: "It is worth noting that some *arrondissements*, Rach-gia and Soc-trang, for example, are, from the land point of view, in a very special situation. Their villages are composed exclusively of communal lands and do not include a single landowner" (Dossier "Assemblée des villages de Cantho," 1869, ANVN). See also R. Pinto, "Les assemblées des villages convogées par l'admiral gouverneur Ohier," BSEI, 1st trimester (1944).

[70]Colonial Council, discussion session of 28 September 1917.

[71]It was also argued that such an endowment would reduce the need to raise village taxes. See Colonial Council, 2d session, 3 March 1925.

[72]Colonial Council, 4th session, 3 August 1927.

[73]*Tribune Indochinoise*, 2 June 1930.

[74]Cited in ibid., 20 June 1930.

[75]Henry, *L'économie agricole*. Even in Chau-doc, only 50 landowners out of 2,979 had entered into contracts with sharecroppers in 1929 (ibid., 157).

[76]Ibid., 55. These intermediaries also had a bad reputation in Tonkin (see Dumont, *La culture du riz*, 55).

[77]Henry, *L'économie agricole*.

[78]Ibid.; Gourou, *L'utilisation des sols.*
[79]Ibid.

Chapter 3

[1]On 24 November 1880, in Le Myre de Vilers, *Les institutions civiles de la Cochinchine, 1879–1881* (Paris, 1908), 140.

[2]Record of a general report by the governor of Cochinchina for the period 1902–7 (ANVN). As late as 1931, the warnings were still being sounded: "It is nevertheless essential not to hide the fact that the rapid development of Cochinchina, which has caused you to foster, and indeed has justified, brilliant hopes, is vulnerable to serious damage because it seems to rest on only a single crop" (Minister of the Colonies Jaureguiberry to the Governor of Cochinchina, reproduced in the *Courrier Saigonnais*, 4 July 1931).

[3]A. Normandin, "Rapport sur les travaux d'hydrographie agricole à étudier et entreprendre en Cochinchine," BCAC, no. 143 (April-May 1913).

[4]J. Biard, in BEI (March 1947); J. Benabenq, "Note sur l'hydraulique agricole," BAISS (October 1920).

[5]Report of Inspector of Agriculture Magen, published in BCAC (1910). Another observer noted, however, that "the agricultural function of the canals remained in the background; or rather it was considered that this situation could be improved rapidly through the efforts of the landowners. The latter could, it was said, by easily executed works, extend into the heart of their estates the beneficial action of the tides moving through the canals. . . . In fact, the action of the tides still only benefits small areas of rice land which lie along certain principal canals" (Robequain, *L'évolution économique*, 245–46).

[6]"Enquête sur le matériel agricole en Cochinchine en 1926," BEI (1927); Henry, *L'économie agricole.*

[7]L. H. Jammes, *Au pays d'Annam*, BSEI, 4th fasc. (1897), 5.

[8]BCAC (1909):235.

[9]Tran Nguon Hanh, "Rapport concernant les divers travaux agricoles," BCAIC (1876).

[10]See, for example, G. Hickey, *Village in Vietnam* (New Haven, 1964), 136. For more on this plough, see Magen, "Extrait d'un rapport," BEI (1921); and J. Delvert, *Le paysan cambodgien* (Paris and The Hague, 1963).

[11]American anthropologist G. C. Hickey recorded oral histories on this subject in a village situated between Tan An and Saigon (see Hickey, *Village in Vietnam*). "Enquête sur le matériel agricole" reported the existence in the provinces of Soc-trang and Chau-doc of an implement that was actually the Cambodian plough. Its design was identical to that described by Delvert in *Le paysan cambodgien*. The descriptions diverge on only one point: the "Enquête" describes a prop on the plough while Delvert states that there was no prop.

[12]This description is drawn from Henry and Devismes, *Documents de démographie*; Y. Coyaud, "Le riz"; and A. Coquerel, *Les paddys et riz de Cochinchine* (Lyon, 1911). On floating rice, see Tran Van Huu, "Note sur la culture du riz flottant en Cochinchine," BAISS (February 1920). Huu corrects the assertion of Pauchont that the threshing was done on flooded ground.

[13]G. Garros, *Les usages de la Cochinchine* (Saigon, 1905), 190.

[14]Ibid.

[15]On 1 March 1915, Dang Tan Dieu, a teacher at the canton school of Cai Von, wrote the following to the chief administrator of the province of Can-tho: "I have the honor of informing you that school begins again today at the normal time. The pupils who are currently attending the school number thirty-eight. The number of pupils will increase to a hundred after the rice harvest" (Can-tho E., Public Education, ANVN).

[16]Henry, *L'économie agricole*, 49–51.

[17]Report of Magen, BCAC (1910).

[18]Response of the administrator of Bac-lieu, minute 1252, 30 December 1869, ANVN.

[19]The popular literature confirmed the use of fertilizers. One common saying had it that *ruong khong phan nhu than khong cua* [A paddy field without manure is like a person without assets]. Other proverbs are to be found in Duong Dinh Khue, *La littérature populaire vietnamienne* (Saigon, 1968), 45. Dumont, in *La culture du riz*, also mentions *nhut nuoc, nhi phan, ba can, bon giong* [First water, second fertilizer, third effort, fourth seeds].

[20]The story is related in Tran Van Huu, "Note sur la culture du riz." The variety was known as Hue-ky, or Hoa-ky, meaning "the United States."

[21]Chamber of Agriculture, session of 21 April 1899, reproduced in BCAC (1899):270.

[22]Session of 24 February 1899, ibid., 205.

[23]Ibid., 206.

[24]Report of the administrator of Can-tho Province, 5 April 1910, reproduced in BCAC, no. 118 (April 1910).

[25]BCAC (June 1932):321.

[26]Garros, *Usages de la Cochinchine*. The *Tribune Indochinoise*, 13 February 1931, gives the same prices.

[27]Colonial Council, 5th session, 2 September 1927.

[28]According to Magen, "Extrait d'un rapport"; and BAISS (February and August 1920).

[29]Colonial Council, 3d session, 10 October 1924.

[30]*Revue Indochinoise* (1927).

[31]BCAC (1909):568.

[32]President of the Chamber of Agriculture of Cochinchina, in BCAC, no. 117 (March 1910):75.

[33]Magen, "La monoculture aux colonies," BAISS (March 1920).

[34]According to the BCAC (October 1932):542.

[35]Rear Admiral Lagrandière, "Commerce de la Basse-Cochinchine," 1 January 1864 (CAOM, Indochine, no. 1[3], C236).

[36]On milling and commerce, see Henry, *L'économie agricole*; A. Coquerel, *Les paddys et riz*; and P. Estebe, *Le problème du riz en Indochine* (Toulouse, 1934).

[37]*L'Opinion*, 18 August 1934.

[38]One picul of paddy is the equivalent of sixty kilograms.

[39]The most common boats in the West were the *ca vom*. Poujade writes: "The *ca vom* are very widespread in all of western Nam Bo, in general those which trans-

port charcoal go up to Saigon, those with rice transfer the cargo to junks" (*Pirogues et ca vom de l'Ouest cochinchinois* [Saigon, 1946]).

⁴⁰Estebe, *Le problème du riz.*

⁴¹Various documents of the province of Bac-lieu, housed in ANVN.

⁴²Lagrandière, "Commerce de la Basse-Cochinchine."

⁴³The interrogation of a Chinese accused of membership in a secret society known as Heaven and Earth is revealing of the business and family connections that united them. Linh Cu, a miller of paddy in Bac-lieu, possessed six mortars and employed seven coolies. For his business he borrowed from his cousin who was registered as a rice broker at Cholon. He also rented a boat with a capacity of 150 piculs from this cousin, at the rate of thirty piasters per month. This miller took payment in fabric, which he resold (CAOM, Indochine, NF 445, carton 31, 1883).

⁴⁴Colonial Council, ordinary session, 1907.

⁴⁵ Magen, "Rapport d'inspection d'avril 1909," BCAC (1910).

⁴⁶In Nam Bo, Mien Tay occupied a special niche. Recently settled, from the economic point of view it had not had time to integrate itself within the national whole. Prior to French development most of its trade was with the Indianized states of Cambodia and the Malaysian region, and with Hai Nam and Hong Kong in China.

⁴⁷J. Chesneaux, *L'Asie orientale aux XIXe et XXe siècles* (Paris, 1973), 248. Chesneaux was comparing the traditional and modern capitalist sectors of the colony.

⁴⁸Another question was posed by Chesneaux (ibid.) on the subject of the role of the colonial currency as an instrument of domination wielded by the colonizing interests: who benefits from an expensive piaster and who benefits from a cheap piaster?

⁴⁹On credit and usury, see G. Khérian, "La position du problème du crédit," RIJE (1941):1, 2; and Henry, *L'économie agricole.*

⁵⁰On the *dien mai*, see Vu Van Mau, "Le dien mai et le nantissement immobilier," RIJE (1940):2.

⁵¹On the Chinese merchants and moneylenders, see Robequain, *L'évolution économique;* Estebe, *Le problème du riz;* P. Bernard, *Le problème économique indochinois* (Paris, 1934); Henry, *L'économie agricole;* and Khérian, "La position du problème."

⁵²Various dossiers (ANVN).

⁵³See G. Dürrwell, *Ma chère Cochinchine: Trente années d'impressions et de souvenirs, 1881–1910* (Paris, 1910); and Bernard, *Le problème économique.*

⁵⁴The *chetty* method for forcing debtors to repay their loans was, in certain respects, analogous to the technique common in the countryside of northern Vietnam, the *khach no* or *nac no.* See Dumont, *La culture du riz,* 68; and P. de Feyssal, *L'endettement agraire en Cochinchine* (Hanoi, 1933).

⁵⁵See P. Bernard, *Le problème économique,* which cites figures for the period 1901–30 (pp. 111–14). A typical case of usury is cited on page 61. See also de Feyssal, *L'endettement agraire en Cochinchine.*

⁵⁶P. Melin, *L'endettement agraire en Indochine* (Paris, 1939), 64, 1n.

⁵⁷P. D'Enjoy, *La colonisation de la Cochinchine* (Paris, 1898), 38.

⁵⁸Letter dated 21 December 1916, CAOM, Indochine, N 20 (3), C.242.

[59]Concerning interest rates, see Bernard, *Le problème économique*, de Feyssal, *L'endettement agraire en Cochinchine*, and Henry, *L'économie agricole*.

[60]Cao Van Cuu, personal communication. It is certainly to this system that Bernard refers when he writes that: "advances in kind, after having been favored by the large landowners during the increase in paddy prices, tended to become more parsimonious after the prices for this cereal collapsed" (*Le problème économique*, 8, n.1).

[61]Ch. Leonardi, "L'usure en Cochinchine," *Extrême-Asie* 5 (1926):229.

[62]See W. Oualid, *Le privilège de la Banque de l'Indochine et la question des banques coloniales* (Paris, 1923), 89, 92.

[63]Postal note, dated 9 January 1912 (no. 22, "Records of Loans Secured on Harvests," Bac-lieu, 1912, ANVN).

[64]"Records of Loans Secured on Harvests," Ha-tien, 1880–81 (ANVN).

[65]"Records of Loans Secured on Harvests," Rach-gia, 1907, 1908, 1910, 1911 (ANVN).

[66]J. Queinnec, *Les prêts sur récoltes en Cochinchine, Annam, Tonkin* (Paris, 1930).

[67]Letter to the Lieutenant Governor (ANVN).

[68]Note of the administrator of Rach-gia in the margin of a letter from the *cai tong* of Thanh Giang, dated 13 April 1907 ("Records of Loans Secured on Harvests," Rach-gia, 1907, ANVN). E. Outrey, lieutenant governor of Cochinchina, justified this interpretation when he wrote to the chief of the province of Rach-gia that the mayor and the *notables* were jointly responsible for deficits in the collection and payment of taxes and also responsible for loan requests made to the bank (Rach-gia, E.3, ANVN).

[69]Huynh Xuan Canh, *Le crédit indochinois: essai sur l'organisation du crédit en Indochine* (Paris, 1929), 14.

[70]See letter from the Annamite *conseillers coloniaux* to the president of the Colonial Council (session of 15 December 1885), which was published as a pamphlet in Saigon in 1886.

[71]Extract from the report of the administrator of Bac-lieu Province, reproduced in BCAC (1913):100.

[72]Oualid concluded that the credit provided by the Banque de l'Indochine "is above all meant for the European clientele. . . . Agriculture benefits from hardly one-tenth of the credit facilities of the bank. Of this tenth, half goes to Europeans and half to natives. But, while the former obtain more than 9 million in advances against about 1,200,000 francs discounted, the latter only receive 1,200,000 in advances for 10 million francs discounted and loans secured on the harvest. Normal means of credit for them are nearly unknown" (*Le privilège de la Banque*, 108).

[73]Letter to the Lieutenant Governor, minute no. 354, 1 May 1909, folder: Banque de Cochinchine (ANVN). This folder, in fact, contains only the one letter. To my knowledge the only author who has drawn attention to the Banque de Cochinchine to date is A. Sabès, in *Le renouvellement du privilège de la Banque de l'Indochine* (Paris, 1931). He imputes the failure of this establishment to the competition of Chinese lenders; the agricultural chaos that hindered effective guarantees; and the fact that "one could not, without danger, lend a native more than his income, and it was impossible to ask him to repay annually more than a tenth of his

income if one wanted to attain the real aim of the advances on harvests, that is, to allow the native to improve his cultivation without having recourse to the very expensive aid of the Chinese or Annamite lenders. Thus it was necessary to reckon on about fifteen years for the repayment of an advance and the interest involved. One sees what amount of capital [would be] tied up for some length of time and what circulating capital it would be necessary for a bank to put into these sorts of operations" (p. 118).

[74]Lieutenant Governor Rodier, "Discours au Conseil Colonial, session ordinaire" (1907).

[75]For the SICAMs, see Henry, *L'économie agricole*; Huynh Xuan Canh, *Le crédit indochinois*; and a pamphlet, *Le crédit agricole mutuel en Cochinchine en 1934* (Saigon, 1934).

[76]On the SICAM, see Estebe, *Le problème du riz*; and issues of the *Bulletin du Syndicat Agricole Français* (1930–38).

[77]*Courrier Saigonnais*, 11 August 1930.

[78]De Feyssal, *L'endettement agraire en Cochinchine*, 46.

[79]M. Rivoal, Confidential report on agricultural credit in Cochinchina, 24 September 1942, no. 2029-C (ANVN).

[80]*Tribune Indochinoise*, 18 June 1934.

[81]For example, on 31 December 1934, there were 1,421 SICAM members in Bac-lieu alone but only 5,974 in the seven provinces of the West (*Le crédit agricole mutuel en Cochinchine en 1934*, table 1). The distribution by province was: Bac-lieu, 809; Can-tho, 1,421; Chau-doc, 373; Ha-tien, 211; Long-xuyen, 1,157; Rach-gia, 1,242; and Soc-trang, 761.

[82]*Monographie de Ha-tien* (1937), ANVN.

[83]*Le Progrès Annamite*, 7 April 1928.

[84]Memorandum no. 135, Governor of Cochinchina to the Chiefs of the Provinces, 30 May 1924, reproduced in BCAC, no. 200 (July 1924).

[85]Bernard, *Le problème économique*, 79.

[86]De Feyssal, *L'endettement agraire en Cochinchine*.

[87]Revenue from salt and opium ranged from 40 to 29 percent of the general budget between 1899 and 1920 but diminished to 18 percent by 1930. In 1935, it was 19 percent, and in 1938 it was16 percent (J. Dumarest, *Les Monopoles de l'opium et du sel en Indochine* [Lyon, 1938], 7).

[88]One could say the same about the diet of the Khmer peasant, for fish was the source of *pra hoc*. Delvert described this as a kind of fish paste, the "national food for the peasant . . . a paste of pinkish color, [with] a very strong odor . . . the juice for its preparation is used like *nuoc mam*" (*Le paysan cambodgien*, 150).

[89]"It's at Rach-gia that one can see the most rudimentary seagoing boats in all of Indochina. They are built of the minimum number of pieces for making a planked boat, and seem to represent the cultural stage immediately superior to the elevated pirogue but below the level of the completely planked boats. . . . These boats are used for fishing in the shallow waters of the Gulf" (Poujade, *Pirogues et ca vom*, 5).

[90]Ibid.

[91]Brière, "Rapport sur la circonscription."

[92]*Monographie de Chau-doc* (1937), ANVN.

[93]*Monographie de Ha-tien* (1937), ANVN. *Mam ruoc* is a paste made of crushed shrimp and salt. Almost all of the substantial output of Duong Dong (on the island of Phu Quoc) was exported to Siam and Singapore. The *mam ruoc* of Phu Quoc, famous throughout Indochina, was described by the author of the *Monographie*. He wrote that better organization would be needed, however, "to permit the producer to free himself of Chinese intermediaries who, without risk, keep the greatest part of the profits for themselves" (p. 188).

[94]Provincial Council of Ha-tien, 2d session, 6 November 1922, ANVN.

[95]Ibid.

[96]Governor of Cochinchina to the Minister of the Navy and the Colonies, 8 November 1887, CAOM, Indochine, M90 (1), C.235.

[97]Decree of the Governor General, 28 June 1922.

[98]"An attempt at trawling undertaken in 1921–22 by a Saigon firm yielded no result and it does not appear that it will be repeated soon. . . . At the present time, for fishing on the high seas with ordinary junks, which is the first step toward the industrialization of fishing . . . there is no Indochinese boat practicing it. The only junks exploiting the sea shelves are Chinese or even Japanese boats manned by Chinese from Hainan or Japanese from Singapore and provided with English fishing licenses" (*Monographie de Ha-tien* [1937], ANVN).

[99]Dumarest, *Les monopoles*, 173.

[100]Ibid.

[101]Ibid.; *Monographie de Bac-lieu* (1937), ANVN.

[102]Decree of 10 November 1930, reproduced in Dumarest, *Les monopoles*, 238–40; Decree of 14 December 1931, reproduced in ibid. Payments were fixed for three years.

[103]M. Dugros, in *Asie Nouvelle*, 29 February 1936; M. Dugros, in EA, 29 February 1936, and 30 April 1936.

[104]Decree of 2 January 1931, paras. 51, 56, 57.

[105]Decree of the Governor General, 13 June 1915.

[106] M. Dugros, in EA, 30 June 1936.

[107]*Monographie de Ha-tien* (1937), ANVN.

[108]Ibid.

[109]Governor General Paul Doumer, economic report of 30 November 1897, CAOM, Indochine, no. 1(11), C.237.

[110]Report of the *huyen* of Hon-chong, reproduced in BCAC (1909):255.

[111]*Monographie de Ha-tien* (1937), ANVN.

[112]Although M. Guillaume (in BEI [1925]:274) claimed that there was nothing to this, and that the Chinese were ignorant of "the first word about cultivation," this seems improbable.

[113]A. Chevalier, "Le poivrier et sa culture en Indochine" (Paris, 1925); Biard, in BEI (1942).

[114]BCAC (September 1913).

[115]Arrondissement Council of Ha-tien, Record of Deliberations (ANVN).

[116]Ibid., session of 27 February 1909.

[117]Ibid., session of 5 March 1910.

[118] *Tribune Indochinoise*, 12 January 1927.

[119]See Delvert, *Le paysan cambodgien.*

[120]Son Nam, *Tim hieu dat Hau Giang* (Saigon, 1959), 41, 1n.

[121]BCAC (October 1931).

[122]Speech by Vo Hieu De, published in the *Courrier Saigonnais*, 11 August 1930.

[123]Minutes of the meetings of the Arrondissement Council of Ha-tien, 1906, 1910, and 1917 (ANVN).

[124] *Tribune Indochinoise*, 23 August 1926.

[125] *L'Appel*, 31 May 1924.

[126]Les Galeries de l'Ouest, economic report, 1918, CAOM, Indochine, NF 1516.

[127] *Courrier Saigonnais*, 11 August 1930.

Chapter 4

[1]Le Myre de Vilers, *Institutions civiles*, 140.

[2]"On the whole, without the will, and even against its secret desire, the white colonization in Indochina has led to the multiplication of what one could call the 'proletarians', while noting the impossibility of likening them to what the same term designates in the Occident. . . . To the criterion of dispossession from the land must be added that of uprooting—of 'detribalization', one would say, if the Annamites had not long ago escaped the framework of the tribe" (Robequain, *L'évolution économique*, 97).

[3]Delvert, in *Le paysan cambodgien*, notes the presence of Khmer Krom, or natives of Nam Bo, in the Cambodian provinces of Battambang and Kampot, where their settlement dates from 1924, but he makes no reference to their numbers. It is probable that the Khmers emigrated slowly and in small groups.

[4]*Annuaire de Cochinchine* and *Annuaire de l'Indochine*, in the *Monographie de Chau-doc* (1937), ANVN.

[5]The Khmer social structure is loose and very mobile. The *khum* (commune) does not correspond to the Vietnamese *xa* but is an administrative unit based on the *phum* (village or hamlet). There is no village community as such, the "peasant mass is unorganized, even inorganic," and the pagoda is "the center of village life. It is a true common house" (Delvert, *Le paysan cambodgien*, 199).

[6]The written complaint was published in *L'Alerte*, nos. 3–4, 8–9, and 10–11 (1937).

[7]*Monographie de Bac-lieu* (1937), ANVN. Some Khmers also adopted one-story dwellings instead of houses on pilings (Delvert, *Le paysan cambodgien*, 181). It would be interesting to study the interactions between the Vietnamese and Khmers in the extreme southern part of Vietnam. On this subject we currently have only a few lines from the *Monographie de Tra-vinh* (1901, 39). As far as I know, the sole attempt to catalogue Vietnamese borrowings of Khmer agricultural techniques, crops, and customs is Son Nam, *Nguoi Viet co zan toc tinh khong?* [Have the Vietnamese a national character?] (Saigon, 1969), 89–98.

[8]Head of the administrative office of the chief town of Rach-gia to the Provincial Administrator, 30 April 1912 (Rach-gia, E.7, ANVN). An analogous case that occurred in the village of Mong Tho in 1911 is also recorded in Rach-gia, E.7, ANVN.

[9]Letter of 10 June 1904 (Rach-gia, E.6, ANVN).

[10]Huynh Ngoc Binh (Colonial Council, 6th session, 7 December 1926).

[11]The author of the *Monographie de Chau-doc* (1937, ANVN) observed that "the affluent Cambodian is a rare thing and truly constitutes an exception," a circumstance resulting from the fact that "the Cambodian is not hard to please and, abhorring effort, he applies the formula *vivere parvo*, contenting himself with working for a scanty living from day to day" (p. 78).

[12]In 1886, for example, an administrator in the province of Soc-trang complained of the presence of several Frenchmen of dubious reputation: "[Land] ownership being not yet well established in the *arrondissement*, and the population being mainly Cambodian, a swarm of business agents has descended on Soc-trang" (Administrator Masseau to the Director of the Interior, no. 7, 23 October 1886, ANVN).

[13]*Monographie de Ha-tien* (1937) ANVN; M. Combot (Colonial Council, 8th session, 26 September 1936).

[14]*Tribune Indochinoise*, 30 September 1929.

[15]L. Malleret, "La minorité cambodgienne," BSEI, no. 21, p. 946.

[16]Delvert wrote: "On a people who have a certain depth of primitive violence, Buddhism has imposed the doctrine of nonviolence and love for all life. But Buddhism has also discouraged among the Khmer, who were probably not very inclined to it, the taste for exertion. One imagines in these circumstances that Buddhism has made the Cambodian a being poorly adapted to rigorous modern economic conditions. He believes effort to be evil and is little interested in profit" (*Le paysan cambodgien*, 141).

[17]Phan An, "Mot so van de Kinh te-xa hoi vung nong thon cua nguoi Khome o Dong Bang Song Cuu long," in *Van de Zan toc o Dong Bang Song Cuu long* (Ho Chi Minh City, 1991), 134.

[18]This statement, signed "G.B.," was published in MCI (June 1929).

[19]Administrator of Rach-gia to the Lieutenant Governor, 27 September 1904, Bac-lieu, E.12, ANVN.

[20]Administrator of Ha-tien to the Provincial Council, 3d session, 13 October 1923, Ha-tien, E.7940, ANVN.

[21]Karpelès, "Rapport au Gouverneur de la Cochinchine," Goucoch 2919, ANVN. As a Sanskritist, Karpelès played a role in the founding of the Institut Bouddhique in Phnom Penh, the aim of which was to protect Khmer monks from Bangkok and other Thai influences.

[22]Ibid.

[23]Ibid. See also the report of the administrator of Tra-vinh for 16 April 1937, which says of ninety thousand Khmers gathered around 109 pagodas, under the moral leadership of fifteen hundred monks, that "they faithfully keep their customs and national traditions" (Goucoch 2917, ANVN).

[24]See Colonial Council, 2d session, 3 November 1925; and 4th session, 5 October 1932.

[25]On the size of the population, the statistics are hardly precise, showing eight thousand in 1930 and six thousand in 1936. Ner advanced the figure of twelve thousand (M. Ner, "Les Muselmans de l'Indochine," BEFEO, fasc. 2 [1941]).

[26]Ibid.; *Monographie de Chau-doc* (1937), ANVN.

[27]Bac-lieu, E.12, ANVN.

[28]"Bac-lieu la xu que mua duoi song ca chot, tren bo Trieu Chau," cited by Ta Nhu Khue in *Thanh Nghi*, no. 57 (1944).

[29]Officially there were sixty-two thousand Sino-Vietnamese in Cochinchina in 1936. But Robequain adds, "these figures do not show the extent of the infusion of Chinese blood because those of mixed blood blend rapidly" (*L'économie de l'Indochine*, 49–50).

[30]See Verdeille, "Edits de Minh Mang," BSEI, no. 4 (1933); and Wang Wen Yuan, *Les relations entre l'Indochine française et la Chine* (Paris, 1937).

[31]For the origins and organization of the *congrégations*, see Nguyen Quoc Dinh, *Les congrégations chinoises en Indochine* (Paris, 1941); and R. Dubreuil, *De la condition des Chinois et de leur rôle économique en Indochine* (Paris, 1910).

[32]Laffargue, *L'immigration chinoise en Indochine* (Paris, 1909).

[33]Extraordinary session of the Arrondissement Council of Ha-tien, 16 January 1905, ANVN.

[34] Rach-gia, E.6, ANVN.

[35]Delegate of Long My to the Administrator of Rach-gia, 1913, Rach-gia, F.3, ANVN.

[36]This document is reproduced in appendix 4, this volume.

[37]*Annuaire de la Cochinchine française* (1855), 55.

[38]Confidential letter from the provincial administrator to the lieutenant governor of Cochinchina, 18 January 1908, dossier "Lettres confidentielles," ANVN.

[39]The phrase translates as "head of a chicken, arse of a duck," and was a Vietnamese nickname for these mestizos. "The Chinese settle easily in the interior of the province, especially in the Cambodian villages, where they live with and marry natives." This remark in the *Monographie de Tra-vinh* (1937, p. 30 [ANVN]) agrees with what Delvert writes about Cambodia (*Le paysan cambodgien*, 25) and with W. Willmott, *The Chinese in Cambodia* (Vancouver, 1967).

[40]In most of the latter, the Chinese partner acted as a comprador. The use of compradors allowed European firms to avoid the risks of insolvency on the part of a poorly known native clientele, and to deal more effectively with a native population that was unfamiliar with or suspicious of European methods. The comprador also acted as guarantor and procurer of clients.

[41]*Tribune Indochinoise*, 29 April 1927. Robequain writes that "One needs them, one admires their ability, one comes to esteem them" (*L'évolution économique*, 49). E. Dennery (*Foules d'Asie* [Paris, 1930], 41) discusses the reasons for their success and also for the "popularity" of Chinese merchant-creditors.

[42]Bac-lieu, E.12, ANVN.

[43]This story appeared in the *Courrier de l'Ouest*, 23 May 1918.

[44]Bac-lieu, E.12, ANVN.

[45]The 1911 census, CAOM, Indochine, GO2, 12.

[46]Administrators also were recruited from among the ranks of clerks of the two highest classes of the civil service who had two years of real service in Indochina, were under thirty-five years of age, possessed a certificate of practical knowledge first class for an Indochinese language, and had passed an aptitude test.

[47]Letter no. 559, 20 June 1913, Rach-gia, E.4, ANVN.

[48]Extract from a report reproduced in BCAC (May-June 1912).

[49]Letter no. 538, 19 July 1913, Rach-gia, E.4, ANVN.

[50]Letter no. 336, 15 April 1912, Rach-gia, E.4, ANVN. We do not have a record of the governor's reply.

[51] Memorandum from the administrator of Can-tho Province, no. 347, 1 March 1910, Can-tho, E, ANVN.

[52]In 1888, bonuses were established to reward the acquisition of language proficiency. However, inspectors of the civil service, administrators of the first, second, and third classes, and functionaries of general or local departments with salaries greater than thirteen thousand francs (in 1910) were ineligible. A decree of 8 October 1911 imposed as a condition of advancement knowledge of native languages for certain functionaries in immediate contact with the population (civil service, justice, *garde indigène*, and customs and excise). Of a total of 3,908 functionaries (excluding those of the Justice Department), there were, in 1912 and 1913, 1,047 candidates for advancement of whom 704 were accepted (H. Brenier, *Essai d'atlas statistique,* 62). Although the decrees of 24 June 1912 and 24 April 1913 confirmed the requirement, during World War I its application was suspended. The decree of 20 December 1920, which reorganized the civil services of Indochina, did away with the requirement altogether. Governor General Pasquier reestablished it in a decree of 5 November 1928.

[53]Administrator Cudenet to the Arrondissement Council of Ha-tien, session of 7 September 1905, ANVN. A colleague reaffirmed this: "You are, Messieurs, the intermediaries between the indigenous population and the province chief" (M. Caillard, Arrondissement Council of Ha-tien, session of 30 August 1909, ANVN).

[54]Interview with a *colon* of the delta, published in the *Courrier Saigonnais,* 12 June 1930.

[55] *Tribune Indigène,* 22 September 1921; *Tribune Indochinoise,* 9 May 1927.

[56]A. Schreiner, *Le livre foncier* (Saigon, 1904), 125. The administrator of Rach-gia echoed him in 1917 in his "Rapport du 2ème semestre," reproduced in BCAC (1918).

[57]Ibid.

[58]Exhortation of Nguyen Tri Phuong, cited in Nguyen Xuan Quang, *Les problèmes économiques et financiers du Viet-Nam a l'aube de son indépendance* (Saigon, 1959), 49.

[59]Vu Quoc Thuc, *Epargne et richesse en Asie du Sud-Est.*

[60]Tran Van Giau, *Mot so van de Khoa hoc xa hoi ve Dong Bang Song Cuu long* (Hanoi, 1982), 199.

[61]Henry noted that "In reality, all the small landowners (particularly those of Chau-doc) are more or less in debt. They generally borrow money in order to pay complementary labor during the season and often borrow a quantity of paddy because they have not kept a sufficient amount for the nourishment of the family. . . . This was the usual case for small landowners holding up to five hectares and for middle-sized landowners holding five to twenty hectares" (Henry, *L'économie agricole,* 319).

[62]The result was that the price of a *gia* of paddy, which on average was between 42 and 63 centimes before 1930, rose to between 70 and 85 centimes according to the size of the estate and the indebtedness of the landowner.

[63] *Tribune Indochinoise,* 10 August 1931. The last sentence was addressed to

the colonial authorities. In Bui Quang Chieu's narrative, the image emerges of a family circle in which this *dien chu* would take his evening coffee on the verandah of his residence, his *ta dien* gathered around him to learn and comment upon the news of the larger world, and to listen to records of *hat cai luong* (modern Vietnamese theater) played on a phonograph.

[64]Bui Quang Chieu, Colonial Council, session of 5 November 1936.

[65]As the *Tribune Indochinoise* put it, "The *ta dien* are the humble artisans of common work, revolving in their [*dien chu's*] orbit like satellites around the sun, sharing good and bad fortune with them" (13 October 1937). Dr. Cao Thien Toan, president of the agricultural union of Rach-gia, went further: "If the *ta dien* is one of the pillars of the social edifice, the landowner in his own way represents one of the rafters of the same edifice" (ibid., 28 November 1937).

[66]Speech by the president of the Chamber of Agriculture, delivered at a reception for Bui Quang Chieu, 27 September 1934, reproduced in the *Tribune Indochinoise*, 28 September 1934.

[67]In 1918, Conseiller Provincial Dieu Song Cang had requested the "creation of a system permitting the Indochinese to sell or to mortgage on the market their government bonds of which the total value amounts to several dozens of millions of francs" (speech delivered at a reception for A. Sarraut, Long-xuyen, reproduced in the *Courrier de l'Ouest*, 24 January 1918).

[68]Ibid., 19 April 1917.

[69]*L'Appel*, 15 March 1930.

[70]*Courrier Saigonnais*, 29 September 1930.

[71]*Courrier de l'Ouest*, 1 February 1917.

[72]*L'Appel*, 24 June 1922.

[73]*La Petite Tribune Indigène*, 9 July 1921.

[74]Reproduced in *L'Appel*, 27 December 1924.

[75]*Tribune Indochinoise*, 1 October 1928.

[76]Ibid., 25 November 1936.

[77]*L'Appel*, 12 May 1923.

[78]*La Petite Tribune Indigène*, 20 August 1921.

[79]A letter from the frontier reads: "Nguoi ngheo nan va tu cac noi toi muon dat ma lam ruong, cay lua tot thi no o, lua xau thi no tron di," which translates as "Poor people from everywhere come to rent and till land. If the harvest is good, they stay; a bad harvest makes them fly" (letter dated 20 September 1911, addressed to the administrator of Rach-gia [Rach-gia, E.7, ANVN]).

[80]L. Werth, *Cochinchine* (Mayenne, 1926), 174.

[81]*Tribune Indochinoise*, 18 February 1938.

[82]Ibid., 23 March 1938.

[83]Ibid., 13 October 1937.

[84]Ibid.

[85]Ibid., 28 November 1934.

[86]Ibid., 6 May 1936.

[87]Bui Quang Chieu, Colonial Council, session of 3 November 1936.

[88]Assistant chief administrator of Rach-gia to the lieutenant governor, 11 April 1906 (Rach-gia, E.3, ANVN).

[89]Administrative office chief to the provincial chief administrator, 17

December 1912 (Rach-gia, D.4, ANVN).

[90]Extract from the report of an inquiry by M. Lorin, administrator of the province of My-tho, on conditions in the province of Rach-gia as regards the collection of taxes (25 May 1906, Rach-gia, E.3, ANVN).

[91]Colonial Council, session of 3 November 1936.

[92]The original wording is "Xu Can-tho nam thanh nu tu // Xu Rach-gia vuon hu chim keu" (Tuan Phong, *Ca-Dao giang luan*, 126).

[93]"Cheo ghe so sau can chun Xuong bung so dia len rung so ma" (ibid.).

[94]Report of Administrative Secretary M. Gérard, 21 January 1898, Bac-lieu, E.12, dossier 51, ANVN.

[95]*Courrier de l'Ouest*, 1 March 1917.

[96]Report of Gérard.

[97]*L'Opinion*, 29 June 1928.

[98]On this affair, see *Tribune Indochinoise*, 13 April 1938.

[99]Ibid., 11 April 1938.

[100]Report of Gérard.

[101]See Garros, *Usages de la Cochinchine;* and Henry, *L'économie agricole*.

[102]This is according to ibid. Wages ranged from $70 to $100 according to Bui Quang Chieu (Colonial Council, 10th session, 29 May 1930).

[103]Henry, *L'économie agricole*.

[104]Henry calculated that for tenant farmers the cost in debt servicing per *gia* was between 67 and 83 centimes, "such that he only makes a profit when the purchase price is greater than $1.10 or $1.50, depending on the case" (ibid., 321).

[105]Son Nam, *Tim hieu dat Hau Giang*, 88.

[106]*Tribune Indochinoise*, 7 September 1942.

[107]Son Nam, *Tim hieu dat Hau Giang*, 21.

[108]See BCAC (December 1931); and the *Monographie de Long-xuyen* (1907), ANVN.

[109]Garros, *Usages de la Cochinchine*, 205.

[110]This has been demonstrated by Le Van Hao in the *Revue du Sud-Est Asiatique*, no. 2 (1962); no. 4 (1962); no. 2 (1963); and no. 1 (1964).

[111]For the symbolism of the *nui*, see G. Coulet, *Les Sociétés secrètes en terre d'Annam* (Paris, 1927).

[112]P. Paris, "Note sur les tatouages de la bonzesse Vo Thi Nan," BIIEH (1941).

[113]*Tribune Indochinoise*, 4 March 1940.

[114]This is according to an undated pamphlet by Nguyen Van Tam (copy preserved in the former Bibliothèque de la Cochinchine, Saigon).

[115]For more on religious sects, see A. M. Savani, *Visages et images du Sud-Vietnam* (Saigon, 1953); and A. M. Savani and Lt. Darches, "Le Caodaisme," a report published by the 2ème Bureau du Corps Expéditionnaire Français en Extrême-Orient (Paris, n.d., personal collection). More recent works include J. Werner, *Peasant Politics and Religious Sectarianism: Peasant and Priest in the Cao Dai in Vietnam* (New Haven, 1981); and Hue Tam Ho Tai, *Millenarianism*.

[116]The road sweepers of Ca-mau to the Governor of Cochinchina, reproduced in *Dan Moi*, 28 April 1939; "Resolutions of the Native Dormitory Servants of Chau-doc City," reproduced in *Saigon*, 4 January 1939.

[117]"Demands of the Chinese Brick Makers of Ca-mau," reproduced in *Cong Luan*, 20 June 1939; "Demands of the Worker-tailors and Apprentices of Can-tho," reproduced in *La Lutte*, 8 April 1937.

[118]*Tribune Indochinoise*, 7 October 1936.

[119]Nonetheless, the editor of the *Monographie de Bac-lieu* (1937, ANVN) warned against harboring any illusions about general prosperity: "One is struck by the wealth of the large landowner who travels, is talked about, and visits Saigon, and one infers from this that the province is wealthy without thinking of the still precarious and unsettled existence of the whole of the *ta dien*" (p. 3).

[120]*Tribune Indochinoise*, 10 August 1931.

[121]Le Quang Liem, in ibid., 9 February 1938.

[122]*La Lutte*, 9 November 1936; 10 January 1937; 23 March 1937; 8 April 1937; and *Tribune Indochinoise*, 21 January 1938.

[123]*Saigon*, 28 January 1939; *Dan Chung*, 38 January 1939. *Dan Moi* (17 August 1939) noted the case of twenty-one other peasants who came from Long-xuyen on a similar errand.

[124]Truong Van Ben, speech delivered at the Chamber of Agriculture, BCAC (January 1937).

[125]Report of the administrator of Bac-lieu Province, ibid. (no. 172, 1918):99. The chief of the Service de l'Enseignement in Cochinchina made a similar remark at the Colonial Council session of 29 September 1938.

[126]*Tribune Indochinoise*, 14 March 1927.

[127]Arrondissement Council of Ha-tien, session of 7 September 1905, ANVN.

[128]*L'Appel*, 8 February 1930.

[129]The notice, for a hotel in Can-tho, appeared in 1922. It is mentioned in ibid., 10 June 1930.

[130]Ibid., 18 September 1926.

[131]Ibid., 28 April 1923. *L'Appel* published ten articles on sports and gymnastics in 1927, six in 1928, and five in 1929.

[132]Arrondissement Council of Ha-tien, session of 19 October 1918.

[133]Report to the Colonial Council, session of 26 September 1938.

[134]A *dan* is a raised mound used as an altar when mortals wish to communicate with the spirits, worship them, or solicit guidance, knowledge, or medical advice.

[135]This is suggested in "Le Caodaisme" (see note 115). The diffusion of Caodaism varied according to province. In 1937, there were 3,400 adepts in Chau-doc, concentrated in the canton of Tan Chau where ten private chapels had been built. The *Monographie de Ha-tien* for the same year notes that Caodaism was expanding. At Bac-lieu as early as 1932 the Cao Trieu Phat sect had recruited five thousand members and built five private chapels (*Monographies* of Chau-doc, Ha-tien, and Bac-lieu [1937], ANVN).

[136]These "reactionary" policies were implemented in different ways: Ngo Dinh Ziem applied assimilation (*dong hoa*), which repressed minorities, while the French, the Americans, and General Nguyen Van Thieu isolated them, preventing them from joining in a united front. Recently, in an attempt to develop a state-party policy toward ethnic minorities that would discourage the intervention of neighboring states, Vietnamese social scientists have begun to reassess this question

in the Mekong Delta. Along with emphasizing the unity of Vietnamese, Khmers, and others against colonialism and neocolonialism, recent works on the Khmers have stressed the role they played in developing the Mekong Delta (see, for example, Phan Thi Yen Tuyet and Mac Duong, in *Van de Zan toc o dong bang Song Cuu Long*, 215, 229, 243–82). Dropping the old cliché of Khmer backwardness, these authors underscore the fact that the Khmer Krom had developed their agriculture beyond slash-and-burn cultivation, though it is not clear whether this occurred prior to the arrival of the Vietnamese. It is known that the Cambodians perfected two hydraulic devices. One, called *yo day*, uses the river tides to wash alum from the rice fields. The other keeps reserves of soft water behind weirs (Thach Voi, in *Tìm hieu von van hoa zan toc khmer Nam Bo* [Ho Chi Minh City, 1988], 16; Phan An, "Mot so van de," in *Van de zan toc o Dong bang Song Cuu Long*, 109–70). At least one author has acknowledged that the Khmer Krom are conservative and strongly influenced by religion. He states, though somewhat ambiguously, that they fight not only against economic exploitation but for an equal standing with other ethnic groups (ibid., 193).

Chapter 5

[1]"Mémoires de Phan Boi Chau," trans. G. Boudarel, *France-Asie* (Paris), nos. 194–95 (1968). See also D. Marr, *Vietnamese Anticolonialism, 1885–1925* (Berkeley, 1971).

[2]Ibid.; Son Nam, *Thien Dia Hoi va cuoc Minh Tan* [The Heaven and Earth Society and the New Light] (Saigon, 1971).

[3]Nguyen Van Hau, *Nguyen Quang Zieu: Phong trao Dong Zu Mien Nam* [The movement of the Eastern Trip in South Vietnam] (Saigon, 1974).

[4]P. Brocheux, "Note sur Gilbert Chieu, patriote vietnamien et citoyen français," *Approches-Asie* (Nice), no. 11 (1991).

[5]P. Brocheux, "De l'empereur Zuy Tan au prince Vinh San: l'Histoire peut elle se répèter?" *Approches-Asie* (Nice), no. 10 (1990).

[6]R. Smith, "The Vietnamese Elite of French Cochinchina, 1943," *Modern Asian Studies* 6, no. 4 (1972); M. Cook, *The Constitutionalist Party in Cochinchina: The Years of Decline, 1930–1942* (Clayton, 1977).

[7]P. Brocheux, "Grands propriètaires et fermiers de l'Ouest de la Cochinchine pendant la période coloniale," *Revue Historique*, no. 499 (1971).

[8]Tran Thi Nhuong, in *Chi mot con duong* [There is but one way] (Hanoi, 1974), 37.

[9]Son Nam, *Thien Dia Hoi*.

[10]Hue Tam Ho Tai, *Millenarianism*, 72.

[11]Ibid., 73–74.

[12]Nguyen Van Hau, *Nguyen Quang Zieu*, 86–89.

[13]Werner, *Peasant Politics*.

[14]Ibid., appendix B.

[15]R. Smith, "An Introduction to Caodaism," *Bulletin of the School of Oriental and African Studies* 33, no. 2 (1970):349.

[16]This is my translation of a passage in a 1926 pamphlet distributed by the Cao Dai: "The French and Annamite are my cherished races. I wish them to be

united forever. The new doctrine that I preach aims to place both in a single community of interests and life" ("Thanh Ngon Hiep Tuyen," published in Saigon in 1928, CAOM, Indochine, NF Indo 450[2]).

[17]The practice of invoking the Immortals (*cau tien*) took place on mounds (*dan*) according to the *Monographie de Can-tho* (1937), ANVN. There were two *dan* in the province of Can-tho and one in Ha-tien where it is known that people invoked healing spirits.

[18]In the 1930s, Cao Trieu Phat opposed the French authorities. In 1945, along with his sect (Cao Dai Hiep Nhut), he joined the Viet Minh and acted as a counsellor to the Uy Ban Khang Chien Hanh Chanh Nam Bo. He died in Hanoi where he retired after the partition of the country (CAOM, Service de Protection du Corps Expéditionnaire, 350). Both Cao and Ca are discussed in Werner, *Peasant Politics.*

[19]When Le Van Trung died, the French authorities supported Nguyen Ngoc Tuong of Ben-tre ("faithful and loyal to France" he was called by Governor Rivoal), intriguing to get him elected "Pope," the supreme position in Tay-ninh, in October 1941 (ANVN, TDBCPNV, D.61–76, D.61–79). Nguyen Ngoc Tuong was described as "consistently pro-French" in CAOM, Indochine, PA 14(2).

[20]Circular of 16 June 1941 (ANVN, TDBCPNV).

[21]Phan Dau, report of the ICP in the province of My-tho, 20 July 1936, CAOM, Indochine, SLOTFOM V, 41.

[22]Communist militant Nguyen Thi Thap observed that the Cao Dai achieved much success in her village following the collapse of the peasant uprising of 1930–31. See Nguyen Thi Thap, *Tu Dat Tien Giang* (Ho Chi Minh City, 1986). The ensuing investigation committee was known as the Commission Guernut, after its chairman, Deputy Guernut. Though it never went to Indochina, it collected a variety of letters, leaflets, pamphlets, manifestos, and reports, which may be found in the Guernut files of CAOM. Nguyen Phan Long's letter, dated November 1937, is also in the collection.

[23]Hue Tam Ho Tai, *Millenarianism.* See also Ha Huy Giap, *Su Tien hoa Lien tuc cua Nguyen An Ninh* (Ho Chi Minh City, 1989); Ha Huy Giap et al., *Nguyen An Ninh* (Ho Chi Minh City, 1988); and Hue Tam Ho Tai, *Radicalism and the Origins of the Vietnamese Revolution* (Cambridge, 1992).

[24] Zan Ton Tu, *Chi mot con duong* (Hanoi, 1974), 5–41.

[25]P. Mus, *Vietnam: Sociologie d'une guerre* (Paris, 1952).

[26]Tran Tu Binh, *Phu Rieng Do* [Phu Rieng the red] (Hanoi, 1971). An English translation of this book has been published by Ohio University Press (Athens, Ohio, 1985). See also Nguyen Thi Thap, *Tu Dat Tien Giang* [From the land of Tien Giang]; Nguyen Thi Luu, *Tinh Yeu va Anh Lua* [Love and firelight] (Ho Chi Minh City, 1985); Nguyen Thi Dinh, *Khong con duong nao khac* [There was no alternative] (Hanoi, 1979); Dan Ton Tu and Tran Thi Nhuong, in *Chi mot con duong* [There was but one way] (Hanoi, 1979); and Ha Thi Lan, in *Con duong giai phong* [The path of liberation] (Hanoi, 1979).

[27]Zan Ton Tu, in *Chi mot con duong,* 25.

[28]Except in one case, the social origins of the authors of these succinct biographies are not identified. My hypothesis is that a proper communist militant was expected to be born of poor peasants (witness Mao Zedong's invention of a peasant

father), and if this was not the case it was thought better not to delve too deeply into the activist's social background. Nguyen Thi Luu acknowledges that her parents were landlords but she adds that because of her mother's superstitions she was separated from them and raised by poor tenants until she was seven years old. She claims to have hated her rich, narrow-minded relatives.

[29]Chau Van Liem's obituary was published in *Co Do* [Red Flag] no. 3 (CAOM, Indochine, 7F4/8/14).

[30]"Confession of Nguyen Van Tran, alias Axinovitch, alias Brigorny, to the French Police," 10 June 1931, SHAT, Papiers Goutès, 1 K211/2). Another activist, Ha Huy Tap, alias Sinikine, organized the ICP in the province of Sa-dec. He also was a schoolteacher.

[31]"Nhung nhiem vu can ban cua cuoc cach mang Dong Zuong" [The fundamental tasks of the Indochinese Revolution], 1932, CAOM, Indochine, SLOT-FOM V, 13. See also translated Communist Party documents in SLOTFOM III, 52, 54, 59.

[32]Tran Van Giau, *Lich su giai cap cong nhan Viet Nam* [A history of the Vietnamese working class] (Hanoi, 1958), 550.

Chapter 6

[1]Colonial Council, 1st session, 10 September 1929.

[2]BAEI, February 1934; *Tribune Indochinoise,* 10 February 1930.

[3]A. Hibon, *La crise économique en Indochine* (Paris, 1934), 27. Bernard, in *Le problème économique (p.* 127), is of the same opinion.

[4]On this question, see A. Touzet, *Le régime monétaire indochinois* (Paris, 1939), 98-99; M. Meuleau, *Des pionniers en Extrême-Orient: Histoire de la Banque de l'Indochine, 1875–1975* (Paris, 1990); and a pamphlet by L. Gerville-Réache, "La stabilisation de la piastre indochinoise," in which the opinions of the governors (Doumer, Van Vollenhoven, and Sarraut) and the financial authorities (mainly Homberg) are expressed.

[5]See, for example, the works of Bernard, Hibon, Estèbe, and Touzet.

[6]"In fact, the nearly concurrent effects of the stabilization of the piaster, the accelerated fall of silver prices, and the general decline of world prices were combined in a single conception by the inactivity of the market due to a slump in rice" (Robequain, *L'Evolution économique,* 165).

[7]Melin, *L'endettement agraire en Indochine, 93.*

[8]*Tribune Indochinoise,* 18 November 1932; BCAC (July 1931).

[9]Extract of a letter from Governor Eutrope to the President of the Chamber of Agriculture, reproduced in BCAC (February-March 1932):215.

[10]*Tribune Indochinoise,* 18 June 1934.

[11]BCAC (September 1933).

[12]*Tribune Indochinoise,* 8 August 1934.

[13]BCAC (April 1934).

[14]Ibid. (November 1932, October 1933).

[15]Ibid. (November 1931):488.

[16]Ibid.

[17]Reply of the governor to the president of the Chamber of Agriculture, 21 December 1931, reproduced in BCAC (January 1932).

[18]Ibid. (July 1934).

[19] *Tribune Indochinoise,* 21 November 1932. On the *chettys,* see ibid., 11 April 1932, 7 October 1931, and 22 April 1931.

[20]Ibid., 27 July 1934.

[21]Dated 23 August 1934, and reproduced in *Le Paysan de Cochinchine,* 31 January 1935.

[22]BCAC (April 1933).

[23]Ibid. (August 1933).

[24] *Tribune Indochinoise,* 24 April 1932.

[25]BCAC (April 1933, September 1933).

[26]Ibid. (July1932, April 1932).

[27]Touzet, *Le régime monetaire.*

[28] *Tribune Indochinoise,* 22 May 1931.

[29]Melin, *L'endettement agraire en Indochine;* de Feyssal, *L'endettement agraire en Cochinchine.* Loans made by the treasuries of Chau-doc, Baria, Cholon, My-tho, and Vinh-long together amounted to only $5,915.

[30]Report to the Colonial Council, 1937–38, 161.

[31]The rate of interest was progressively lowered: to 7 percent on 1 November 1934, 6.5 percent on 1 November 1935, and 6 percent on 1 November 1936.

[32]The principal function of the Service des Prêts Fonciers à long terme [Service for long-term land loans] was to encourage amicable dealings between creditors and debtors (Robequain, *L'Evolution économique,* 197). After 1933, the land societies renounced long-term credit operations, and only the Crédit Hypothécaire continued to operate in this sphere (ibid.).

[33]Speech by the governor of Cochinchina to the Colonial Council, 1st session, 1 September 1938.

[34]Decree of 13 March 1933 by the governor of Indochina.

[35]The distribution was as follows: 15 percent to the SICAMs or for taxes, 10 percent to the banks, 10 percent to the Vietnamese, and 60 percent to the *chettys* (de Feyssal, *L'endettement agraire en Cochinchine*).

[36]Memorandum from Governor Pagès, no. 302, 29 August 1934, to the Provincial Administrator, cited in BCAC (September 1934).

[37]Ibid. The poll tax had varied from one province to another but before 1935 it averaged $7.50. Thus, it was both reduced and made uniform.

[38]Memorandum of Governor Pagès. Of this amount, $700,000 came from the general reduction of land taxes not paid in previous years.

[39]"*Bulletin Financier de l'Indochine,"* reproduced in the *Tribune Indochinoise,* 2 September 1932.

[40]A. Touzet, *L'Economie indochinoise et la grande crise universelle* (Paris, 1934).

[41]Nonetheless, Robequain writes that, although the Chinese maintained control over the internal paddy commerce, their stranglehold had been broken in the other areas: "It seems that the Chinese have not regained all the lost ground. . . . They no longer hold the milling monopoly: they are rivaled in this industry by the French and even by the Annamites who, especially in Cochinchina, have multiplied" (Robequain, *L'évolution économique,* 51–52). He adds, in a note (p. 52), that "The

Annamites have also begun making charcoal in the mangrove forest of Ca-mau. . . . This was till then, in fact, a Chinese monopoly," and remarks upon changes in the role of the comprador, stating that "he is no longer the universal informer and tout, responsible for the solvency of his clients, but is very often already an ordinary intermediary assisting in the execution of business prepared by others" (ibid.).

[42]Figures generated by the Saigon Chamber of Commerce.

[43]Colonial Council, session of 3 September 1937. Governor Brévié recognized that the salary increases were less than the increase in the cost of living (opening speech of a session of GCIEFI, 2 December 1937). The periodical *Le Paysan de Cochinchine*, which was edited by M. Chêne, a *colon* of the West, pointed out the dual effect of the devaluation of the franc: the rejuvenation of the price of rice and demands for salary increases by the agricultural workers of the West (*Le paysan de Cochinchine*, 31 December 1936). On the price increases, see also *l'Asie Française* (May 1936):159; and *l'Asie Française* (September-October 1937):251.

[44]Resolution of the Bac-lieu Provincial Council, cited in Touzet, *Le régime monétaire*, 337. The same author also wrote that "the progressive depreciation of the piaster greatly improved the position of debtors. The situation of the service for long-term land loans and of the native [SI]CAM societies of Cochinchina, which was critical, suddenly became nearly normal again. . . . The condition of those debtors who had not fulfilled their obligations before February 1938 is improving due to the extraordinary windfall of a remittance of 56.4 percent prior to May 1936 and of 61.2 percent since that time, on the amount of their debts in gold piasters." As for the rise in prices, "the peasantry in its entirety will have to suffer from it, the well-off class will profit from it" (ibid.).

[45]By 1937, Governor General Brévié could note the improvement in the budgetary situation before the Governor's Council. The quote is from the *Tribune Indochinoise*, 20 July 1937.

[46]Ibid.

[47]Report to the Colonial Council, 1930, 11.

[48]Administrator of Rach-gia to the Governor of Cochinchina, 9 January 1930, ANVN.

[49]*Tribune Indochinoise*, 29 April 1931.

[50]Ibid.

[51]*Monographie de Ha-tien* (1937), ANVN.

[52]For Labasthé's comments, see Report of the Colonial Council, 11th session, 20 October 1932.

[53]Chief Administrator of Chau-doc to the Director of the Bureaux du Gouvernement of Cochinchina, 20 January 1936, no. 208, ANVN.

[54]*Indochine*, 28 January 1943.

[55]Ibid., 10 March 1945.

[56]The newspaper *Saigon*, on 3 August 1939, announced the arrest of ten women and children who had prevented Truong Van Huan, an agent of the land survey, from carrying out boundary work at Ca-mau. They had mistaken the agent in question for a surveyor hired by a landowner in order to deprive them of land. On these occurrences, see also *Cong Luan*, 3 April 1939; *Saigon*, 8 August 1939; *Dan Chung*, 13 January 1939; and *Sang*, 13 January 1939.

[57]*Tribune Indochinoise*, 5 March 1937.

[58]*Dien Tin*, 9 April 1936.

[59]According to the *Monographie de Chau-doc* (1937), ANVN.

[60]Devismes, in *Indochine*, 26 November 1942.

[61]Ibid.

[62]Ibid.

[63]Account of the activities of the Indochinese Rice Office prepared for the Governor General, 1 July 1944, ANVN.

[64]Statement by M. Commun, engineer of the Rice Office, delivered at the agricultural festival of 23 April 1938 in Saigon.

[65]"Rapport sur le Crédit Agricole Mutuel en Cochinchine en 1934," pamphlet prepared by the government of Cochinchina, 1935, Saigon.

[66]This was accomplished through a decree of 15 April 1940.

[67]"Le Crédit Agricole Mutuel en Cochinchine pendant l'année 1934," a pamphlet prepared by the government, published in Hanoi in 1935, Hanoi.

[68]Ibid.

[69]Confidential report of Governor of Cochinchina Rivoal, 24 September 1942, no. 2029c, ANVN.

Chapter 7

[1]*Tribune Indochinoise*, issues of 7 May 1930, 11 June 1930, 13 June 1930, 16 June 1930, 16 July 1930, 6 August 1930, and 25 August 1930.

[2]This reproach was an old one, having been expressed in a speech by the *colon* Labasthe at a reception at the Cochinchinese Chamber of Agriculture for the deputy for Cochinchina, E. Outrey, as early as 1918. Concerning the operations of the Banque de l'Indochine the reader is referred to M. Meuleau, *Des pionniers*, chap. 9, where the author contends that though the bank was not an octopus it had a cold, calculating philosophy and treated its debtors harshly (p. 400).

[3]Descriptions may be found in a statement made by Bui Quang Chieu on 15 February 1931; a motion of the Chamber of Agriculture sent to the governor of Cochinchina in1932; and in a motion by Labasthe to the Rice Commission of 24 March 1933 (all published in the colonial press—*Tribune Indochinoise*, *La Dépêche*, and *Le Populaire*).

[4]The police asked the village *notables* to find out who was going to attend the demonstration from their villages. (The text of the leaflet announcing the demonstration is reproduced in appendix 6). One newspaper printed the instructions of the deputy chief of Cai Rang, Zuong Thanh My.

A letter of the chief of the police at Can-tho reports that some people are urging the landowners to come to Saigon on 17 April to attend a meeting of protest against the policy of the Banque de l'Indochine. Accordingly, *notables* will examine the following questions and reply to the delegation (Bureau of District) on 17 April 1934.

1. Is anyone in your village planning to travel to Saigon on 17 April 1934 to attend the meeting of protest against the Banque de l'Indochine?

2. Did an Annamite or a Frenchman come to your village to promote this meeting?

3. Is a river-transport or motor-transport company giving discounts to the landowners to allow them to attend this meeting? What are their names?

[5]On 25 March 1934, Paul Gannay was head of the bank with the title of *inspecteur général*. Stavisky was a financial swindler arrested in 1933 in France. His case was used by the French extreme right to illustrate the corruption of the parliamentary republic, which was controlled, they suggested, by financiers and Jews.

[6]*Tribune Indochinoise,* 4 April 1934.

[7]For example, see the *Tribune Indochinoise* on Governor General P. Pasquier (10 January 1934); and BSAF (December 1933).

[8]Nguyen Phan Long, in the *Tribune Indochinoise,* 9 April 1934. Maurice Diethelm was also a director of finance for Indochina, and later a Gaullist resistant and a well-known politician.

[9]BCAC (March 1934).

[10]*Tribune Indochinoise,* 5 January 1934.

[11]Vo san hoa: Hoi ky cach mang [Proletarianization] (Hanoi, 1972).

[12]"Le Communisme, 1920–1930" (translated communist documents), Fonds Résidence Supéieure du Tonkin, CAOM, Indochine.

[13]SLOTFOM III, 49, CAOM, Indochine.

[14]P. Brocheux, "L'implantation du mouvement communiste en Indochine: La cas du Nghe Tinh, 1930–1931," *Revue d'Histoire modern et contemporaine* 14 (1977).

[15]Report of the administrator of Long-xuyen, 12 May 1930, CAOM, Indochine, 7F36(2). For Nam Bo, file 7F36(2) in CAOM contains reports of administrators of every province in which demonstrations took place. A chronology of events is provided in SLOTFOM III, 48, 7F24, NF2641.

[16]Report of C. Esquivillon, administrator of Sa-dec, 15 May 1930, CAOM, Indochine, 7F36(2).

[17]Nguyen Thi Thap, *Tu Dat Tien Giang.*

[18]Telegram of Governor General Pasquier to the Minister of the Colonies, 3 June 1930, CAOM, Indochine, NF2641/327.

[19]*Tribune Indochinoise,* 15 November 1929.

[20]Nguyen Van Tran, "Confession," Papiers Goutès 1K211(2), SHAT.

[21]CAOM, Indochine, 7F36(1).

[22]*Contribution à l'histoire des mouvements politiques de l'Indochine française,* Vol. 4, *"Le 'Dong-Duong Cong-San Dang' ou 'Parti Communiste Indochinois,'"* (Hanoi, 1933), 40–41.

[23]*Co Do,* March 1934, CAOM, Indochine, 7F8; *Su That,* 20 September 1936, CAOM, Indochine, SLOTFOM III, 59.

[24]The new political agenda was made explicit in the "Confidential Letter of the Central Committee of the ICP to the Party Members," in PA 28 (Papiers Moutet), CAOM, Indochine.

[25]Quoted from "Resolutions of the Enlarged Conference of the Central Committee of the ICP," held in August and September of 1937 under the presidency of Ha Huy Tap (French translation in CAOM, Indochine, SLOTFOM III, 59).

[26]On 19 October 1937, CAOM, Indochine, SLOTFOM III, 59.

[27]D. Hémery, *Revolutionnaires vietnamiens et pouvoir colonial en Indochine.* Paris, 1975)

[28]Lists of the demonstrations, meetings, and strikes may be found in CAOM, Indochine, 7F26(5); 7F26(6); NF 271; and SLOTFOM III, 52. SLOTFOM V contains translations of many communist newspapers of the period. A nonexhaustive synthesis may be found in Quynh Cu, "Tai lieu tinh hinh dau tranh cua nong zan trong thoi ky Mat tran binh zan (1936–1939)," *Nghien cuu lich su,* no. 60 (1964).

[29]In this regard, CAOM (Affaires Politiques, 25, 26) contains detailed correspondence between the administrators of Long-xuyen and Rach-gia and the governor of Cochinchina.

[30]CAOM, Indochine, 7F26(5); NF 2391; SLOTFOM III, 52.

[31]L. Brasey to the Governor of Cochinchina, 30 June 1937, CAOM, Affaires Politiques, 26.

[32]Governor General Brévié's letter to the governor of Cochinchina dated 10 May 1938, extensively describes the "agrarian malaise" of western Nam Bo (CAOM, Agence FOM 65). The same awareness appeared in Inspector of the Colonies Carbon Ferriere's 1939 report, "Contestations foncieres dans le Transbassac" (CAOM, Indochine, NF 2502).

[33]Governor General Brévié to the Governor of Cochinchina, 10 May 1938 (CAOM, Agence FOM 65).

[34]Vo Nguyen Giap and Truong Chinh (under the pen names Van Dinh and Qua Ninh), *Van de dan cay* [The peasant question] (Hanoi, 1937). An English version was translated and edited by C. White (Ithaca, 1974).

[35]Huynh Kim Khanh, *Vietnamese Communism.* See also *Nhung su kien lich su Dang (1920–1945)* [Historical events in the history of the party] (Hanoi, 1976), 1:481–85.

[36]P. Brocheux, "L'occasion favorable, 1940–1945," in *L'Indochine française, 1940–1945,* ed. P. Isoart (Paris, 1982).

[37]CAOM, Indochine, 7F27.

[38]Tran Van Giau was interned in Ta Lai camp (interview with the author, 1979, Ho Chi Minh City), along with Nguyen Thi Dinh (interview with the author, 1979, Hanoi). See also the latter's *hoi ky, Khong con duong nao khac.*

[39]*Nhung su kien lich su Dank* 485–88.

[40]Brocheux, "L'occasion favorable." The communists were impatient because they were convinced that the insurrection would succeed. For instance, in October 1940, the committee of the northern province of Ha Nam Ninh decided to prepare for armed insurrection, after the defeat of Bac Son and Nam Ky, although the *xu uy* of Bac Ky ordered them to give up the project. Thus, it would appear that all the party members, and not only the southern "adventurers," were in a warlike or romantic frame of mind (*Su kien lich su Dang Ha Nam Ninh* [Historical events in the history of the party in Ha Nam Ninh] (Nam Dinh, 1978), 78.

[41]CAOM, Indochine, 7F27.

[42]Nguyen Thi Thap, *Tu Dat Tien Giang.*

[43]Nguyen Thi Thap related a tragi-comic incident that occurred during these bombings. One plane had the inscription "S.V." painted under its wings and some people, believing that it was a "So Viet" plane, cheered until it began strafing them (ibid.). A set of telegrams from Admiral Decoux to the Vichy government describing Poulo Condor are contained in CAOM, Indochine, NF 1096.

[44]Quoted from ibid. The numbers of prisoners are included in Administrator Brasey's report, TDBCPNV, D 1-366, ANVN.

[45]"Notice sur l'activité des intrigues politiques de tendances subversives dans les milieux indigènes de Cochinchine pendant les mois de novembre et décembre 1940," CAOM, Indochine, 7F27.

[46]Tran Huy Lieu and Van Tao, *Cac cuoc khoi nhia Bac Son, Nam Ky, Do Luong* [The insurrections of Bac Son, Nam Ky, and Do Luong] (Hanoi, 1957).

[47]Bui Quang Chieu, letter of 25 April 1941, opened by French censors and filed in CAOM, Indochine, NF 1198.

Chapter 8

[1]J. Decaudin, "Essais de contrôle du marché du riz en Cochinchine, 1941–1944," CAOM, Indochina, APOM 4 (probably written in 1946, based on the archives of the Committee for the Control of Rice). On economic controls in general, see J. Martin, "L'economie indochinoise pendant la guerre" (CAOM, Indochine, NF 1267). The author was the head of the Economic Department of the Gouvernement Général de l'Indochine during World War II. Decaudin was one of Martin's top assistants.

[2]Decaudin, "Essais de contrôle." On the protest of the rice producers, see CAOM, Indochine, PA 14 (Papiers Decoux).

[3]Governor of Cochinchina's report to the governor general, 21 April 1943, CAOM, Conseiller Politique, 161.

[4]Hue Tam Ho Tai (in *Millenarianism*) has exhaustively followed the thread that runs through the history of Nam Bo from the Buu Son Ky Huong tradition to the Hoa Hao. For the delta at large, see the table covering 1943–44 in Decaudin, "Essais de contrôle."

[5]G. Huet, "Le riz en Indochine" (undated, mimeographed document in the SHAT archives), 8; Werner, *Peasant Politics,* 39.

[6]Hue Tam Ho Tai, *Millenarianism,* 170. The actions of the Hoa Hao sect have also been studied by Lieutenant Lacroix, a French intelligence officer who worked in Mien Tay at the headquarters of the Hoa Hao armed forces. He clearly identifies the legacy of Buu Son Ky Huong in the Hoa Hao sect (lecture delivered at the CHEAM, Paris, on 15 June 1949).

[7]Ibid.

[8]Renou's report of an investigation in Long-xuyen (TDBCPNV, DI-368, ANVN).

[9]Gautier's report on the Hoa Hao in Chau-doc (TDBCPNV, D1-368, ANVN).

[10]Hue Tam Ho Tai, *Millenarianism,* 127–28.

[11]Nguyen Hien Le, *Hoi ky* [Memoirs], 1:308–9 (Van Nghe, 1990).

[12]Inspection reports of Administrator Renou, 1943, TDBCPNV, E.03312, no. 368, and no. 175, ANVN.

[13]Masaya Shiraishi, "La présence japonaise en Indochine," in *L'Indochine française, 1940–1945,* ed. P. Isoart (Paris, 1982).

[14]Hue Tam Ho Tai, *Millenarianism,* 129.

[15]Either Bui Van Zu infiltrated the Hoa Hao sect or he held talks with its

representatives. Infiltration of an alien organization was a common tactic of the communists. In the late 1950s, in the same region, they made their way into armed Hoa Hao units and Ziem's constabulary, the Bao An. In 1943, the French identified Zu as the secretary of the ICP Interprovincial Committee of Mien Tay (see Governor of Cochinchina's report, 25 September 1943, in CAOM, Conseiller Politique, 161). Nguyen Thi Thap, in *Tu Dat Tien Giang*, describes him as a high-ranking leader who helped rebuild the party in 1943–44. Trotskyites and others who lacked mass support tried to anchor themselves in popular movements. These nonconverted outsiders played an essential role in 1946 in creating the political party linked to the Hoa Hao sect, the Zan Chu Xa Hoi Dang (Social Democratic Party).

[16]Ibid., 268–69. Ho Chi Minh convened a conference of the Central Committee of the ICP on 13–15 August 1945 in the village of Tan Trao in Bac Bo. This meeting was followed by a "People's Congress," which created a provisional government headed by Ho.

[17]CAOM, Conseiller Politique, 161.

[18]Quoted later by the French administrator of Chau-doc in a report dated 1948, TDBCPNV, D61–74, ANVN.

[19]CAOM, Conseiller Politique, 161.

[20]Nguyen Thi Thap, *Tu Dat Tien Giang*, 259–69; Tran Van Giau, interviews with the author, Saigon, November 1979, July 1989, and December 1989.

[21]Thap, *Hoi ky*, 284.

[22]*Giai Phong* [Liberation], no. 15 (17 July 1945).

[23]Giau's text reads "Mot cuoc khoi nghia gianh chinh quyen o Nam Ky phai no ra truoc tien va chu yeu la o Saigon, dau nao cua dich, cac tinh tiep sau va dong thoi. . . . Con Bay gio xu uy khong chu truong cuop chinh quyen bang zu kich, bang noi len thinh linh cua mot so can tu, khong chu truong nong thon bao vay va tan cong thanh thi (Tran Van Giau, "Mot so dac diem," 2–4). Giau and Dr. Thach's names were suppressed in communist documents such as Nguyen Thi Luu's *hoi ky* (*Tinh Yeu va Anh Lua*) and *Tran danh ba muoi nam*, vol. 1, edited by generals Hoang Van Thai and Tran Do and published by the Army Publishing House (Hanoi, 1983).

[24]According to Tran Van Giau, Huynh Phu So and the Hoa Hao aimed to install a theocratic state with its capital at Can-tho (interview with the author). We can easily suppose that, once in control of the "rice basket," So might have expected to play a role on the Nam Bo Administrative Committee or even in the central government.

[25]Giau, "Mot so dac diem," 2, 4. On the revolution in Sa-dec, see *Truyen thong cach mang cua Phu nu Nam Bo Thanh Dong* (Ho Chi Minh City, 1989), 106, 107.

[26]Not all the Caodaists entered into the agreement but the powerful Tay-ninh sect did.

[27]Nguyen Hien Le, *Hoi ky*, 1:319, 320.

[28]Ibid, 1:322.

[29]Ibid, 1:342.

[30]M. Solier, "La pacification dans la province de Soc-trang," mimeographed paper in CHEAAM, no. 1858.

[31]H. Loustau, *Les deux bataillons* (Paris, 1987), 107.

[32]Ibid., 126.

[33]General Valluy, "Le problème cochinchinois," note to the High Commissioner, 30 May 1947, SHAT, 10H165, dossier 3.

[34]Nguyen Thanh Son was in charge of the UBK's "foreign relations and of the Cambodian front" (Viet Minh documents, SHAT archives). When Nguyen Binh, military commander of the Resistance in Nam Bo, was attacked and killed on his way to Hanoi in October 1951, the French seized his papers, including a diary dedicated to his wife and a report on the situation in eastern Cambodia. The diary contains interesting opinions on the Cambodians and suggestions for establishing in northeastern Cambodia a rear base for the Vietnamese Resistance of Nam Bo (SHAT, 10H 366).

[35]SHAT, 10H 3757. The French estimated that the Resistance controlled 130,000 tons of rice in 1947 (SHAT, 10H 1043). The French blockade was not completely effective, for the Hoa Hao, the Caodaists, and even the Catholics conducted their own commerce, trading with the Viet Minh through the Chinese intermediaries known as *binh phong* ("folding screens").

[36]Benoit Trong was a member of the Nam Bo elite. Born into a landowning family of Vinh-long, he graduated from the French military academy of Saint Cyr and was commissioned as a French army *lieutenant de réserve*, after which he joined the revolution (see CAOM, Service de Protection du Corps Expéditionnaire, 378).

[37]For the military history of the war, see P. Davidson, *The History, 1946–1975: Vietnam at War* (Presidio, Calif., 1988); and C. Gras, *Histoire de la guerre d'Indochine* (Paris, 1979).

[38]In *Sa-dec Thong tin,* 16 July 1950 (SHAT, 10H 3995). Dr. Pham Ngoc Thach was a member of the Xu Uy Nam Ky of the IPC, a leader of the Vanguard Youth, the spearhead of the revolution in Saigon in 1945. He died in Mien Dong, Nam Bo, on 7 November 1968, during the Second Indochina War, while serving as the minister of health for North Vietnam.

[39]Captured UBK document from Rach-gia, 1951 (ibid.).

[40]Captured UBK documents from the provinces of Soc-trang, Can-tho, and Tan-an, 1950–51 (ibid.). The term *provisional* is used in one of the official documents, although such a condition is denied by the official history, which states that as early as 1948, in Rach-gia and Ha-tien at least, the distribution of land was permanent. See *Buoc mo dau thoi ky lich su ve vang* [The beginnings of a glorious period of history] (Hanoi, 1987), 276. For the government decrees, see Lam Quang Huyen, *Cach mang ruong dat o Mien Nam Viet Nam* [The agrarian revolution in South Vietnam] (Hanoi, 1985).

[41]According to a self-critical speech by Pham Van Bach, delivered in 1952, entitled "Cong tac thue nong nghiep o phan Lien Khu Mien Tay, mua 1951-52" [The collection of agricultural tax in the interzone of Mien Tay, harvest campaign, 1951–52] (SHAT, 10H 3994). Originally from Tra-vinh, Bach was a graduate of the Law Faculty of Lyon, France, and chairman of the UBK.

[42]Ibid.

[43]Document of the Uy ban of Vinh Tra (in Rach-gia), dated November 1952 (SHAT, 10H 39).

[44]Pham Van Bach, "Cong Tac Thue."

[45]Captured UBK documents in SHAT, 10H 3994–3995. Bach observed that preferential treatment of the Khmers stirred up jealousy and hatred ("Con Tac Thue").

[46]See directives of the Economic Committee of Resistance of the province of Can-tho, 24 February 1954 (SHAT, 10H 3996).

[47]Huyen, *Cach Mang Ruong,* 25.

[48]Thayer, *War by Other Means,* 15.

[49]Ladejinsky, *Agrarian Reform* (especially the appendixes). For a good analytical summary of Ziem's domestic policy, see Thayer, *War by Other Means,* 112–29.

[50]*Buoc mo dau.*

[51]Ibid., 274–80.

[52]D. Dacy, *Foreign Aid, War, and Economic Development: South Vietnam, 1955–1975* (Cambridge, 1986). Dacy notes that "Most of the financing for resettlement was supplied by U.S. aid, $93 million in the first two years, and much of the organizing and administration work by Catholic relief organizations" (pp. 2–3).

[53]*Van Kien Dang ve khang chien chong thuc zan Phap* [Party documents on the resistance against the French colonialists], vol. 2: *1945–1951* (Hanoi, 1988), 327.

[54]Ibid.

[55]*Buoc mo dau,* 162.

[56]Ibid., 280, 284, 300.

[57]Ladejinsky, *Agrarian Reform.* According to the *Buoc mo dau,* 60,000 tenancy contracts were signed in 1956, and 63,638 in 1957. The same source states that 270 *dien chu* owning more than 100 hectares recovered a total of 81,204 hectares (p. 227).

[58]On the Chinese, see Tsai Maw Kuey, *Les Chinois au Sud Vietnam* (Paris, 1968). The campaign among the highlanders and the founding of BAJARAKA are treated in G. Hickey, *Free in the Forest* (New Haven, 1982). BAJARAKA is an acronym formed from the names of the principal highland tribes—the Bahnar, Jarai, Rhade, and Koho. Later it was replaced by the Front Uni de Libèration des Régions Opprimées (FULRO). On the oppression of the Khmers, see *Buoc mo dau;* and *Van de Zan Toc DBSCL* (Ho Chi Minh City, 1991), 55.

[59]Ladejinsky, *Agrarian Reform; Buoc mo dau;* W. Andrews, *The Village War: Vietnamese Communist Revolutionary Activities in Dinh Tuong Province, 1960–1964* (Columbia, Mo., 1973). Dinh Tuong is the former province of My-tho.

[60]Thayer, *War by Other Means.* See also Truong Nhu Tang, *A Viet Cong Memoir* (New York, 1985), a rich source of information on life within the communist camp.

[61]R. Sansom, *The Economics of Insurgency in the Mekong Delta of Vietnam* (Cambridge, Mass., 1970). Jeffrey Race's *War Comes to Long An: Revolutionary Conflict in a Vietnamese Province* (Berkeley, 1972) is also a useful guide to understanding the events of the Second Indochina War.

[62]*Buoc mo dau,* 276.

Chapter 9

[1]Tran Van Giau. "Mav dac tinh cua nong zan dong bang Song Cuu Long" in

Mot so van de khoa hoc xa hoi ve dong bang Song Cuu Long, 199.

[2]The "Last Confucian" is the title given to Ngo Dinh Ziem by Denis Warner in *The Last Confucian: Vietnam, South East Asia and the West* (Baltimore, 1964).

[3]A. Varenne, Speech delivered to the French Chamber of Deputies, reprinted in the *Journal Officiel de la République Française, 28* January 1930.

[4]J. H. Boeke, *Economics and Economic Policy of Dual Societies as Exemplified by Indonesia* (New York, 1953).

[5]J. C. Scott, *The Moral Economy of the Peasant: Rebellion and Subsistence in Southeast Asia* (New Haven, 1976); in contrast, see S. Popkin, *The Rational Peasant* (Berkeley, 1979). For a discussion of both theories as they apply to Vietnam, see P. Brocheux, "Moral Economy or Political Economy? The Peasants are Always Rational," *Journal of Asian Studies* 42, no. 4 (1983).

[6]In *Weapons of the Weak: Everyday Forms of Peasant Resistance* (New Haven, 1985), J. C. Scott reminds us of the capacity of individuals to resist oppression and exploitation without resorting to strikes, armed rebellion, trade unionism, or political activism. Scott's theory is quite applicable to the social relationships of Nam Bo, at least those prevailing prior to 1930.

[7]See Tran Van Giau, "May doc tinh," 205; and, more recently, Do Thai Dong, "Nhung Van De Lich su cua Nam Bo" [Questions concerning the history of Nam Bo], a paper delivered at the conference on Phat Trien Nong Thon Nam Bo [The development of the countryside in Nam Bo], held in 1990 in An Giang City, Vietnam.

[8]W. Ladejinski, *Agrarian Reform,* 258.

Bibliographies, Atlases, and Dictionaries

A Bibliography on Land, Peasants, and Politics for Vietnam, Laos, and Cambodia, comp. J. Scott and H. Leichter. New Haven, 1972.

Boudet, P. *Bibliographie de l'Indochine (1930-1935).* Paris, 1967.

Boudet, P., and P. Bourgeois. *Bibliographie de l'Indochine française.* 3 vols. Hanoi, 1931-1943.

Brebion, A., and A. Cabaton. *Dictionnaire de bio-bibliographie générale ancienne et moderne de l'Indochine française.* Paris, 1935.

Brenier, H. *Essai d'atlas statistique de l'Indochine française.* Hanoi, 1914.

Nguyen Huyen Anh. *Viet Nam danh nhan tu dien* [Bibliographical dictionary of Vietnam]. Saigon, 1967.

Nguyen Quang Thang and Nguyen Ba The. *Tu dien nhan vat lich su Viet Nam* [Dictionary of historical biography of Vietnam]. Saigon, 1967.

Nguyen The Anh. *Bibliographie critique sur les relations entre le Vietnam et l'Occident.* Paris, 1967.

Phan Thien Chau. *Vietnamese Communism: A Research Bibliography.* Westport, Conn., 1975.

Thu Muc Dong Bang song Cuu Long [Bibliography of the Cuu Long delta]. Ho Chi Minh City, 1981.

Vuong Hong Sen. *Tu vi Tieng Viet Mien Nam* [Dictionary of the Vietnamese Language of South Vietnam]. Hanoi, 1933.

Whitfield, D. *Historical and Cultural Dictionary of Vietnam.* Metuchen, NJ, 1976.

Primary Sources

Archives

Archives d'Outre-mer, Centre des Archives d'Outre-mer (CAOM), Aix en Provence, France. The principal holdings consulted were:

Agence de la France d'Outre-mer (Agence FOM)
Conseiller Politique
Direction des Affaires Économiques
Indochine
Nouveau Fonds Indochine (NF)
Papiers Agents (PA)
Service de Liaison avec les Originaires des Territoires d'Outre-mer (SLOT FOM)
Sûreté Indochinoise (7F)

Archives du Service Historique de l'Armée de Terre (SHAT), series 10H. The most interesting files are those of the intelligence service of the French Army, the 2ème Bureau, but access to them is subject to authorization.

National Archives of Vietnam, Ho Chi Minh City (formerly Saigon). The principal holdings consulted were

Archives of the provinces of Bac-lieu, Ha-tien, Rach-gia, Can-tho, and Long-xuyen, 1874–1925

Files L and M (Crédit Agricole; and Immigration Tonkinoise, Main d'Oeuvre)

Goucoch (Gouverneur de la Cochinchine)

Toa Dai Bieu Chinh Phu Nam Viet, or TDBCPNV (files from Goucoch originally assembled for the reference of the Assembly of representatives of the government of South Vietnam)

Official Publications

Angladette, A. *Les statistiques agricoles en Indochine*. Paris, 1958.

Annuaire Economique de l'Indochine, various issues.

Annuaire Générale de l'Indochine, various issues.

Archives de l'Office Indochinois du Riz. Hanoi, 1932–41.

Aubaret, G., ed. and trans. *Histoire et description de la Basse Cochinchine (Pays de Gia-Dinh),* by Trinh Hoai Duc. Paris, 1863. The original Vietnamese, in Chinese script, with an accompanying *quoc ngu* version, has been published more recently. See Trinh Hoai Duc, below.

Bulletin Administratif de la Cochinchine, 1865–1944.

Bulletin de l'Agence Economique de l'Indochine. Paris, 1928–37.

Bulletin Agricole de l'Institut Scientifique de Saigon. Saigon, 1919–21.

Bulletin de la Chambre d'Agriculture de Cochinchine, 1898–1940.

Bulletin du Comité Agricole et Industriel de la Cochinchine, 1865–83. Later the name was changed to the *Bulletin de la Société des Etudes Indochinoises.*

Bulletin Economique de l'Indochine. Paris and Hanoi, 1898–1951.

Cochinchine, 1931. Booklet prepared for the Exposition Internationale Coloniale de 1931, Paris.

La Cochinchine: Notice à l'usage des émigrants. Paris, 1904.

La Cochinchine Agricole, 1927–31.

Contribution à l'histoire des mouvements politiques de l'Indochine française. Vol. 4, *Le "Dong-Duong Cong-San Dang" ou "Parti Communiste Indochinois" 1925-1933.* Hanoi, 1933. Published by the Gouvernement-Générale d'Indochine, Direction des Affaires Politiques et de la Sûreté Générale.

Dai Nam Thong Chi, Luc Tinh Nam Bo [Monograph of Dai Nam, the six provinces of Nam Bo]. 3 vols. Saigon, 1972.

Discours des Gouverneurs Généraux de l'Indochine, 1915, 1934.

Etat de la Cochinchine française pendant les années 1878 à 1902. 6 vols. Saigon, 1878-1902

Guide-annuaire de la Cochinchine (later *Guide-annuaire Illustré de la Cochinchine*), 1899–1905.

Guide Touristique de la Province de Ha-tien, n.d.

Laurence, F. "Etude statistique sur le développement économique de l'Indochine." BAEI, 1925, 1927–28,11930–32.

Monographie dessinée de la Cochinchine. Paris, 1938.

Monographie de la province de Bac-lieu, 1937. Typescript.

Monographie de la province de Chau-doc, 1937. Typescript.

Monographie de la province de Ha-lien, 1937. Typescript.

Monographies des provinces de la Cochinchine. Annual *monographies* published by the Société des Etudes Indochinoises (Saigon, 1901–8) and the *Revue Indochinoise* (Saigon, 1907).

Proès-verbaux du Conseil Colonial de la Cochinchine, 1880–1942.

Rapports sur la Situation en Cochinchine devant le Conseil Colonial, various issues. Also known as *Le Livre Vert.*

Smolski, T. *Les statistiques de la population de l'Indochine.* Paris, 1938.

Souverains et notabilités d'Indochine. Hanoi, 1943.

Statistiques Commerciales. Published by the Saigon Chamber of Commerce.

Trinh Hoai Duc. *Gia-Dinh Thanh Thong-Chi* [Gazetteer of Gia Dinh]. Includes the original Vietnamese version in Chinese characters, as well as a *quoc ngu* translation by Tu Trai Nguyen-Tao. 3 vols. Saigon, 1972. A French translation was published in 1863. See G. Aubaret, above.

Miscellaneous Primary Sources

Abel, H. *La question de Cochinchine au point de vue des intérêts français.* Paris, 1864.

Bao Dinh Giang, ed. *Tho van yeu nuoc Nam Bo nua sau the ky XIX* [Patriotic poetry of Nam Bo in the second half of the nineteenth century). Ho Chi Minh City, 1977.

Barrow, J. *A Voyage to Cochinchina.* London, 1806.

Bouillevaux, C. *Voyage dans l'Indochine.* Paris, 1858.

Boilloux, N. *Etude sur l'assiette de l'impôt foncier et sur la constitution de la propriété en Cochinchine.* Saigon, 1879.

Boudet, P., and A. Masson. *Icnographie historique de l'Indochine française.* Paris, 1931.

Boudillon, A. *La réforme du régime foncier indochinois.* Paris, 1927.

———. *Le régime de la propriété foncière en Indochine.* Paris, 1915.

Brière, A. "Rapport sur la circonscription de Camau." ER, no. 1. Saigon, 1879.

"British Missions to Cochinchina, 1778–1822," ed. Alastair Lamb. JMBRAS 34 (1965).

Chapman, Ch. *Relation d'un voyage en Cochinchine en 1778.* BSEI (1948).

Chi Mot con Duong: Hoi ky [There was but one road: Memoirs]. Hanoi, 1974.

La Cochinchine. Saigon, c. 1930. Album of 456 copperplates from Atelier Nadal.

Combanaire, A. *Exploration scientifique et monographie des régions françaises du golfe du Siam.* Saigon, 1929.

Con Duong Giai Phong: Hoi ky [The road to liberation: Memoirs]. Vol. 1. Hanoi, 1979.

Cooke, N., and L. Tana, eds. *Water Frontier: Commerce and the Chinese in the Lower Mekong Region, 1750–1880.* Lanham, Md., 2004.

Danguy, H. *Le nouveau visage de la Cochinchine.* Saigon, 1929.

Decoux, J. *A la barre de l'Indochine.* Paris, 1953.

"Documents pour servir à l'histoire de la Cochinchine française, 1859–1865." BSEI 3, no. 1 (1928).

Doumer, P. *Rapport sur la situation de l'Indochine, 1897–1901.* Hanoi, 1902.

Dürwell, G. *Ma chère Cochinchine: Trente années d'impressions et de souvenirs, 1881–1910.* Paris, 1910.

Empis, Ph. *La colonisation et ses perspectives d'avenir en Indochine.* Paris, 1940.

de Feyssal, P. *L'endettement agraire en Cochinchine: Rapport au gouvernement général de l'Indochine.* Hanoi, 1933.

Goudal, A. *Problèmes du travail en Indochine.* Geneva, 1937.

Henry, Y. *L'Economie agricole de l'Indochine.* Hanoi, 1932.

Henry, Y., and M. Devismes. *Documents de démographie et de riziculture en Indochine.* Hanoi, 1928.

Ho Bieu Chanh. *Con nha ngheo* [Born poor]. Paris, n.d.

Indochine 1947: Règlement politique ou solution militaire. Papers and documents presented to Cdt. G. Bodinier, SHAT. Paris, 1989.

Le Tien Giang. *Cong giao khang chien Nam Bo, 1945–1954* [The Catholics of Nam Bo in the anti-French resistance]. Saigon, 1972.

Lemonnier de la Bissachère, J. *Essai statistique du Tonkin, de la Cochinchine et du Cambodge.* 2 vols. London, 1811.

Louvet, A. *La Cochinchine religieuse.* 2 vols. Paris, 1885.

Magen, L. "Rapport sur une tournée dans l'Ouest cochinchinois." BCAC (1910).

Le Myre de Vilers. *Les institutions civiles de la Cochinchine, 1879–1881.* Paris, 1908.

Nghiem Xuan Yem. "Dieu tra nho, nhung to dien" [A brief survey of the tenants]. *Thanh Nghi* 62 (1944).

Nguyen Hien Le. *Bay ngay trong Dong Thap Muoi* [Seven days in Dong Thap Muoi]. Houston, 1976.

Nguyen Thi Dinh. *Khong con duong nao khac* [There was no other road]. Hanoi, 1979.

Nguyen Thi Luu. *Tinh Yeu va anh lua* [Love and firelight]. Ho Chi Minh City, 1985.

Nguyen Thi Thap. *Tu dat Tien Giang* [From the land of Tien Giang]. Ho Chi Minh City, 1986.

1945–1946: Le retour de la France en Indochine. Papers and documents presented to Cdt. G. Bodinier, SHAT. Paris, 1987.

Pham Quynh. *Mot thang o Nam Ky* [One month in Nam Ky]. Saigon, 1918.

Poivre, P. *Voyage d'un philosophe.* Paris, 1768.

Quelques vues de Baclieu et Camau. N.p., n.d. Photographs.

Solier, M. *La pacification dans la province de Soctrang.* Paris, 1947.

Ta Nhu Khue. "Dieu tra nho, day Baclieu" [A brief survey of Bac-lieu]. *Thanh Nghi* 57 (1944).

Taboulet, G. *La geste française en Indochine.* 2 vols. Paris, 1955–56.

Trinh Dinh Khai. *Décolonisation du Vietnam: Un avocat témoigne, Mᵉ. Trinh Dinh Thao.* Paris, 1994.

Truong Nhu Tang: *A Vietcong Memoir: An Inside Account of the Vietnam War and its Aftermath.* New York, 1985.

Van Kien Dang ve khang chien chong thuc zan Phap tap II (1951–1954) [Party documents on the Resistance against the French colonialists, II (1951–1954)]. Hanoi, 1988.

Vial, P. *Les premières années de la Cochinchine.* Paris, 1874.

Viollis, A. *Indochine S.O.S.* Paris, 1949.

Viviès, A. *L'âme de la Cochinchine.* Saigon, 1924.

Vo Nguyen Giap and Truong Chinh. *Van de zan cay* [The peasant question]. 2d ed. Hanoi, 1959.

Vuong Hong Sen. *Hon nua doi hu* [Half a life wasted]. Ho Chi Minh City, 1992.

Werth, L. *Cochinchine.* Mayenne, 1926.

White, J. *A Voyage to Cochinchina.* London, 1824.

Newspapers and Periodicals

L'Alerte, 1934–37.

An Ha Nhat Bao (Can-tho), 1917, 1919, 1922–24, 1932–33. Vietnamese edition of *Le Courrier de l'Ouest.*

L'Appel (Can-tho), 1922–32.

L'Avenir de la Cochinchine, 1891–92.

Bulletin de la Société des Etudes Indochinoises.

Le Courrier de l'Ouest (Can-tho), 1917, 1919, 1922–24, 1932–33.

Le Courrier de Saigon (later *Le Courrier Saigonnais*), 1899–1933.

La Dépêche Coloniale.

La Dépêche Coloniale Illustrée.

La Dépêche d'Indochine, 1921–43.

Duoc Nha Nam, 1928–32.

L'Echo Annamite, 1920–22, 1939, 1941, 1943.

L'Ere Nouvelle, 1920–29.

L'Eveil Economique de l'Indochine, 1918–34.

Excursions et Reconnaissances.

L'Impartial, 1917–40.

Indochine.

La Lutte, 1934–39.

Nong Cong Thuong, 1939–40.

L'Opinion, 1899–1944. Merged in 1933 with *Le Courrier Saigonnais* under the title *L'Opinion.*

La Paysan de Cochinchine, 1934–42.

Populaire d'Indochine, 1930–40.

Le Progrès Annamite, 1925–31.

Le Réveil Saigonnais, 1892–1929.

La Revue Indochinoise.

La Revue Indochinoise Juridique et Economique.

La Revue du Pacifique.

Saigon Républicain, 1924–6.

La Tribune Indigéne, 1917–25 (later *La Tribune Indochinoise,* 1926–42).

Ve Nong Bao.

La Voix de l'Ouest (Long-xuyen), 1941.

Secondary Sources

Materials in Vietnamese

Buoc mo dau thoi ky lich su ve vang [The beginnings of a glorious period in history]. Hanoi, 1988.

Cach mang ruong dat o Viet Nam [The agrarian revolution in Vietnam]. Hanoi, 1968.

Chung mot bong co (Ve Mat tran zan toc giai phong Mien Nam Viet Nam) [United under a single banner (on NFLSVN)]. Hanoi, 1993.

Cong An Nam Bo trong khang chien chong thuc zan Phap xam luoc [The Nam Bo Security Agency during the Anti-French Resistance]. Ho Chi Minh City, 1993.

Giang Minh Doan. *Nguyen Trung Truc*. Ho Chi Minh City, 1991.

Ha Huy Giap. *Nguyen An Ninh: Mot lanh to cach mang* [Nguyen An Ninh: A revolutionary leader]. Ho Chi Minh City, 1989.

Hanh Trinh. *Mot doi nguoi: Bac si Nguyen Van Huong* [One man's life: Doctor Nguyen Van Huong]. Ho Chi Minh City, 1991.

Huynh Lua, ed. *Lich su khai pha vung dat Nam Bo* [A history of the colonization of Nam Bo]. Ho Chi Minh City, 1987.

Huynh Minh. *Camau xua va Anxuyen nay* [Ca-mau in ancient times and An-xuyen today]. Saigon, 1972.

———. *Sadec xua va nay* [Sa-dec in ancient times and today]. Saigon, 1971.

———. *Gocong xua va nay* [Gocong in ancient times and today]. Saigon, 1969.

———. *Dinhtuong xua va nay* [Dinhtuong in ancient times and today]. Saigon, 1968.

———. *Baclieu xua va nay* [Bac-lieu in ancient times and today]. Saigon, 1966.

———. *Cantho xua va nay* [Can-tho in ancient times and today]. Saigon, 1966.

Lam Quang Huyen. *Cach mang ruong dat o Mien Nam Viet Nam* [The agrarian revolution in South Vietnam]. Hanoi, 1985.

Luu Nhat Vu, ed. *Zan ca Kien Giang* [Popular songs of Kien Giang]. Ho Chi Minh City, 1985.

Mac Duong, ed. *Van de zan toc o Dong Bang song Cuu Long* [The nationalities problem in the Cuu Long delta]. Ho Chi Minh City, 1991.

Mot so van de khoa hoc xa hoi ve Dong Bang song Cuu Long [Some problems of social science in the Cuu Long delta]. Hanoi, 1982.

Nguyen An Ninh. Ho Chi Minh City, 1988.

Nguyen Cong Binh, ed. *Van hoa va cu zan Dong Bang song Cuu Long* [Cultures and peoples of the Cuu Long delta]. Ho Chi Minh City, 1990.

Nguyen Dinh Dau. *Che do cong dien cong tho trong lich su khan hoang lap ap o Nam ky Luc tinh* [The regime of communal lands in the historical process of land clearing and the establishment of villages in the southern Six Provinces] Hanoi, 1992.

———. "Thu tim hieu dat nuoc va zan toc qua 10,044 tap dia bo" [To understand our country and nation through 10,044 land registers]. *Tap Chi Khoa Hoc Dai Hoc Tong Hop Ha Noi* 4 (1988).

———. "Gop phan Nghien cuu van de do, dong, can, dem cua Viet Nam xua"

[Research on measures, currencies, and weights of ancient Vietnam]. *Nghien Cuu Kinh Te* 5 (1978).

Nguyen Ngoc Tran, ed. *Truyen co Kho-me Nam Bo* [Old Khmer tales of Nam Bo]. Hanoi, 1983.

Nguyen Phan Quang and Le Huu Phuoc. *Khoi Nghia Truong Dinh* [Truong Con Dinh's uprising]. Ho Chi Minh City, 1989.

Nguyen Quang Thang. *Tien trinh van nghe Mien Nam* [The evolution of arts and literature in South Vietnam]. Ho Chi Minh City, 1990.

Nguyen Van Hau. *Nguyen Quang Zieu: Phong trao Dong zu Mien Nam* [Nguyen Quang Zieu: The Eastern Trip movement in South Vietnam]. Saigon, 1974.

———. *Le Thanh Hau Nguyen Huu Canh: Nguoi co ky cong o trong viec khai thac Mien Nam* [Nguyen Huu Can: The man who showed prowess in colonizing South Vietnam]. Saigon, 1970.

Nguyen Van Huy. *Nguoi Hoa tai Vietnam* [The Chinese in Vietnam]. Costa Mesa, Calif., 1993.

Nguyen Van Sam. *Van chuong Nam Bo va cuoc khang Phap, 1945–1950* [The literature of Nam Bo and the anti-French resistance, 1945–1950]. Saigon, 1972.

Nguyen Zuy Oanh. *Tinh Ben tre trong lich su Viet Nam to 1757 den 1945* [The province of Ben-tre in the history of Vietnam, 1757 to 1945]. Saigon, 1971.

Nhu Hien Nguyen Ngoc Hien. *Le Thanh Hau Nguyen Huu Canh voi cong cuoc khai san Mien Nam nuoc Viet cuoi the ky thu XVII* [Le Thanh Hau and Nguyen Huu Canh and the colonization of the southern part of Vietnam at the end of the seventeenth century]. Hanoi, 1993.

Nhung su kien lich su Dang, 1920–1945 [Events in the history of the party, 1920–1945]. Vol. 1. Hanoi, 1976.

Pham Cao Zuong. *Thuc trang cua gioi nong zan Viet Nam zuoi thoi Phap thuoc* [Peasant conditions under French domination]. Saigon, 1968.

Phan An. "Mot so van de kinh the xa hoi nong thon cua nguoi Khome o Dong Bang song Cuu Long" [Economic and social questions in the Khmer village in the Cuu Long delta]. In Mac Duong, ed., *Van de zan toc*. Ho Chi Minh City, 1991.

Son Nam. *Dong Bang song Cuu Long hay la van minh Miet vuon?* [The Cuu Long delta or a Polders civilization?]. Houston, 1976.

———. *Ca tinh cua Mien Nam* [The personality of South Vietnam]. Saigon, 1974.

———. *Lich su khan hoang Mien Nam* [The history of settlement in South Vietnam]. Saigon, 1973.

———. *Mien Nam dau the ky XX: Thien Dia Hoi va cuoc Minh Tan* [South Vietnam at the turn of the twentieth century: The Heaven and Earth Society and the New Light Movement]. Saigon, 1971.

———. *Nguoi Viet co zan toc tinh khong?* [Do the Vietnamese have a national character?]. Saigon, 1969.

———. *Tim hieu dat Hau Giang* [Understanding the land of Hau Giang]. Saigon, 1959.

Su Kien Lich su Dang Ha Nam Ninh [Historical events of the party in Ha Nam Ninh Province]. Nam Dinh, 1978.

Thach Phuong, ed. *Van hoa zan gian nguoi Viet o Nam Bo* [Folk culture of the Vietnamese people of southern Vietnam]. Hanoi, 1992.

Thach Phuong and Doan Tu, eds. *Dia chi Ben tre* [Guide to Bentre]. Hanoi, 1991.

Thach Voi. "Khai quat ve nguoi Khmer o DBSCL" [General remarks concerning the Khmers of DBSCL]. In *Tim hieu von van hoa zan toc Khmer Nam Bo*. Hau Giang, 1988.

Thai Bach. *Bon vi Anh hung Khang chien Mien Nam* [Four heroes of the resistance of the South]. Saigon, 1957.

Tieng not Troi manh thu [Broadcasts of anti-French colonial resistance by the "Voice of Nam Bo," 1945–1954]. Ho Chi Minh City, 1993.

Tim hieu von van hoa zan toc Khmer Nam Bo [Understanding the cultural foundations of the Khmer nation in Nam Bo]. Hau Giang, 1988.

Tran Bach Dang. *Dong Bang song Cuu Long 40 nam* [The Cuu Long delta during the last forty years]. Ho Chi Minh City, 1986.

Tran Huy Lieu and Nguyen Khac Dam, eds. *Xa hoi Viet Nam trong thoi Phap Nhat* [Vietnamese society in the French-Japanese period]. Hanoi, 1957.

Tran Huy Lieu and Van Tao, eds. *Cac cuoc khoi nghia Bac son, Nam ky, Do luong* [The uprisings of Bac Son, Nam Ky, and Do Luong]. Hanoi, 1957.

Tran Quang Hao. *Cao lanh den 1954* [Cao Lanh to 1954]. Saigon, 1963.

Tran Tu Binh. *Phu Rieng Do* [Phu Rieng, the red]. Hanoi, 1971.

Tran Van Giau. "Mot so dac diem cua Khoi nghia Thang Tam 1945 o Nam Bo Saigon" [Some specifics concerning the August 1945 Revolution in Nam Bo Saigon]. *Tap Chi Khoa Hoc Xa Hoi* 5 (1990).

———. *He y thuc tu san* [Bourgeois thought systems]. Hanoi, 1975.

———. *He y thuc phong kien* [Feudal thought systems]. Hanoi, 1973.

——— *Giai cap cong nhan Viet Nam* [The Vietnamese working class]. Hanoi, 1958.

Truong Ba Can, ed. *Ky niem 100 nam ngay Phap chiem Nam ky* [Remembering 100 years of the French conquest of Nam Ky]. Saigon, 1967.

Truong Luu, ed. *Van Hoa Nguoi Khmer vung Dong Bang song Cuu Long* [The culture of the Khmers of the Cuu Long delta]. Hanoi, 1993.

Truyen thong cach mang cua Phu nu Nam Bo thanh long [The revolutionary tradition of the women of Nam Bo]. Ho Chi Minh City, 1989.

Vo Tran Nha, ed. *Lich su Dong Thap Muoi* [A history of Dong Thap Muoi]. Ho Chi Minh City, 1993.

Western-Language Materials

Adas, M. *The Burma Delta: Economic Development and Social Change on an Asian Rice Frontier, 1852–1941*. Madison, 1974.

Anderson, M., et al. "Insurgent Organizations and Operations: A Case Study of the Vietcong in the Delta, 1964–1966." N.p., 1967. Typescript. Rand Corporation memorandum.

Andrews, W. *The Village War: Vietnamese Communist Revolutionary Activities in Dinh Tuong Province, 1960–1964*. Columbia, Mo., 1973.

Aurillac, H. *Cochinchine, Annamites, Mois, Cambodgiens*. Paris, 1870.

Auriol, R., and Lam Van Lang. "Etudes sur les terres et eaux alunées." BCAC (1934).

Baurac, J. *La Cochinchine et ses habitants, provinces de l'Ouest*. Saigon, 1894.

Benabenq, J. "Note sur l'hydraulique agricole." BAISS (1920).

Bernard, P. *Nouveaux aspects du problème économique indochinois*. Paris, 1937.

———. *Le problème économique indochinois*. Paris, 1934.

Bineteau, H. "Divisions territoriales et agricoles par provinces." BSG (1864).

Boeke, J. *Economics and Economic Policy of Dual Societies as Exemplified by Indonesia*. New York, 1953.

Bonnaud, A. "Etude sur les voies navigables de la Cochinchine." ER (1881).

Boudet, P. "La conquête de la Cochinchine par les Nguyen et le rôle des émigrés chinois." BEFEO (1943).

Bourbon, A. *Le redressement économique de l'Indochine, 1934–1937*. Paris, 1937.

Bray, F. *The Rice Economies: Technology and Development in Asian Societies*. Oxford, 1986.

Brocheux, P. "Elite, Bourgeoisie ou la difficulté d'être." In *Saigon, 1925–1945, de la "Belle colonie," à l'éclosion révolutionnaire ou la fin des dieux blancs*. Paris, 1992.

———. "Portrait en blanc et noir d'un bourgeois mal aimé: Bui Quang Chieu." In *Saigon, 1925–1945, de la "Belle colonie," à l'éclosion révolutionnaire ou la fin des dieux blancs*. Paris, 1992.

———. "Note sur Gilbert Chieu, patriote vietnamien et citoyen français." *Approches-Asie* 11 (1991).

———. "De l'empereur Zuy Tan au prince Vinh San: L'Histoire peut-elle se répèter?" *Approches-Asie* 10 (1990).

———. "Moral Economy or Political Economy? The Peasants are Always Rational." *Journal of Asian Studies* 42, no. 4 (1983).

———. "'L'occasion favorable', 1940–1945: Les forces politiques vietnamiennes pendant la seconde guerre mondiale." In P. Isoart, ed., *L'Indochine Française, 1940–1945*. Paris, 1982.

———. "Les communistes et les paysans dans la révolution vietnamienne." In *Révoltes, réformes, révolution en Asie du Sud-est*. Lille, 1981.

———. "L'implantation du mouvement communiste en Indochine française, le cas du Nghe Tinh (1930-1931)." *Revue d'Histoire Moderne et Contemporaine* 24 (1977).

———. "Crise économique et société en Indochine française." *Revue Française d'Histoire d'Outre-mer* 232–33 (1976).

———. "Vietnamiens et minorités en Cochinchine pendant la période coloniale." *Modern Asian Studies* 6, no. 4 (1972).

———. "Grands propriétaires et fermiers dans l'Ouest de la Cochinchine pendant la période coloniale." *Revue Historique* 246 (1971).

Bruzon, E., and P. Carton. *Le climat de l'Indochine et les typhons de la Mer de Chine*. Hanoi, 1930.

Bunout, R. *La main d'oeuvre et la législation du travail en Indochine*. Bordeaux, 1936.

Bussy, P. "Etude agricole des terres de la Cochinchine." BAISS (1920).

Cady, J. *The Roots of French Imperialism in Eastern Asia*. Ithaca, 1954.

Caratini, J. *Le statut des missions en Indochine*. Hanoi, 1941.

Chandler, D. *A History of Cambodia*. 2d ed. Boulder, 1992.

Chau Kiem Thanh. *Essai d'une réforme sur le crédit agricole mutuel en Cochinchine*. Paris, 1940.

Chesneaux, J. *Contribution à l'histoire de la nation vietnamienne.* Paris, 1955.

Chesneaux, J., G. Boudarel, and D. Hémery, eds. *Tradition et révolution au Vietnam.* Paris, 1971.

Chevalier, A. *Le poivrier et sa culture en Indochine.* Paris, 1925.

Cook, M. *The Constitutionalist Party in Cochinchina: The Years of Decline, 1930–1942.* Melbourne, 1977.

Coquerel, A. *Paddys et riz de Cochinchine.* Lyon, 1911.

Coulet, G. *Les sociétés secrètes en terre d'Annam.* Paris, 1927.

Dacy, D. *Foreign Aid, War, and Economic Development: South Vietnam, 1955–1975.* Cambridge, 1986.

Davidson, P. *The History, 1946–1975.* Presidio, Calif., 1988.

Delvert, J. *Le paysan cambodgien.* Paris and The Hague, 1963.

Dennery, E. *Foules d'Asie.* Paris, 1930.

Deschaseaux, E. "Note sur les anciens don dien annamites de la Basse Cochinchine." ER (1889).

Descours-Gatin, C. *Quand l'opium finançait la colonisation en Indochine.* Paris, 1992.

Devillers, P. *Histoire de l'Indochine de 1940 à 1952.* Paris, 1952.

Dubreuil, R. *De la condition des Chinois et de leur rôle économique en Indochine.* Paris, 1910.

Dugros, M. "Le domaine forestier inondé de la Cochinchine." BEI (1937).

———. "La mangrove et l'arrière-mangrove." *L'Asie Nouvelle* (February/April/June 1936).

Dumarest, J. *Les monopoles de l'opium et du sel en Indochine.* Lyon, 1938.

Dumont, R. *La culture du riz dans le delta du Tonkin.* Paris, 1934.

d'Enjoy, P. *La colonisation de la Cochinchine.* Paris, 1898.

Estèbe, P. *Le problème du riz en Indochine.* Toulouse, 1934.

Evans, Grant. "The Accursed Problem: Communists and Peasants." *Peasant Studies* 15, no. 2 (1988).

Fraisse, A. "Note de géographie humaine sur la province de Longxuyen." BIIEH 5 (1942).

Garros, G. *Les usages de la Cochinchine.* Saigon, 1905.

Gaspardonne, E. "Un Chinois des Mers du Sud: Le fondateur de Ha Tien." *Journal Asiatique* (1952).

Gerville-Réache, L. "La stabilisation de la piastre indochinoise." Paris, 1928. Pamphlet published by *La Dépêche Coloniale.*

Gonjo, Y. *Banque coloniale ou Banque d'affaires: La banque de l'Indochine sous la IIIième République.* Paris, 1993.

Gourou, P. "La population rurale de la Cochinchine." *Annales de Géographie* 51 (1942).

———. *L'utilisation du sol en Indochine française.* Paris, 1940.

———. *Le paysan du delta tonkinois.* Paris, 1936.

de Grammont, L. "Notice sur la Basse Cochinchine." BSG (1864).

Grandjean, Ph. *Le statut légal des missions catholiques et protestantes en Indochine française.* Paris, 1939.

Gras, Y. *Histoire de la guerre d'Indochine.* 2d ed. Paris, 1992.

Hémery, D. *Révolutionnaires vietnamiens et pouvoir colonial en Indochine.* Paris, 1975.

Henry, A. *Etude sur les forêts de la Cochinchine*. Saigon, 1891.

Hibon, A. *La crise économique en Indochine*. Paris, 1936.

Hickey, G. *Free in the Forest*. New Haven, 1982.

———. *Village in Vietnam*. New Haven, 1964.

Hoselitz, B., and R. Lambert, eds. *Le rôle de l'épargne et de la richesse en Asie du Sud-est et en Occident*. [Paris], 1963.

Huard, P., and M. Durand. *Connaissance du Vietnam*. Paris, 1955.

Hue Tam Ho Tai. *Radicalism and the Origins of the Vietnamese Revolution*. Cambridge, Mass., 1992.

———. *Millenarianism and Peasant Politics in Vietnam*. Cambridge, Mass., 1983.

Huynh Kim Khanh. *Vietnamese Communism, 1925–1945*. Ithaca, 1982.

Huynh Xuan Canh. *Le crédit indochinoise: Essai sur l'organisation du crédit en Indochine*. Paris, 1929.

Isoart, P. *Le phénomène national vietamien: De l'indépendance unitaire à l'indépendance fractionée*. Paris, 1961.

Jammes, H. *Au pays d'Annam*. Paris, 1900.

Kahin, G. McT. *Intervention: How America Became Involved in Viet Nam*. New York, 1986.

Kartodirdjo, S. *Protest Movements in Rural Java*. Singapore, 1973.

Kerkvliet, B. *The Huk Rebellion*. Berkeley, 1977.

Khérian, G. "La position du problème du crédit en Indochine." RIJE (1941).

Kolko, G. *Anatomy of a War*. New York, 1985.

Ladejinsky, W. *Agrarian Reform as Unfinished Business*. Oxford, 1977.

Laffargue, H. *L'immigration chinoise en Indochine*. Paris, 1909.

Lansdale, E. *In the Midst of Wars: An American Mission to South East Asia*. New York, 1972.

Le Thanh Khoi, *Le Vietnam: Histoire et civilisation*. Paris, 1955.

Leclerc et l'Indochine, 1945–1947: Quand se noua le destin d'un empire. Paris, 1992.

Lefeuvre, E. "Etude des terres de Cochinchine." BSEI (1903).

Leonardi, C. "L'usure en Cochinchine." EA (1926).

Lim Teck Ghee. *Peasants and Their Cultural Economy in Colonial Malaya, 1874–1941*. Kuala Lumpur, 1977.

Le Louet, M. "Note sur le barbone en Cochinchine." BAISS (1921).

Loustau, H. *Les deux bataillons*. Paris, 1987.

Malleret, L. *L'archéologie du Delta du Mekong*. 4 vols. Paris, 1959–63.

Marr, D. *Vietnamese Tradition on Trial, 1920–1945*. Berkeley, 1981.

———. *Vietnamese Anticolonialism, 1885–1925*. Berkeley, 1971.

Mathieu, E. *Le prêt usuraire et le crédit agricole en Cochinchine*. Paris, 1912.

———. *Essais sur l'organisation et le régime de la propriété rurale en Cochinchine*. Paris, 1909.

Melin, P. *L'endettement agraire en Indochine*. Paris, 1939.

Meuleau, M. *Des pionniers en Extrême-Orient: Histoire de la Banque de l'Indochine, 1875–1975*. Paris, 1990.

Moreau, M. "Les cours d'eau de la presqu'île de Camau." ER (1881).

Morel, J. *Les concessions de terre au Tonkin*. Paris, 1912.

Murray, M. *The Development of Capitalism in Colonial Indochina, 1870–1940*. Berkeley, 1980.

Mus, P. *Vietnam: Sociologie d'une guerre.* Paris, 1952.

Ner, M. "Les Musulmans de l'Indochine." BEFEO (1941).

Nguyen Anh Tuan. *South Vietnam, Trial and Experience: A Challenge for Development.* Athens, Ohio, 1987.

Nguyen Quoc Dinh. *Les congrégations chinoises en Indochine.* Paris, 1941.

Nguyen Thanh Nha. *Tableau économique du Vietnam au XVII–XVIIIème siècles.* Paris, 1972.

Nguyen Xuan Quang. *Les problèmes économiques et financiers du Vietnam à l'aube de son indépendance.* Saigon, 1959.

Nonini, D. *British Colonial Rule and the Resistance of the Malay Peasantry, 1900–1957.* New Haven, 1992.

Normandin, A. "Rapport sur les travaux d'hydrographie agricole à étudier et à entreprendre en Cochinchine." BCAC (1913).

Osborne, M. *The French Presence in Cochinchina and Cambodia: Rule and Response, 1859–1905.* Ithaca, 1969.

Oualid, W. *Le privilège de la Banque de l'Indochine et la question des banques des coloniales.* Paris, 1923.

Paige, J. *Agrarian Revolution: Social Movements and Expert Agriculture in the Underdeveloped World.* New York, 1975.

Paris, P. "Note sur les tatouages de la bonzesse Vo Thi Nan." BIIEH (1941).

Pinto, R. "Les assemblées de villages convoquées par l'amiral-gouverneur Ohier." BSEI (1944).

Popkin, S. *The Rational Peasant.* Berkeley, 1979.

Poujade, J. *Pirogues et ca vom de l'Ouest cochinchinois.* Paris, 1946.

Pouyanne, A. "Les dragages de Cochinchine et l'inauguration du canal Rachgia-Hatien." EA (1930).

_____. *Les voies d'eau de Cochinchine.* 2 vols. Saigon, 1911.

Purcell, V. *The Chinese in South East Asia.* 2d ed. Oxford, 1964.

Queinnec, J. *Les prêts sur récolte en Cochinchine, Annam, Tonkin.* Paris, 1930.

Race, J. *War Comes to Long An: Revolutionary Conflict in a Vietnamese Province.* Berkeley, 1972.

Robequain, Ch. *L'évolution économique de l'Indochine française.* Paris, 1939.

Sabès, A. *Le renouvellement du privilège de la Banque de l'Indochine.* Paris, 1931.

Sansom, R. *The Economics of Insurgency in the Mekong Delta of Vietnam.* Cambridge, Mass., 1970.

Sarraut, A. *La mise en valeur des colonies françaises.* Paris, 1923.

Schreiner, A. *Le livre foncier.* Saigon, 1904.

_____. *Les institutions annamites en Basse Cochinchine avant la conquête française.* 3 vols. Saigon, 1900–1902.

Scott, J. *Weapons of the Weak: Everyday Forms of Peasant Resistance.* New Haven, 1985.

_____. *The Moral Economy of the Peasant: Rebellion and Subsistence in Southeast Asia.* New Haven, 1976.

Shiraishi, M. "La présence japonaise en Indochine (1940–1945)." In P. Isoart, ed., *L'Indochine française, 1940-1945.* Paris, 1982.

Skocpol, T. *States and Social Revolutions: a comparative analysis of China, Russia, and France.* Cambridge, 1979.

Smith, R. *An International History of the Vietnam War.* 3 vols. London, 1983.

_____. "The Vietnamese Elite of French Cochinchina, 1943." *Modern Asian Studies* (1972).

_____. "Introduction to Caodaism." *Bulletin of the School of Oriental and African Studies* (1970).

Smith, R., and W. Watson, eds. *Early South East Asia: Essays in Archaeology, History and Historical Geography.* Oxford, 1979.

Steinberg, D., ed. *In Search of South East Asia.* 2d ed. Sydney, 1989.

Sturtevant, D. *Popular Uprisings in the Philippines, 1840–1940.* Ithaca, 1976.

Taylor, K. *The Birth of Vietnam.* Berkeley, 1983.

Thayer, C. *War by Other Means: National Liberation and Revolution in Vietnam, 1954–1960.* London, 1989.

Thiollier, L. *La grande aventure de la piastre indochinoise.* Saint Etienne, 1930.

Tonnesson, S. *The Vietnamese Revolution of 1945: Roosevelt, Ho Chi Minh and de Gaulle in a World at War.* London, 1991.

Touzet. A. *Le régime monétaire indochinois.* Paris, 1939.

_____. *L'économie indochinoise et la grande crise universelle.* Paris, 1934.

Tran Nguon Hanh. "Rapport concernant les principaux travaux agricoles." BCAIC (1876).

Tran Van Huu. "La riziculture en Cochinchine." BAEI (1927).

_____. "Note sur la culture du riz flottant en Cochinchine." BAISS (1920).

Tsai Maw Kieuw. *Les Chinois au Sud Vietnam.* Paris, 1968.

Turton, A., and Shigeharu Tanabe, eds. *History and Peasant Consciousness in South East Asia.* Osaka, 1984.

Verdeille, H. "Deux édits de l'empereur Minh Mang concernant les Chinois de Cochinchine." BSEI (1933).

Vu Quoc Thuc. "Épargne et richesse en Asie du Sud-est." In Hoselitz and Lambert, eds., *Le rôle de l'épargne et de la richesse en Asie du Sud-est et en Occident.* [Paris], 1963.

_____. *L'économie communaliste du Vietnam.* Hanoi, 1951.

Vu Van Hien. *Communal Property in Tonkin: A Contribution to the Historical, Judicial, and Economic Study of Cong Dien and Cong Tho in Annam.* New Haven, 1955.

Vu Van Mau. "Le dien mai et le nantissement immobilier." RIJE (1940).

Wang Wen Yuan. *Les relations entre l'Indochine française et la Chine.* Paris, 1937.

Warner, D. *The Last Confucian: Vietnam, South East Asia, and the West.* Baltimore, 1964.

Werner, J. *Peasant Politics and Religious Sectarianism: Peasant and Priest in the Cao Dai in Vietnam.* New Haven, 1981.

Willmott, W. *The Chinese in Cambodia.* Vancouver, 1967.

Wolf, E. *Peasant Wars of the Twentieth Century.* New York, 1969.

Woodside, A. *Community and Revolution in Modern Vietnam.* Boston, 1976.

_____. *Vietnam and the Chinese Model: A Comparative Study of Vietnamese and Chinese Government in the First Half of the 19th Century.* Cambridge, Mass., 1971.

Young, M. *The Vietnam Wars, 1945–1990.* New York, 1991.

BOOKS OF RELATED INTEREST

From Rebellion to Riots: Collective Violence on Indonesian Borneo
Jamie S. Davidson

Amazons of the Huk Rebellion: Gender, Sex, and Revolution in the Philippines
Vina A. Lanzona

An Anarchy of Families: State and Family in the Philippines
Edited by Alfred W. McCoy

Pretext for Mass Murder: The September 30th Movement and Suharto's Coup d'État in Indonesia
John Roosa

The Social World of Batavia: Europeans and Eurasians in Colonial Indonesia
Jean Gelman Taylor

Việt Nam: Borderless Histories
Edited by Nhung Tuyet Tran and Anthony Reid

Modern Noise, Fluid Genres: Popular Music in Indonesia, 1997–2001
Jeremy Wallach